D1593651

The Long Road Home

Mass. MOLLUS, USAMHI

George E. Welles

Adjutant, Major, Lieutenant Colonel
68th Ohio Veteran Volunteer Infantry

Brevet Brigadier General

The Long Road Home

Ten Thousand Miles
Through the Confederacy with the 68th Ohio

Myron B. Loop

Edited by Richard A. Baumgartner

BLUE ACORN PRESS
Huntington, West Virginia

BLUE ACORN PRESS
P.O. Box 2684
Huntington, W.Va. 25726

ISBN 978-1-885033-34-5

THE LONG ROAD HOME
Ten Thousand Miles Through the Confederacy with the 68th Ohio

Illustrated. Includes bibliographical references and index

History — American Civil War 1861-1865

Manufactured in the United States of America

CONTENTS

ACKNOWLEDGMENTS

Sincere gratitude is extended to all who assisted in this book's compilation, particularly the following individuals whose contributions merit special notice:

Daniel A. Masters, Whitehouse, Ohio; Craig V. Fisher, Toledo, Ohio; Larry M. Strayer, Kettering, Ohio; Roger D. Hunt, Gettysburg, Pa.; Steven H. Ward, Dayton, Ohio; Jerry B. Everts, Lambertville, Mich.; Dennis M. Keesee, New Albany, Ohio; Karl Sundstrom, North Riverside, Ill.; Dr. Richard A. Sauers, Williamsport, Pa.; Margaret Wilkins, West Covina, Calif.; Mark Warren, Bloomfield, Iowa; Marilyn Levinson, manuscripts curator, and Stephen M. Charter, reference archivist, Center for Archival Collections, Jerome Library, Bowling Green State University, Bowling Green, Ohio; Randy Hackenburg, photo historian, and Stephen Bye, research technician, Army Heritage and Education Center, U.S. Army Military History Institute, Carlisle Barracks, Pa.; Amanda Aikman, reference assistant, Bentley Historical Library, University of Michigan, Ann Arbor; Mary Michals, audio-visual curator, Abraham Lincoln Presidential Library, Springfield, Ill.; and Bill Markley, reference archivist, Ohio Historical Society Library, Columbus.

ABBREVIATIONS

AGR	Adjutant General's Report.
BHL	Bentley Historical Library, University of Michigan, Ann Arbor.
CAC	Center for Archival Collections, Jerome Library, Bowling Green State University, Bowling Green, Ohio.
CSR	Compiled Service Record.
Mass. MOLLUS	Massachusetts Commandery, Military Order of the Loyal Legion of the United States.
NARA	National Archives and Records Administration, Washington, D.C.
OHS	Ohio Historical Society, Columbus.
OR	*War of the Rebellion: A Compilation of the Official Records of the Union and Confederate Armies.*
RG	Record Group.
USAMHI	U.S. Army Military History Institute, Carlisle Barracks, Pa.

INTRODUCTION

Shriveled leaves still clung to branches of northwest Ohio's ash, maple and white oak trees when Ira M. Kelsey welcomed a familiar face to his Bowling Green recruiting office on Nov. 13, 1861. He instantly recognized the young man's blue eyes and auburn hair. Both were residents of Woodville in neighboring Sandusky County, and both had served together in the same infantry company during one of the Civil War's opening campaigns in western Virginia. Three months had elapsed since their discharge, but Kelsey well appreciated the worth of the individual standing before him. He also discovered little inducement was required to convince him to reenter the army. Shaking his recruiter's hand, Myron Loop signed enlistment papers for the second time. Within days, he and Kelsey found themselves reunited again — this time as members of Company I, 68th Ohio Volunteer Infantry Regiment.[1]

In the late summer and fall of the war's first year, Loop was among 84,116 Ohioans answering President Abraham Lincoln's appeal for 500,000 men to enlarge the Federal Army and suppress rebellion in the confederacy of Southern states.[2] Stinging Union defeats at Bull Run in Virginia and Wilson's Creek in Missouri clearly dashed Northern hopes for the conflict's quick conclusion. A protracted war meant the North needed more soldiers in the field, far more than the 75,000 raw, untrained volunteers who flocked enthusiastically to their national banner after the fall of Fort Sumter the previous spring. Most belonged to regiments raised for just three-months' service, a reflection of prevailing early belief that any fighting would be short and decisive. The July 1861 confrontation at Bull Run abruptly dispelled this notion. In the battle's wake, thousands of Union three-month troops mustered out. A majority, however, soon reenlisted and were reorganized in three-year regiments and batteries. Following Lincoln's call another enlistment wave rolled through the North, vastly increasing army manpower. In Ohio, recruiters fanned out across the state to harvest a fresh crop of enlistees. Competition was fierce. The most successful recruiters usually gained commissions for themselves, whether or not they possessed any military knowledge.

At the end of September 1861 Governor William Dennison, the first of Ohio's three wartime chief executives, authorized two prominent Henry County businessmen to raise the 68th Regiment from the state's 10th Congressional District. Fifty-seven-year-old Samuel Harris Steedman was appointed lieutenant colonel. Born in Northumberland County, Pa., Steedman moved in 1837 to Ohio, where he contracted to build portions of the Wabash & Erie Canal. A Democrat, he was elected a representative to the state's General Assembly in 1850, at one time serving as chairman of five different committees. For several years before war's outbreak he operated a dry goods store in the Henry County seat of Napoleon. Although Steedman's background was bereft of military experience, his nephew, James Blair Steedman, had become colonel of the 14th Ohio Infantry Regiment in April 1861. The younger Steedman eventually distinguished himself in the battles of Perryville, Chickamauga and Nashville, finishing the war as a major general of volunteers.[3]

Another native Pennsylvanian, Robert Kingston Scott, was appointed major. His Irish grandfather had fought as a teenager in the American Revolution, and his father was a veteran of the War of 1812. Born July 8, 1826, Scott arrived in Ohio at age 16, supplementing a common-school education by studying at Central College and Starling Medical College. During 1850-51 he prospected for gold in California, Mexico and South America, then returned to Ohio where he practiced medicine at Napoleon. Like Steedman, Scott also engaged in merchandising, while shrewd real estate and land investment prior to the Civil War made him one of Henry County's wealthiest citizens.[4]

The two new field officers immediately began raising and organizing companies for the 68th Regiment from Henry, Paulding, Defiance, Williams, Fulton, Lucas, Wood and Sandusky counties. Their efforts were greatly augmented by at least a half dozen recruiters who already served three months as line officers in the 14th or 21st Ohio regiments. A camp of rendezvous and instruction was established November 21 a half mile outside Napoleon on a farm adjoining the Maumee River's north bank. It was christened Camp

Latty to honor Alexander S. Latty, a former common pleas court judge of the district who was "a staunch Union man and true friend" of the regiment. Upon arriving, Myron Loop found Camp Latty "pleasantly located on high and dry ground." The recruits "were provided with a complete outfit of large Sibley tents ... and roomy wall tents for the officers, each of which was furnished with an abundant supply of clean straw by the neighboring farmers, and together with warm woolen blankets provided us by our Uncle Samuel we were as warm and comfortable as heart could wish." [5]

By the end of November Steedman and Scott were promoted and mustered as colonel and lieutenant colonel, respectively. While they were absent much of December closing business affairs, Major John S. Snook assumed regimental command. Snook, 46, was the father of two young children, a Mason and merchant in the small Paulding County town of Antwerp. In April 1861 he was among the first in northwest Ohio to raise a company, leading it that summer when the 14th Ohio tramped the hills of western Virginia between minor fights at Philippi, Laurel Hill and Carrick's Ford. At Camp Latty Snook was assisted by a freshly minted lieutenant less than half his age. Born July 4, 1840 at Elyria, Ohio, Adjutant George E. Welles was a Napoleon wholesale drug company clerk whose enthusiasm, it was said, surpassed even Snook's. Both were "noble men and good disciplinarians," thought Myron Loop, "and at once entered into a regular system of camp rules, frequent roll calls and daily drill." Welles was destined to command the regiment later on, receiving a brigadier general's brevet in 1867. Snook, however, did not survive the war.[6]

Like Snook, Private Loop recognized "the importance of being well versed in military tactics and thoroughly understanding their duties as soldiers of the Republic." It was gratifying to be among some of the old crowd again — Lieutenant Kelsey, Jim Vorhes, Mike Burgermeister, Henry Spafford, Sergeant Jim Crego — all having "seen the elephant" in the Kanawha Valley as former members of the 21st Ohio. In early December Loop's older brother William, a new enlistee, also turned up in the 68th's camp, and promptly was assigned as Company I's wagoner. There were hundreds of others Loop did not know, but he learned a large majority were farmers like himself, men "accustomed to the hard work incident to clearing off and making fertile fields from the forest of that part of the State." There was even a small contingent of non-Ohioans, Loop discovered. "Near the village of Pioneer, Williams Co., our recruiting officers got over the State line and captured one Robert Masters, and through him a number of men were enrolled from Hillsdale Co., Mich." Masters was appointed Company G's first lieutenant and in 1864, promoted to captain of Company B.[7]

Possessing an inquisitive nature, Loop acquainted himself with some of the regiment's recruits by strolling company streets and "studying the many strange faces surrounding me." It amused him to read inscriptions scrawled on the camp's Sibley tents, designating them "Social Hall," "Fiddler's Green," "Tigers' Ranch," "Lions' Den" and the "Howling Wilderness." A few tents bore placards warning that "There shall be no swearing or card-playing allowed here" — an admonition that all but disappeared three months later. Several of the boys (as the soldiers referred to themselves, irregardless of age) brought violins from home. Smokers lit pipe bowls and cigars, nearly everyone "talking, laughing, singing and watching the artistic rings of smoke as they ascended and were lost in the smoky haze" permeating the tents' conical forms.[8]

Loop's prior military service was beneficial, yet he considered himself almost as raw as most of those gathered at Camp Latty. After Colonel Steedman procured Enfield rifle-muskets for the regiment, "our young hearts thumped with delight when we ... marched out of our camp, keeping step to the soul-stirring music of fife and drum. How fierce our officers looked as with swords a-port they gave the command, 'Attention — company, Shoulder — arms!' And, presto, how those guns would immediately find a lodgment on our shoulders in all conceivable ways, just as we used to carry our rifles when hunting game in the Maumee woods."[9]

Drilling and maneuvering by companies and battalions on the parade ground just east of camp occupied much of December and the first three weeks of January 1862. Initially, wrote Loop, "we thought that another day of such hard soldiering and marching would make us fit subjects for a coroner's inquest, as we were quite sure ... our organs of locomotion would drop off, and our arms be pulled out of their sockets. Thankful we were when we turned our faces toward camp, where we threw ourselves down on last night's couch, and meditated upon the uncertainties of life."[10]

Constant repetition of evolutions on the drill field soon transformed the 68th's "awkward squads" into a homogeneous body of men, their progress critically monitored in large part by Major Snook, Adjutant Welles and Company H's captain, James J. Vorhes, a Sandusky County veteran of the Mexican War. On several occasions groups of local citizens and dignitaries braved the season's biting winds and cold temperatures to observe the trainees at work. One assemblage from Henry County's Florida township "came loaded with provisions" on New Year's Day "and urged us to partake," recorded Sergeant William A. Ward of Company H. "When we had indulged as long as prudence dictated and in some instances even to satiety, we formed into companies and repaired to the parade ground where we made several manoeuvres on double quick to the apparent satisfaction of [the] spectators." Carrying a regimental flag presented on Christmas Day by these same citizens, the 68th concluded its exercises by forming a hollow square. In the center, the Florida delegation presented Lieutenant Colonel Scott with a "splendid" sword and scabbard. Scott promised "that the sword will ever be drawn in defense of right, and in opposition to wrong, in defense of the cause we are going forth to defend, against all that oppose us, from whatever quarter they may come." [11]

Noble rhetoric, the enlisted men agreed, but as January's gray, overcast days passed they chafed for relief from the "dull monotony of 'camp life,' and bread and pork and pork and bread." During the new year's first weekend 13 men slipped past the guard and "made tracks for the 'rural deestricks'," although all returned to camp within 24 hours. Neighboring farmers complained of missing fowl, especially chickens. Most of these, undoubtedly, found their way into Camp Latty's cooking kettles. "Suffice it to say," admitted Private Loop, "that some of the boys who had seen service in the 21st and 14th Ohio ... had learned well how to forage." [12]

Such perceived depredations prompted Thomas Morrison, editor of the Napoleon *North-West,* to urge marching orders for the 68th "at the earliest possible moment" (all 10 companies had been mustered into Federal service by Christmas Eve). Morrison claimed "The boys are positively 'spoiling for a fight,' and are getting so obstreperous as to cause their officers no little trouble and annoyance. Their presence here also is thought to have an unfavorable effect upon the longevity of poultry. By all means give the boys an early chance at the secesh." [13]

The opportunity moved a step closer January 22 when the regiment struck tents, loaded baggage and boarded railcars at Napoleon's depot. With its departure Camp Latty's existence came to an end. Traveling first to Toledo, the regiment arrived in Columbus the next morning. "The 68th," reported the *Ohio State Journal,* "made a splendid appearance, and we heard several persons declare that it was the finest looking regiment that has passed through our city." The men continued west on foot to Camp Chase via the National Road, ordinarily a good turnpike, but that afternoon covered with almost three inches of oozing mud.[14]

It was "rather disagreeable marching," Company C sergeant Jacob Bruner informed his wife by letter in the evening. On the other hand, he wrote, "Camp Chase is as much ahead of Camp Latty as a mansion is ahead of a hovel. We don't use tents but every mess has a frame house. It looks more like a village than a camp. We have 6 bunks 3 high one above the other. We have rough tables to write upon and very good benches to set upon with stoves &c. We can take care of our things now. It was a great bore on me to keep my things in order at Camp Latty but now there is no trouble."[15]

In common with everyone else in the regiment, Bruner, a 29-year-old Antwerp attorney and father of three, waited impatiently for the paymaster's first visit. Money matters were a constant topic in his early correspondence; even the trifling amount paid for each bar of soap he shipped in a package to Paulding County was mentioned. An amateur lyricist, Bruner began composing patriotic songs at Camp Latty for Companies C and E, then penned a nine-stanza ditty with chorus titled "The Sixty-Eighth," sung to the air "We're Camped Here in the Wilderness." During off-duty hours at Camp Chase he parlayed his talent into supplemental income, as related home with considerable ardor: "I send you a copy of a song which I wrote last week called 'Root hog or die.' I got 1,000 printed at Columbus for $2.00 and sold Twelve dollars and 84 cents worth in one day! I got over $6.00 in silver and the rest in writing paper, stamps, envelop[es] & Sutler tickets which I can sell now and get cash. I have a fellow selling and peddling for me to day. Altogether I have sold Thirteen dollars and fourteen cents worth and have 5 or 6 hundred [copies] left. I expect to clear $20.00 on it which is $3.00 a verse or 76 cents a line! or 10 cents a word not counting chorus."[16]

Bruner's entrepreneurial venture had merit, but to Sergeant Ward of Company H there was another fellow in camp whose business, he believed, was a decided demerit. This was the regimental sutler, a civilian contract merchant who sold non-issue "luxury"

***Opposite:* A stained copy of "Root Hog Or Die," written in late January 1862 by Sergeant Jacob Bruner of Company C.**

Ohio Historical Society

ROOT HOG OR DIE.

BY ONE IN THE SIXTY-EIGHTH.

All the papers say Johnny Bull had a notion
Not to let Uncle Sam's vessels sail upon the ocean;
But he mustn't do it again, and I will tell you why,
If he does, Uncle Sam will make him root hog or die.

CHORUS—For the whole Yankee Nation has raised a mighty cry,
B-i-g pig, little pig, root hog or die.

Old Jeff and Beauregard hate the Constitution,
They thought they'd act sharp and get up a revolution;
Says old Jeff to Beauregard, "We'll do it on the sly!"
But we're just the boys to make 'em root hog or die.

CHORUS—For the whole Yankee Nation has raised a mighty cry,
"By the Eternal," they shall root hog or die.

In the month of April, Eighteen and sixty-one,
Jeff Davis took Fort Sumpter from Major Anderson!
But says old General Scott, "My boys I guess we'll try
And see if we can't make 'em root hog or die."

CHORUS—The whole Yankee Nation, &c.

He sent us to Virginia, their chivalry to try:
We routed them at Carrick's Ford and at Phillippi!
It would have done you good I think, to see the rascals fly;
The music which we gave them there was root hog or die.

CHORUS—The whole Yankee Nation, &c.

Down to Fort Hatteras, General Butler went,
To take 'em down a peg or two, he was fully bent;
He knocked 'em in a cocked hat, and didn't half try,
But every ball he sent 'em said "Root hog or die."

CHORUS—The whole Yankee Nation, &c.

Zollicoffer thought he could flog us all himself,
But a ball from Colonel Fry just laid him on the shelf;
At this all the rebels set up a mighty cry,
But we told 'em "Just to dry up, and root hog or die."

CHORUS—The whole Yankee Nation, &c.

The Ohio 57th, Colonel Mungen, can't be beat;
The 58th and 72d 'll thrash the rebels quite complete;
And with the 68th, Colonel Steedman's bound to try,
To give 'em some instructions in root hog or die.

CHORUS—The whole Yankee Nation, &c.

items to the troops — foodstuffs, tobacco, stationery and writing supplies, sometimes liquor — almost always at inflated prices. The soldiers invariably grumbled, but most laid down their money anyway and the sutler turned a tidy profit. Ward, a school teacher, called the sutlery the "Golgotha of the Camp," opining in late January to *The Perrysburg Journal:* "Since the Sixty-eighth went into camp they have spent at the sutler's over five thousand dollars; and that, too, for things that were an injury, rather than an advantage, to the men. Some of the boys have spent one half their wages, and are far worse off than if they had not received such miserable trash. Many of them have spent enough to have kept them at a first class hotel; and instead of receiving a just equivalent for their money, they have had it dealt out to them in raisins, figs, lager-beer, and candies containing poison enough to poison all the rats in Wood Co. If Congress does not rid our camps of these pests, it is time public sentiment should." [17]

Little time remained for further complaint. On the morning of February 9, 892 officers and men departed Camp Chase's barracks, marched to Columbus' train station and again climbed aboard railcars, this time destined for Cincinnati.[18] Before leaving Ohio's capital city, Myron Loop purchased the first of several pocket diaries (whether acquired from post sutler William Jamison or another source is unknown),[19] in which events of future days with the regiment were recorded. Ahead lay the most memorable, defining period of Loop's life. He scarcely imagined, while boarding the steamer *Lebanon* at Cincinnati's crowded levee, that his duty to "Uncle Samuel" would last another three years and five months.[20] Nor did he contemplate that one day his diaries would provide the basis for an engaging narrative history of the 68th Ohio Volunteer Infantry — among the most solid regiments to serve in the western theater of operations under Generals Grant, Sherman, McPherson, Logan and Howard in the Army of the Tennessee.

Myron Benjamin Loop was born October 8, 1838 at Perrysburg, Ohio, the youngest of Jediah and Betsey Loop's four children. The Loops had moved from Cayuga County, N.Y. about 1830, settling on rich farmland near the Maumee River in northern Wood County, Ohio. Jediah Loop died when Myron was a boy; consequently, his mother resettled 17 miles to the southeast on a Sandusky County farm outside Woodville. There, Myron grew to manhood. He was 22 years old when the war's first shots were fired at Fort Sumter, and responded to the government's initial call for volunteers by enlisting April 26, 1861 in Company I, 21st Ohio.[21]

The regiment's three-month service in western Virginia culminated July 17 with a bayonet charge against Confederate forces at Scary Creek in the Kanawha Valley. Blunders were committed by both sides in the five-hour fight that cost two 21st officers their lives. Colonel Jesse S. Norton, regimental commander, was severely wounded in the hips and captured. Less than a month later the 21st mustered out at Columbus.[22]

Loop returned home to Woodville unscathed by bullets, which he also eluded in his subsequent service with the 68th Ohio. He was hospitalized twice for brief bouts with diarrhea (a common Civil War malady), and required medical attention December 2, 1864 from the regimental surgeon. While tearing up railroad track near Millen, Ga., during Sherman's celebrated March to the Sea, Loop badly injured two fingers of his right hand. They were splinted and Loop wore his right arm in a sling when Sherman's troops occupied Savannah three weeks later.[23]

Two months after his July 1865 discharge Loop married Mary L. Jay of Toledo. By 1883 the couple produced five daughters (two other children died in infancy) while living in Woodville and Steuben County, Ind. They divorced in January 1886, Mary receiving full custody of the girls who ranged in age from 2 to 19. Loop packed his trunks and headed west, finding a new residence in the central Kansas hamlet of Geneseo, 12 miles from the Rice County seat of Lyons. In August 1887 he married a local woman, Sadie A. Piper, at Lyons' United Presbyterian Church. They had no children, but eventually three of Loop's daughters also moved to Kansas, ostensibly to be closer to their father.[24]

The aging farmer continued working, though manual labor became increasingly difficult to perform due to his right hand's crippled fingers. He began devoting more time to affairs of the Grand Army of the Republic, the nation's largest organization of Union Civil War veterans. Obtaining equitable pensions for wounded, injured or disabled soldiers was a major concern to G.A.R. membership, whose advocacy was championed through the pages of *The National Tribune,* published as a weekly newspaper beginning in August 1881. Furthermore, *The Tribune* encouraged ex-soldiers and sailors to send in editorial matter "of historical interest, incidents, or amusing anecdotes of the war." Initial response was slow, but in the two decades between 1885 and 1905 contributions from readers flooded the newspaper's Washington, D.C. office.[25] Among those writing was Myron Loop.

His first article was printed December 1, 1898 — 32 paragraphs topped by the headline "Sounding the Alarm. The 68th Ohio's Trying Time at the Battle of Atlanta." A second, shorter piece describing his regiment's May 1863 actions at Champion Hill, Miss., followed four weeks later. About this time (or possibly earlier), Loop began composing a much longer, comprehensive, chronological memoir of service with the 68th. He relied largely on entries from his wartime diaries, which escaped an 1879 fire in Woodville that consumed most of his books, personal papers and family records.[26] The manuscript was offered to *Tribune* editor John McElroy, who determined its length required serialization. Beginning September 27, 1900, the first half of Loop's account appeared in 11 of the next 12 issues under the title "Campaigning with the Buckeyes. Ten Thousand Miles with the 68th Ohio." These "sketches," using a phrase popular at the time, traced early days at Camps Latty and Chase to veteran furlough in the spring of 1864. Publication of the narrative's final 10 installments, covering the Atlanta Campaign, March to the Sea, Carolinas Campaign and muster-out, did not resume until May 9, 1901, when it was retitled "Rounding-up the Confederacy. Veteran Campaigns of the Gallant 68th Ohio, Under Uncle Billy Sherman." The following week the subtitle was shortened to "Veteran Campaigns of the 68th Ohio," which was retained until the series concluded July 11, 1901.

Although the extent of editing performed on the original manuscript by McElroy or his colleagues is not known, Loop's chronicle as published in *The Tribune* painted a vivid picture of life as a private soldier in a well-respected Western regiment. Blessed with keen wit and sharp powers of observation, he effectively captured the collective experience of his comrades as well. Historian Richard A. Sauers, who has indexed Civil War material in *The Tribune,* labeled Loop's account an Army of the Tennessee "classic," fully "deserving to be brought to a wider audience."[27]

For this Blue Acorn Press presentation some further minor editing was applied. Spelling of proper names has been standardized and in some cases corrected. More complete identification of certain individuals, places and dates is supplied within brackets, but punctuation has been left essentially intact. Chapter divisions have been created that do not necessarily match content breaks of separate installments in the original series.

Additionally, a Notes section follows each chapter. These feature excerpts from wartime diaries, letters and official reports written by 40 other regimental personnel that corroborate, enhance or explain incidents described by Loop. Together, they represent the largest assemblage to date of 68th Ohio narratives gathered in one place.

In the wake of his articles' publication, Loop likely took pride in the approbation of surviving veterans who, in dwindling numbers, continued to attend reunions, reminisce about past glories, erect monuments and lobby for increased pensions. "To further introduce myself," he wrote to the U.S. Commissioner of Pensions in 1913, "cite to the files of the National Tribune." Nine years later, on May 26, 1922, Myron Loop passed away at his central Kansas home. He was 83.

Richard A. Baumgartner
Huntington, West Virginia

Notes to Introduction

1. M.B. Loop and I.M. Kelsey CSR, RG 94, NARA; M.B. Loop pension records, RG 94, NARA; *Official Roster of the Soldiers of the State of Ohio in the War of the Rebellion, 1861-1866* (Akron, Cincinnati, Norwalk, 1886-1895), vol. I, p. 439-440, vol. V, p. 661, 663. Hereafter referred to as *Ohio Roster.*

2. Whitelaw Reid, *Ohio in the War. Her Statesmen, Generals and Soldiers* (Cincinnati: The Robert Clarke Company, 1895), vol. II, p. 4.

3. Samuel H. Steedman obituary, *The Perrysburg Journal,* April 15, 1887; Myron B. Loop, "Campaigning with the Buckeyes. Ten Thousand Miles with the 68th Ohio," *The National Tribune,* Sept. 27, 1900; Reid, vol. I, p. 785-786.

4. *The National Cyclopaedia of American Biography,* vol. XII (New York: James T. White & Company, 1904), p. 175-176.

5. Robert B. Roberts, *Encyclopedia of Historic Forts: The Military, Pioneer, and Trading Posts of the United States* (New York: MacMillan Publishing Company, 1988), p. 643; O. Morrow & F.W. Bashore, compilers, *Historical Atlas of Paulding County, Ohio* (Madison, Wis.: The Western Publishing Company, 1892); Loop, "Campaigning with the Buckeyes," *The National Tribune,* Sept. 27, 1900.

6. S.H. Steedman, R.K. Scott, J.S. Snook and G.E. Welles CSR, RG 94, NARA; Reid, vol. II, p. 103-104; *Paulding Independent,* June 25, 1863; Loop, "Campaigning with the Buckeyes," *The National Tribune,* Sept. 27, 1900; Roger D. Hunt & Jack R. Brown, *Brevet Brigadier Generals in Blue* (Gaithersburg, Md.: Olde Soldier Books, Inc., 1997), p. 657.

7. W.H. Loop and R. Masters CSR, RG 94, NARA; Loop, "Campaigning with the Buckeyes," *The National Tribune,* Sept. 27, 1900.

William Loop, 34, served only four months with the regiment. Hospitalized in April 1862 at Cincinnati, he died at his Sandusky County home May 31, 1862 of typhoid fever.

8. Loop, "Campaigning with the Buckeyes," *The National Tribune*, Sept. 27, 1900.

9. *Ibid.* The regiment's weapons were issued on New Year's Day 1862. *The Perrysburg Journal,* Jan. 16, 1862. Prior to receiving their Enfields "we used clubs in place of guns," recalled Company E private Oscar B. Lingle. "Before we drew our guns they put guards around the camp to keep the boys from going to town. But the boys would fool the guards by pretending they were going for water. Then they would hide their pail and go off up to town. I remember one night they put me out near the spring with an old flint-lock gun with orders [that] if any one started off to halt them, and if they failed to halt, shoot. It was safe to say no one tried to go that night." *Henry County, Ohio,* vol. 1 (Napoleon: Henry County Historical Society, 1976), p. 302-303.

10. Loop, "Campaigning with the Buckeyes," *The National Tribune*, Sept. 27, 1900.

11. J.J. Vorhes CSR, RG 94, NARA; William A. Ward, Jan. 1, 1862, to *The Perrysburg Journal*, Jan. 16, 1862.

12. *The Perrysburg Journal,* Jan. 16, 1862; *Toledo Blade,* Jan. 18, 1862; Loop, "Campaigning with the Buckeyes," *The National Tribune,* Sept. 27,

1900.

13. *Toledo Blade,* Jan. 18, 1862.

14. Roberts, p. 643; *Ohio State Journal,* Jan. 24, 1862.

15. Jacob Bruner to Martha Bruner, Jan. 23, 1862, J. Bruner Papers, OHS.

16. Bruner letters of Jan. 23 and 29, 1862, OHS.

17. William A. Ward in *The Perrysburg Journal,* Feb. 13, 1862.

18. The figure of 892 was reported by Col. Steedman in the regiment's Record of Events. See Janet B. Hewett, editor, *Supplement to the Official Records of the Union and Confederate Armies* (Wilmington, N.C.: Broadfoot Publishing Company, 1997), pt. II, vol. 53, serial no. 65, p. 509. Loop stated regimental strength when leaving Ohio was 950.

19. David E. Schenkman, *Civil War Sutler Tokens and Cardboard Scrip* (Bryans Road, Md.: Jade House Publications, 1983), p. 63.

20. Jacob Bruner to Martha Bruner, Feb. 11, 1862, OHS; *Ohio Roster,* vol. V, p. 663.

21. M.B. Loop pension records, RG 94, NARA; *Ohio Roster,* vol. I, p. 440.

22. Reid, vol. II, p. 148-149; Stan Cohen, *The Civil War in West Virginia: A Pictorial History* (Missoula, Mont.: Gateway Printing & Litho, 1976), p. 21.

23. M.B. Loop pension records, RG 94, NARA.

24. Ibid.

25. Richard A. Sauers, *"To Care For Him Who Has Borne the Battle": Research Guide to Civil War Material in the National Tribune* (Jackson, Ky.: History Shop Press, 1995), p. xv-xvi.

26. M.B. Loop pension records, RG 94, NARA.

27. Richard A. Sauers to the editor, Sept. 21, 2004.

1

'Our hopes and fears, our highly-wrought excitement'

Sunday night [Feb. 9, 1862] found us sweeping down the beautiful Ohio.[1] The next morning we reached Madison, Ind. Here a short stop was made to take on some comrades who, while we were at Camp Chase, had made a flying trip to their homes. Soon after leaving Madison occurred the accidental drowning of J. Ferree, Co. H.[2]

The remainder of our trip down the Ohio was uneventful. We passed Louisville, Ky., Evansville, Ind., and on Tuesday, Feb. 11, found ourselves in company with a portion of Gen. Grant's army at Paducah, Ky. We were assigned to a brigade commanded by Col. Thayer, 1st Nebraska.[3] Tuesday evening we, in company with several other boats loaded with troops, started up the Tennessee River to Fort Henry, to reinforce the troops that had preceded us. Tuesday night we met a dispatch boat, and were informed that our gunboats had silenced Fort Henry, and were in possession of the only rebel stronghold on the Tennessee. We then turned around and started on our return to Paducah. Some of the boys became very enthusiastic, and declared the surrender of Fort Henry had settled the whole shooting match, and we were going home. Eager inquiries were heard on all sides as to why we were going back down the river, but the only answer among my comrades was, "The war is ended; Fort Henry finished it."

We remained at Paducah until Wednesday evening, the 12th, when we started back up the Ohio River. "There, I told you so," said a comrade; "we are going home."

When we reached Smithland, a few miles up the Ohio, the *Lebanon's* prow turned toward the Kentucky side and was soon plowing its way through the waters of the Cumberland. The gunboats *Tyler* and *Lexington* were cautiously leading the way, with a heavy fleet of transports loaded with human freight following in their wake. The heavy laboring of the engines awoke the echoes of either shore, and amid a wild tumult of wind and water a hoarse command assailed our ears: "Attention, 68th. Be ready to land at any moment. We are nearing Fort Donelson."

Our boat carefully felt its way to the west shore, the gang-plank was run out, and early on the morning of Friday, Feb. 14, the 68th Ohio landed on the soil of Tennessee. In plain view, but out of range, were the big guns of Fort Donelson.

After breakfast we engaged in studying our surroundings, and the sight that met our eyes was worth going many miles to see. The gunboats were firing. Our meditations were brought to an abrupt close by a shrill voice of command. Never did a body of men obey with more alacrity, and in less time than it takes to tell it we were in line ready to move upon the foe. We took a road leading out among the hills to the right, but about 12 o'clock returned to the boats. Soon after we moved to the left, and with the rest of Thayer's Brigade[4] took a position about half a mile from the river, forming the extreme left of Gen. Grant's line investing the fort. Here a detail was made, and we had our first experience in realities of war.

Extending all along our entire front was a deep and heavily wooded ravine, on the opposite side of which the ground ascended sharply. On the top of this high ground could be seen a long line of Confederate rifle pits, from which came whistling unpleasantly near the deadly minie balls.

A body of sharpshooters[5] was now ordered forward, and for a time there was more or less firing at long range between the pickets of friend and foe. Meantime our regiment remained standing in line of battle, watching our front, and listening to the heavy guns of our gunboats and the Confederate fort.

Such was about the position of things on our portion of the line on the night of Feb. 14. On that memorable Friday night we were the recipients of a pearly white valentine sent down from Heaven. Several inches of snow had fallen, which made our first night's experience on the soil of Tennessee an extremely cold and trying one.

On Saturday afternoon we witnessed a most gallant and successful charge by an Iowa brigade of Gen. C.F. Smith's Division. Silently we stood and watched those proud columns, saw them waver, then rush onward and upward in the face of a withering fire, and as they reached the top a loud cheer broke from our lips. This hill commanded the interior works of the enemy.[6]

Meantime we were engaged in holding an assigned position on

the extreme left of Gen. Grant's line, where we remained until night wrapped her mantle of darkness around us. After having fully prepared ourselves, being without tents, to weather the trials of another stormy night, we lay down on the frozen ground. We passed the night much better than the previous one.

Early on Sunday morning we marched well around to the right, and were placed in the front line of battle in Gen. Smith's command. Soon after reaching the position we were ordered to fix bayonets, the rumor being that we were assigned to a heavy column whose purpose was to make a grand assault upon the Confederate works. Our hearts were beating high with suppressed excitement, as we stood there in the early morning hours waiting for orders to move forward, expecting every moment that the wild crash of artillery and musketry would assail our ears.[7]

A heavy fog hung over the country which shut from our view surrounding objects; yet we maintained a close watch along the dusky horizon in our front. Suddenly the fog lifted. In our front we saw a white flag, and off to our right another; to our left another. Only a moment to satisfy ourselves of its meaning, and then a glad shout was heard as the glorious truth flashed through our minds. Fort Donelson had surrendered.

This was the first great victory for the Union. There were surrendered, besides a Confederate force of several thousand, nearly 70 heavy guns and an immense amount of supplies.[8]

Fort Donelson was located on a high bluff on the south side of the Cumberland River, about 100 feet above the waters of the beautiful river that flowed at its foot. There were heavy water batteries commanding the river, while the upper batteries were of lighter caliber, and were strongly posted in defense of the rear. There was also an elaborate system of earthworks, which extended in a semicircle nearly up to the village of Dover, one mile above the fort.

Soon after the surrender we marched inside the Confederate works, and after viewing the heavy guns we returned to the rear, where, exposed to the elements, we braved another night in Tennessee. Early on Monday morning we moved up to the eastern extremity of the works and made our camp on a sloping hillside near the village of Dover. Here it was we received our tents, which we had not seen since leaving our camp at Napoleon, O.

After going into camp, our rations being nearly exhausted, we were ordered to supply our wants from the Confederate supplies stored at Dover. Eating too heartily of rice and molasses thus secured made many of the boys dangerously ill. This caused a report that the Confederate stores had been poisoned. But upon careful examination by a board of medical men it was determined that such was not true, but that the sickness in camp was due to exposure and other causes incident to our hard campaigning.

Our first loss at Dover was Isaac Hooker, Co. C, who died Feb. 19.[9] During the few days following occurred a loss of nearly 100 comrades, many of whom died and were buried at Dover, or were removed on hospital boats to breathe their lives away in different hospitals and among strangers. During the months of March, April and May 1862 the mortality in our regiment exceeded our total loss from all causes during any succeeding six months of our service.[10]

On Tuesday, March 4, we were the happy recipients of our first pay as soldiers of the Republic.

Passing over the many incidents of the camp, our hopes and fears, our highly-wrought excitement, and then our deep dejection, we arrive at March 7, when we received marching orders. Night found us in camp in a dense wood, having crossed a tract of country void of timber, which had been used in iron works near where we passed. The following day we marched a short distance and made camp near a place named Metal Landing, on the Tennessee River, there to await transports to convey us farther into the heart of rebellion. When leaving our camp on the Cumberland, Serg't. L. W. Richardson, Co. G, was detailed to take command of those unable to march, who were sent around on the transports, and again joined the regiment at Metal Landing.[11]

We remained in camp till the morning of March 15, when we were set in motion and went on board the transport *Minnehaha.* We remained at the landing until Sunday morning, the 16th, when our boat dropped down the river to Fort Henry, and after loading with commissary stores, started back up the beautiful Tennessee. We continued on our course up the Tennessee all day and night, and early on Monday morning found ourselves at a place which afterward became famous in history as Pittsburg Landing.

I think I am safe in saying that, with the exception of a small body of cavalry which had disembarked at the upper landing and had engaged a force of the enemy that same afternoon, our regiment was among the first Union troops to set foot upon the soil of Pittsburg Landing. The proof of this was a number of hogs we found quietly feeding in a field nearby, which did not take fright upon our approach.

During the day, having been previously assigned to the command of Gen. Lew Wallace,[12] we were ordered to return to the boats, after which we dropped down to a place called Crump's Landing. Here our boat forced its way through brush and saplings fringing the shore until near enough for the gang-plank to reach land.

During the landing of artillery and horses at this place a horse fell overboard, which after swimming round the boat boldly struck out and crossed to the east side of the river, apparently heartily enjoying its bath. After landing we went into camp in a beautiful grove a short distance from the river. Our camp at Crump's was a great contrast to our camp at Dover. A warm southern sun beamed upon us, and a balmy southwind, which had taken the place of the cold, chilly blasts from the frozen north, made us feel happy and contented.

My memory often reverts to our first night at Crump's, when it seemed by one consent the boys opened their hearts, and our great National anthem, "The Red, White and Blue," floated on the shores of the Tennessee. One and all joined in the grand chorus. Our merrymaking continued long into the night, when an approaching storm of wind and rain, accompanied by vivid flashes of lightning and crashing of Heaven's artillery, burst in its wildest fury upon us. Not an eye was closed in sleep that long night, as a flood of water swept down the hillside, forcing its way into our sleeping room. As another day dawned upon us the sun came out, and its warm, cheerful rays soon made us forget our trials of the preceding night.

On Tuesday night, March 18, our regiment was called out for picket duty. After a hasty inspection we were marched away and soon reached a position bordering a heavily-wooded ravine, where a heavy picket guard was put out, the regiment remaining posted in reserve. It had been reported during the day that a force of the enemy had been seen on the road leading from Crump's Landing to Purdy. This report kept the picket line on the alert.

During the still hours of the night the noise of a man or beast moving about in the shadows in front was distinctly heard, and occasionally a shadowy form could be seen. The picket was wide awake. One of Co. K watched with eagle eye the movements of the shadowy form pictured in the darkness. At last, tired of further suspense, and not wishing to be captured by a Johnny, he sent a whole broadside into the bushes. The shot aroused the whole camp, as well as the reserve, who sprang to their feet, thinking the whole rebel army was near at hand. After a while all became quiet, save for the squeal of a hog that had attempted to pass the picket line without giving the countersign.

The comrade had in his make-up the vein of the humorous, so when the picket officer censured him for disturbing the quiet of the camp by willfully shooting at a hog, he replied: "That darn hog had no business to be monkeying around, no how." This response wrung a smile from the picket officer, who said no more.

The succeeding 10 days we engaged in the daily routine of the camp. Our first loss while here was L.K. Neer, Co. K, who died March 18.[13]

We remained at Crump's Landing until March 30, when we were ordered to break camp. We marched out on the Purdy road about four miles, where we again pitched our tents, being then north of Shiloh about five miles. The days were pleasant and the air full of balmy influences of Spring. Nature had begun to robe herself in garbs of green, pink and white. But there came a change, as on April 4 a terrific storm of wind and rain burst upon us. A tree blew down, which fell on a tent in Co. K, severely injuring two comrades.

On the ever memorable day of Sunday, April 6, we were in camp near Crump's plantation, and were busily engaged in preparing our breakfast, when the morning breeze wafted to our ears the heavy boom of a cannon, then another, and another, until there seemed hardly a second between the sounds, accompanied by the sullen roar of volley upon volley of musketry.

We were ordered to "fall in." A large force of the enemy was reported in our front. Batteries went sweeping into position, and all was excitement and everything in motion. But no enemy put in an appearance.

The terrible roar of battle still continued with unabated fury, which meantime appeared to be moving farther to our left. What did it mean? was the all-absorbing question.

About the hour of noon, Gen. Wallace, with a portion of his command, moved away in the direction of the sound of battle near Pittsburg Landing.[14] But Sunday night found our regiment near our camp of the morning. The flood-gates of heaven were open, the rain fell in torrents, and it almost seemed that we could reach forth our hands and grasp the bolts of electric fire. The awful thundering of heaven's artillery, interspersed with the bellowing of the gunboats on the Tennessee, made weird music to us who were not familiar with the state of affairs on Shiloh's field.

At last Monday morning came with long arrows of electric fire shooting back over the heavens, and with it came a renewal of battle. From beyond the green hills came the crash of battle — a rippling roar of musketry punctuated by the deep boom of artillery. The sound of battle gradually drew nearer the direction whence it came on the previous morning, which told us the enemy was being forced back. About 3 o'clock in the afternoon the sound of conflict suddenly died away, the enemy hastily retiring to their intrenchments at Corinth [Miss.].

During the second day's battle Lieut. Col. Scott and Capt. Richards were Aids to Col. Thayer on the field, and were highly commended for meritorious services. Col. Scott's horse was shot under him.[15]

We remained in camp until April 16, when we took up our line of march back to the Tennessee River. Next day we passed through our late camp, and as night came upon us went into camp in a large cottonfield. On the following day we marched over a portion of the recent battlefield, and pitched our tents in an oak grove on the west side of a deep and boggy ravine, known as Snake Creek. Here we remained for some days. After going into camp we gave our attention to peeling bark and cutting poles, which we converted into camp sofas and settees.

When not on duty we rambled over different portions of the battlefield and stood beside the little mound where slept some dear comrade who went down on that fateful Sunday. Here it was noticed, and the trees were our silent witnesses, that had the leaden balls swept the ground from two to six feet, the same as from 10 to 20 feet, few could have escaped.

On Monday, April 21, we were engaged in cutting timber and building a corduroy road across the low, swampy ground between our camp and the high grounds on the east. We were amateurs in building causeways, yet we soon completed our work, which enabled our commissary trains to move forward.

Nothing of special interest occurred until Monday, April 28, when we moved about eight miles in the direction of Corinth. A heavy rain began to fall early in the evening and continued through the night.[16] We remained in camp until the evening of the next day, when we were ordered forward to the support of the picket line, which was hotly engaged with the enemy. On April 30 we were in motion at the break of day. We moved to the right about three miles, and then retraced our steps to camp, where we remained three days. A few more days of preparation seemed necessary to the slow-going Halleck.[17] The days had been in many respects the same. But now they began to grow heavy with the signs of an approaching storm — a meeting of the giants around Corinth.

On Sunday, May 4, we received orders to march. At an early hour we were in motion and moved about four miles through a heavy rain, which continued throughout the day. May 5 rain was still falling. We started to march, but made slow progress. During the day a portion of the regiment was engaged in assisting the mules to drag our wagons through the mud. In the evening we went into camp on Pea Ridge — also called Stony Lonesome — wet, muddy and cold. Those were times that tested our endurance.

Day after day we advanced our line and then engaged in throwing up earthworks throughout the night.[18]

Early on May 15 we moved out to within one mile of Purdy, where we remained until dark, when we retraced our steps one mile and went into bivouac for the night. On the following morning we returned to our old position on the line confronting the enemy. On May 18 we were ordered out on the double-quick, and away we went, jumping logs and dodging the overhanging brush to support the picket line, which was warmly engaged. On the 19th and 20th there was heavy cannonading all along our front, after which all became quiet except the incessant firing of the pickets. And thus, day after day, the great siege of Corinth progressed.

On May 28 a warm engagement took place on our left, which caused us to grip our guns more firmly and watch our front with jealous care. Early the following day we were called into line and hastily moved off in the direction of Corinth. Indications were that a struggle for the possession of Corinth was about to take place. We moved forward with slight resistance until we could look over the enemy's line of works and see the village of Corinth in the distance, after which a halt was ordered. On May 30 we were called into line on our front. Orders were issued to be in readiness to march at a moment's notice. Yet we remained in idle expectancy, and were informed later on of the cause of the heavy explosions in our front. The rebels were engaged in blowing up their magazines and evacuating Corinth.

During the siege of Corinth we were assigned to the Army of the Reserve, under Gen. McClernand, whose duty was to construct roads, keep our cracker line open and watch any force of the enemy that might be operating on flank or rear.[19]

We also furnished large details of working parties, engaged in constructing earthworks and bastions to cover and protect our front, which no sooner completed than a new line would be established a half mile or less in advance in the direction of the besieged rebel hosts at Corinth; the cutting of large trees and hauling or rolling heavy logs to build breastworks, only to be abandoned as soon as finished, and the same tedious work to be repeated on some newly-selected portion of the line. Thus the great advance on Corinth was conducted, under the direct command of Maj. Gen. Halleck, commander-in-chief, which resulted in the safe withdrawal of the Confederate forces, without the loss of a man, gun or any supplies, leaving nothing but a little straggling Southern village the trophy of that long and trying campaign.

Our ranks were very far from being a matter of congratulation, as we had suffered a loss of two-thirds by death and otherwise of the number that went up the Cumberland River less than four months previous.

On Sunday, June 1, we remained quietly in camp and held regimental inspection, after which the regiment stacked arms. The writer then and there walked along the line and counted the guns. Two hundred and eighty-four was the number, not including a light picket guard. Three hundred and fifty at the most were all that were left of nearly 1,000 men who landed at Donelson.

Our total loss by death since leaving Camp Latty, a period of 120 days, was 104. Up to this time about 100 others had been discharged from different hospitals as unfit for military service. Add to the above the 350 that were with the regiment on June 1, and we have a total of 554, leaving a balance of 400 in hospitals, sick. A number of the latter joined the regiment at Bolivar, Tenn., while others were discharged from the service, or died in the hospitals.

Notes to Chapter 1

1. The 68th Ohio's 10 companies left Cincinnati equally divided aboard the steamers *Lebanon* and *Hazel Dell.*

2. Pvt. John C. Ferree was 39 years old. According to Sergt. William Ward, Co. H, Ferree was survived by a family of seven children. Sergt. Jacob Bruner, Co. C, wrote that "several said they saw him fall [overboard] and heard him holler for help but when the skiff went out all was quiet. Poor fellow!" *Ohio Roster,* vol. V, p. 659; *The Perrysburg Journal,* Feb. 20, 1862; Bruner to Martha Bruner, Feb. 11, 1862, OHS.

3. Col. John M. Thayer, a native of Massachusetts, had moved to Nebraska Territory in 1854 and gained some renown as an Indian fighter before the Civil War. He was promoted to brigadier general in 1863 and brevet major general in 1865. Ezra J. Warner, *Generals in Blue: Lives of the Union Commanders* (Baton Rouge: Louisiana State University Press, 1993), p. 499-500.

4. At Fort Donelson, Thayer's 3rd Brigade of Brig. Gen. Lew Wallace's 3rd Division consisted of the 58th, 68th and 76th Ohio, and 1st Nebraska Infantry. Temporarily attached to Thayer were the 46th, 57th and 58th Illinois. *The War of the Rebellion: A Compilation of the Official Records of the Union and Confederate Armies* (Washington: Government Printing Office, 1882), series I, vol. VII, p. 169. Hereafter referred to as *OR.*

5. Loop referred to Birge's Western Sharpshooters, later designated the 66th Illinois Infantry.

6. Brig. Gen. Charles F. Smith commanded Grant's 2nd Division. The "Iowa" brigade mentioned by Loop was led by Col. Jacob G. Lauman, consisting of the 2nd, 7th and 14th Iowa, 25th Indiana and Birge's Sharpshooters. *OR,* vol. VII, p. 168.

Lt. Ira M. Kelsey, Co. I, 68th Ohio, wrote of Lauman's assault: "On the afternoon of [Feb.] fifteenth the second Iowa, supported by the seventh and fourteenth Iowa and twenty-fifth Indiana made a splendid charge in full view of our lines, on the enemies outworks, driving him from his battery and rifle pit, over a half mile nearer his main fort. I saw the whole manoever through a spy glass. Every minute as they ascended the hill on which the battery they were charging was situated, their gallant ranks were thinned by a murderous fire, but on they went never flinching, halting or firing, until they arrived at the first entrenchment, when they po[u]red in a destructive fire. ... Did they stop, no, on they went to the battery that was flanked by rifle-pit[s], loading and firing as they went, until the hill was cleared of every traitor able to get away. Night closing in, they rested on their arms, maintaining the ground taken." Kelsey, Feb. 20, 1862, in *The Perrysburg Journal,* March 13, 1862.

7. Twelve days later, regimental quartermaster James G. Haly reported: "About 6 o'clock in the evening [of Feb. 15], Gen. Grant, having been informed that ours was a 'No. 1' regiment, notified Col. Steedman to hold himself in readiness to move at daylight to the right, for the purpose of engaging the enemy. This was what the boys had been waiting for for two days, and all were delighted. You ought to have seen 'Old Harry's' eyes light up at the prospect of storming the entrenchments of the enemy. Steedman ... remained on his horse during the whole of the first night, throwing out his pickets and reconnoitering parties to the front, to prevent surprise, notwithstanding the regiment [was] in full view of the enemy's works, and almost within range of their rifles. ... Colonel Scott was on hand at every point, giving orders and encouraging the boys, and aching all over for the moment to come when we would be ordered up to the enemy's breastworks." Haly to his wife, Feb. 27, 1862, in the Napoleon *North-West,* March 12, 1862.

8. About 12,000 Confederates under Brig. Gen. Simon B. Buckner surrendered at Fort Donelson. E.B. Long, *The Civil War Day by Day: An Almanac 1861-1865* (Garden City, N.Y.: Doubleday & Company, Inc., 1971), p. 172.

After Donelson's capitulation, Sergt. William Ward, Co. H, wrote: "We took about sixty cannon, as nearly as I can learn ... but I have been all around the fortifications and have seen but forty-two. We took about six hundred horses, four hundred cattle, and three hundred hogs, and about $40,000 worth of ammunition and other stores, twenty-five thousand stand of arms. ... I have conversed with quite a number of the prisoners, and they all claim to have been misled. Several of them expressed the hope that this would end the war, and some even cheered the stars and stripes as we came in. One fellow said it was four months since he enlisted, and he had not been so well satisfied since, as he was when he found he was a prisoner. Some said they never would have enlisted if they had known [we] were not fighting to free the 'niggers.' Others said their leaders told them we wished to make slaves of them, and their women, and they seemed greatly surprised to find us so humane. They said they expected to be butchered as soon as they fell into our hands. One poor fellow with tears in his eyes, said the time of his enlistment would be out in three days, and he had intended to go home, and stay there." Ward, Feb. 21, 1862, in *The Perrysburg Journal*, March 6, 1862.

9. Pvt. Isaac Hooker, a 20-year-old laborer, enlisted Nov. 20, 1861 at Antwerp, Paulding County. His death was attributed to pneumonia. I. Hooker CSR, RG 94, NARA.

10. By the end of February, according to Quartermaster Haly, "We have over 200 of our Regiment sick, mostly measles and diarrhoea. This has been caused, no doubt, by exposure on the field during the battle [of Fort Donelson]." Haly to his wife, Feb. 27, 1862, in the Napoleon *North-West,* March 12, 1862.

"The Regiment is nearly all sick with diarrhoea," observed Sergt. Jacob Bruner, Co. C, early in March. "We are no account at present." Two weeks later he wrote that "from 100 to 150 are sick ... under the Doctors hands. More than 20 men are dead. Co. C has lost 4 men." Bruner to Martha Bruner, March 4 and 18, 1862, OHS.

Fifer Eli M. Bundy, Co. G, also wrote in mid-March to his family in Henry County: "the health of the regiment is very poor   our regiment is reported as not fit for laborious duty consequently will not go in frunt   day befour yesterday the physician reported but 240 Sound men in the regiment mostly dyarie and fevors   among the dead is John Meikesel [John B. Mikesell] our fife major   he died [March 11] at Donelson." Bundy himself died of typhoid fever July 16, 1862 at Bolivar, Tenn. Bundy to his wife, March 17,

1862, CAC; E.M. Bundy CSR, RG 94, NARA.

Using the pen name "Sixty-Eighth Regiment," an unidentified member of Co. B wrote April 4: "We have found an enemy here more potent than the Confederates, and which is wasting our energies and our numbers daily. I mean sickness, and of this we have had almost all kinds that 'flesh is heir to' —measles, mumps, diarrhoea, and of fevers, typhoid, remitting, intermitting and continued. Palsies, agues, and joint-racking rheums, they too have had their victims. It was as appalling a sight as ever I witnessed, when we arrived at this place [Crump's Landing, Tenn.] two weeks ago. Two-thirds of our Regiment were sick, in hospitals, or prostrate upon the steamboat, and some were dying. We had no way to make the sick comfortable, and nothing except the hard bread and salt pork for them to eat. God help the sick soldier! for if he does not, there is no hope for him. The whole surgical staff of the army is good for nothing in the treatment of disease. They carry their knives, saws, and probes, and would be ready to amputate a limb or trace the direction of a ball, but consider it beneath their dignity to see to the comfort of the sick, who lie in some ill-ventilated hospital, dying for lack of care, nourishment and treatment. I wish they were all away, and some good old woman in their place, to nurse and properly treat the sick and we should save lives thereby. I hope the State authorities will think seriously of this, for I speak of it in all seriousness. Our armies always lose in Southern latitudes, ten by sickness to one in battle, and it is for the treatment of disease that we need physicians. Now, the doctors have not been of the least service to us since we came here, and the friends of deceased soldiers will no doubt require of them a reason for this conduct. I cannot explain it. Our Regiment has lost about fifty men by disease and they are dying still — it is our stoutest men that die." *Defiance Democrat,* April 26, 1862.

In just one group of 28 sick 68th Ohio soldiers transported to hospitals at Cairo, Ill. immediately after Fort Donelson's surrender, 12 died, most of them in March. *Toledo Blade,* March 10, 1862; *Ohio Roster,* vol. V, p.. 796-803.

11. A resident of Napoleon, Lay Whitney Richardson had been first sergeant of Co. F in the 14th Ohio's three-month organization. In the 68th Ohio he eventually was promoted to first lieutenant of Co. G. *Ohio Roster,* vol. I, p. 307; L.W. Richardson CSR, RG 94, NARA.

12. Brig. Gen. Lewis "Lew" Wallace, an Indiana native and Mexican War veteran, was promoted major general to rank from March 21, 1862. He is best known as the author of *Ben Hur: A Tale of the Christ.* Warner, p. 535-536.

"Gen. Wallace seems to be a gentleman of fine ability, industrious and very attentive to business, and not much given to display," thought a member of the 68th's Co. B. "He is much respected in the Division," but "not having received a military education, he is not held in high esteem by those boasting the prestige of an education at the West Point Academy." *Defiance Democrat,* April 26, 1862.

13. Corp. Lewis K. Neer, a Williams County farmer, died of typhoid fever. L.K. Neer CSR, RG 94, NARA.

14. Pvt. Simeon Gillis, Co. K, spent the night of April 5 on picket. Years later he recalled: "At about 9 o'clock, forenoon of the 6th, we of the picket guard were called in. Joining the reserve we marched into camp. To reach our camp we passed through the entire brigade. We found that all the tents had been struck and rolled up, ready to be loaded on wagons, for removal if necessary. The guns of the infantry regiments were stacked at the side of the road, the horses were harnessed to the artillery guns and caissons, and were strung out in the road, headed toward the battlefield; the men of all arms were fully accoutered, ready and anxiously awaiting the command, Forward! On arrival at our camp we found our tents, like the others, ready for shipment; the guns were stacked on the color line, but the men were not accoutered; they stood around in groups looking gloomy and dissatisfied. We soon learned that our regiment, in company with the 56th Ohio [of the division's 3rd Brigade], was to be left to guard the camp equipage, and if necessary to convey all to the landing at Crump's." Simeon Gillis, "The First Gun at Shiloh," *The National Tribune*, Aug. 15, 1901.

15. At Shiloh, Thayer commanded the 2nd Brigade of Lew Wallace's 3rd Division, Army of the Tennessee. In his after-action report, Thayer praised volunteer aides Scott and Capt. Lewis Y. Richards, Co. A, "for their prompt conveyance and execution of orders in the face of all danger." He also cited Dr. Eugene B. Harrison, 68th Ohio and brigade surgeon, for "prompt attention to the wounded. [He] labored at the hospitals with ceaseless devotion for days and nights after the battle in administering relief." Writing a week after Shiloh, Scott simply stated, "It was a grate [*sic*] fight." *OR,* vol. X, pt. 1, p. 102, 195; Scott to P. Chanse, April 15, 1862, R.K. Scott Papers, OHS.

16. Having been promoted regimental quartermaster sergeant a week before Shiloh, Jacob Bruner elaborated on the April 28 excursion: "our Reg. and 4 or five others with a battery of brass cannon (6) went out 6 or 7 miles toward Purdy to 'clean out' a secesh camp but before we got there the cowardly curs ran away as usual! We only took one prisoner. I believe the rest made tracks for the main camp. We had 2 days rations in our haversacks and expected to have a fight but we had to face about and march back to camp where we arrived a little before sundown. It rained on us all day and was not pleasant at all but I had my oil cloth and did not get wet. Every morning at 4 o'clock we have to form in line of battle to prevent the rebels from surprising us as they did before [at Shiloh]." Bruner to Martha Bruner, April 28, 1862, OHS.

17. At the time, Maj. Gen. Henry W. Halleck commanded the Department of the Mississippi. A brilliant administrator, his personal direction of Union field forces in the Corinth campaign was marked by extreme caution resulting in snail-like movement. This was in sharp contrast to statements made to his troops shortly after Shiloh. On April 17 Sergt. William Ward, Co. H, wrote: "General Halleck delivered a speech a few evenings ago in which he said: 'If the heroes of Fort Donelson, and the heroes of Pea Ridge, and the heroes of Pittsburg Landing stand by me I am sure of success in this battle, which will soon be a part of history, and you will be on your way home in eight weeks.' " Warner, p. 196; *The Perrysburg Journal,* May 7, 1862.

18. The terrain traversed by the 68th Ohio as it inched toward Corinth, thought Capt. Hiram H. Poe, Co. I, was "as beautiful a country as God ever made. The land is undulating, and delightful springs gush forth from every hillside and supply the brooks which course along the bottom of every valley, clear as crystal, and cool and refreshing to the thirsty soldier after his day's toilsome marching." Poe, May 10, 1862, to the Napoleon *North-West,* May 21, 1862.

19. During the Union advance upon and siege of Corinth, Maj. Gen. John A. McClernand commanded the Army of the Tennessee's Reserve Corps.

2

'A grabbing for guns and rubbing of eyes'

On June 1 we received orders to be ready to move at 6 o'clock the following morning. The appointed hour found us in motion, and after a march of 12 miles we went into bivouac for the coming night. Early in the morning of June 3 we resumed our march, and, as usual, in the midst of a fall of rain. We marched 15 miles, and as the day began to wane went into camp near a village consisting of half a dozen straggling houses. We drew rations of flour, which meant to the rank and file of our regiment root, hog or die. We must prepare that wheat flour for our suppers or go to bed hungry. We decided to do the former, and began to stir up a pancake batter of flour and creek water. Meantime, others of our comrades turned their attention to making biscuits, which, after being rolled up in forms like those our mothers made, were deposited in the hot embers of our campfire. In due time our supper was ready. But, oh! Officers and men declared that those pancakes struck the soles of their boots with a dull, sickening thud; and as to our improvised biscuits — well, a hog would have backed off, shook his head and squealed in distress.

While the boys were engaged in preparing this flour for supper Col. Scott, who took great interest in his men, viewed the effort with nervous anxiety. Taking a position centrally among his men he shouted: "Men of the 68th Ohio, don't you know that Col. Scott has a number of hogs in the wood over yonder? Don't shoot, but outrun them — if you can." The hint was immediately acted upon, and pork was supplied in profusion.

Early on the 4th we were in motion. We marched 10 miles and made camp. The next day, after a march of eight miles, we reached Bolivar, Tenn. The weather was lovely and a fine country surrounded us, which did much to remove all thoughts of sore trials from Shiloh to Corinth. The citizens with whom we came in contact tried to be friendly toward us, yet we could plainly see their friendship was to some extent assumed. On Friday, June 6, we received three months' pay.

We established our camp one mile north of Bolivar, near the Tennessee & Ohio Railroad, where we remained most of the time until the following November.

About this time a number of our officers were sent north on recruiting service, and as the balmy summer days passed away we commenced to make a better showing, as our ranks began to fill up with new men.

On June 22 six companies of the regiment [including Co. I] were ordered to Grand Junction, 20 miles from Bolivar. However, we did not leave Bolivar until the 29th, reaching the Junction about dark, and made camp in the woods a short distance south of the place. Bolivar being our base of operations, we made frequent marches in different directions for the purpose of chastising any roving bands of the enemy infesting the country around us. In fact, we kept up a regular game on the military chess-board with Price and Van Dorn all summer, and often it got interesting to all parties.[1] Price was a sly old fox, and often played a sharp game, but he never made a move — with one exception — in which he was not checkmated, and quite often he was glad to get out of any hole that was large enough to let him pass through.

Independence Day found us still at Grand Junction, near the Mississippi line, where we were treated to a Fourth of July oration by Col. W.Q. Gresham, Commander of the Post.[2] On the 7th our camp equipage and the other four companies of the regiment arrived from Bolivar, after which we established our camp near the railroad crossing, where we remained until July 24.[3]

All remained quiet around the Junction until July 14, which was the beginning of many exciting days. The enemy was reported in force on our front. Late in the night a rumor was circulated that the enemy was forming to attack us, when a heavy reconnoitering party was ordered out, returning the next day and reporting no enemy in our front.

The three succeeding days were quiet. On the 19th, William and James Badger, of Co. K, and William Glime, of Co. G, while engaged in picking blackberries, ventured a little too far outside of the picket line, when they were captured by the enemy. Two days later they were released and returned to camp.[4]

On July 23 we marched 10 miles in the direction of Bolivar, and went into bivouac. Rumors were current that another rebel force was in our vicinity, which caused a heavy guard to be posted and all precautions taken to guard against a surprise. Before morning we were again in motion, reaching our old camp at Bolivar about 10 o'clock. Here we found a body of men engaged in building heavy earthworks. We were assigned a position in the new-made works. All was excitement about us. A rebel force was in our front, and we were momentarily expecting an attack. Artillerists were standing by their guns with lanyards in hand earnestly watching for any puff of smoke in the timber beyond. Our wall of blue and steel gave no encouragement to those rebel hosts. On July 27, the enemy having retired from our front, everything assumed its usual quiet.

During August we were engaged in the usual daily routine of the camp. After the morning detail for guard came a season of company drill. Twelve o'clock was our dinner hour. Four o'clock in the afternoon dress parade, after which was our supper hour.[5]

The cares of the day passed, now came the evening's amusements. And what dances we had, our partners appearing with a blanket pinned around the waist to give force and variety to the scene. In one of our camp quadrilles was embodied a whole drama of lovemaking. There was never a scene on any theatrical stage that equaled the coquetry of the "gal" who danced away from her lover and seemingly tormented and mocked him, only to be won in the end and kindly escorted to a seat on the ground.

About this time an influx of colored men began.[6] Many were the colored boys that waded swamps during the dark hours of night to notify our commanders of the approach of the enemy. Of these, Little Dick, Big Tom and several others are inseparably connected with the history of our regiment. Dick was a quick-witted fellow, and always had a ready answer when a joke was attempted at his expense. He was unlike Tom and Simon, who were always bubbling over with merriment. These boys made a full team and were the source of much amusement to us.

At the battle of the Hatchie one of our colored boys took a position behind a stump. A six-pound shot struck the stump. The next moment he was headed for the rear, and as he disappeared in a cloud of dust the boys yelled, "Run, Sambo, it's after you!" This increased his gait, and it was said he never stopped until he got back to Bolivar.

During the days of August the regiment gradually increased in strength. Comrades who had been recuperating in Northern homes, or lying in some army hospital, were returning.

While at Bolivar, Maj. Welles came into possession of his war horse, "Polk." Capt. [Marshall T.] Polk, the former owner of the horse, was a wealthy rebel planter. He furnished the horses to equip his artillery battery, which lost so heavily at Shiloh that the battery was disbanded and the horses sent to his plantation near Bolivar. They fell into our hands and were sold at public auction. Maj. Welles paid $60 for Polk. He rode him in 12 general engagements and numerous skirmishes. Polk learned all the bugle calls and was very fond of music, and loved to prance and dance as well as a little darky. At the close of the war Welles brought him home.

During our sojourn at Bolivar the utmost vigilance was maintained, as there was every indication the enemy would make an effort to gain some advantageous position, or to destroy the railroad north of us. The early morning of Aug. 30 we were called to arms. The picket line on the south side of Bolivar had been attacked by rebel cavalry. The picket line held the enemy in check until support came up, which ended the difficulty.

The following day, Sunday, heavy skirmishing took place along the railroad between Bolivar and Jackson. The railroad was torn up, bridges burned, and our cracker line cracked, if not broken. Sept. 1 the 30th Ill. engaged the enemy at Britton Lane. Our regiment was called into line at 4 o'clock in the morning, but our comrades of the 30th Ill. needed no assistance.

Early on the morning of Sept. 2 assembly was sounded, followed a moment later by a shrill voice of command, "Battalion — fall in!" In an incredibly short space of time we were peering over earthworks looking for the enemy, who was said to be on our front and flank. We soon learned that the force in our front was a body of the enemy's cavalry, which, after feeling our outposts, withdrew in haste.

Friday, Sept. 5, we received marching orders. We left camp early and marched out to Whitesville, 12 miles northwest of Bolivar. We reached there about noon and remained until the evening of the next day, when we silently marched five miles in the direction of Bolivar. Sunday morning we again moved forward, reaching camp at Bolivar that afternoon. This march, though a short one, may be mentioned as the most dusty of any during our service.

Many comrades were overcome by dust and heat. We had no water to quench our thirst. At one place we tried to get water from a deep well by the roadside, but the effort was abandoned on account of a hole in the well-bucket. Much of the way one in the ranks could not see the fences on either side of the road, yet we pressed forward and late in the day reached Hatchie River.

Sept. 15 there came a change. We were ordered into line and late in the day boarded a train on the Tennessee & Ohio Railroad. Early the next morning we rolled into Jackson, Tenn. We remained at Jackson until 3 o'clock in the afternoon, when we left [via the Mobile & Ohio Railroad] for Corinth. Late that night we reached Corinth, where we left the train and under cover of darkness pushed on in the direction of Iuka, Miss. Our brigade moved out about two miles, when a halt was ordered to wait for the line to close up. At Corinth George McCoy, our Adjutant's Orderly, and our colored boy, Dick, were left behind with orders to bring on the officers' horses, which were coming on the next train. During our halt the horses came up. Little Dick sprang from the Major's horse and passed around to the opposite side to untie the Quartermaster's mule, when the latter's rear pedals shot out in the darkness, and Dick landed in the bushes some distance away. Dick landed on his head and then came to a halt on his back. We thought he had come to an untimely end, but he jumped to his feet and shouted, "Dum, dum, who dat knock me down?" It was a miraculous escape for Dick, as an army mule's heels were considered almost sure death.

The early morning of Sept. 17 found us in motion. About 2 o'clock in the afternoon we reached Burnsville, 17 miles from Corinth. We remained there until the afternoon of the following day, when we formed in line of battle and cautiously moved forward. We had advanced but a short distance when our skirmishers became warmly engaged. The whole division, under command of Gen. Ord, was now pushed forward, the enemy retiring as we moved upon them; nor did we stop until about 10 o'clock at night, when a halt was ordered to wait for the dawn of another day.[7]

Tired and weary, we lay down beside our guns. About 2 o'clock we were awakened by heavy firing on the picket line. Then there occurred a grabbing for guns and rubbing of eyes. We looked and looked until every stump and bush seemed an enemy. However, no enemy appeared; the firing died away and we resumed our sleep.

The morning of Sept. 19 our attention was called to the enemy, whose line was marked by the smoke of their campfires. We remained quiet until about 4 o'clock in the afternoon when a general advance was ordered. Our skirmishers having brushed away the enemy, we went forward about a mile, when a halt was ordered and we went into bivouac for the night.

The following morning our regiment was detailed to form the skirmish line, and had advanced about one mile in the direction of Iuka, expecting every moment to be fired upon by a concealed foe, when we met a colored man, who informed us “dat de rebils was dun gone; dar was a battle an’ de rebils dun got whipped.” This was the first information we received of the battle of Iuka, fought by Gen. Rosecrans’ forces the previous afternoon. The heavy wind blowing from the west carried the roar of battle away from our position. Nevertheless, we thought it quite singular, considering our close proximity to the field. The colored man was taken to Gen. Grant, to whom he told his story. The skirmishers were called in, the regular order of the march was again taken up, and about noon we stacked our arms in the streets of the straggling village of Iuka and ate our dinner. That same afternoon we marched back to Burnsville, and as night came on made our camp near a large field of green corn.[8]

Our supplies having run low, we made our suppers of corn and beans, which we converted into an old-fashioned succotash, with pumpkin sauce for dessert. There were great yellow pumpkins in abundance.

Early morning of Sept. 21 found us headed for Corinth, which place we reached late in the afternoon. The following afternoon we boarded a train and started on our return to Bolivar. All went well until, while rounding a curve at Jackson, Tenn., three cars near the rear of the train left the track, causing a wreck and the fatal injury of five men — two of the 61st Ill., two of the 12th Mich., and one of our regiment, N. Lyman, Co. A — besides a number of others who were more or less injured.[9]

Upon our return to Bolivar we again took up the daily routine of the camp, which remained unbroken till the morning of Oct. 3. The uneventful days and weeks in camp at Bolivar were by no means unprofitable to us. It was while here, by the vigorous and skillful efforts of Col. Scott, Lieut. Col. Snook and Maj. Welles, with the enthusiastic support of the company officers, that the men devoted a large part of each day to perfecting themselves in military drill. Companies vied with each other in the manual of arms, and in skirmish and battalion drill, which soon placed the 68th Ohio among the crack regiments of the army in points of evolution and discipline, a reputation we ever after maintained.

Friday, Oct. 3, Gen. Hurlbut,[10] having been ordered to the relief of Corinth, called upon Gen. Ross,[11] then in command at Bolivar, for two regiments to supplement his command, and the 68th Ohio and 12th Mich. were designated. The following morning we moved out of our camp. About 8 o'clock in the evening, after a march of about 24 miles, we reached the vicinity of Pocahontas, where, after a sharp skirmish with the enemy, we went into bivouac.

On Oct. 5 the 68th Ohio and 12th Mich., [jointly] commanded by Col. R.K. Scott, moved cautiously forward toward the Hatchie River, and for a time held a position near what was known as Davis Bridge. To the left front of our position, about 500 yards distant, was a large building occupied by the enemy's sharpshooters. The whiz of rebel balls made unpleasant music. Our artillery planted a few shells in the building, causing the enemy to flee to the wood beyond.

Our brigade was ordered to make a flank movement. In the meantime the enemy's shot and shell flew thick and fast around us, but on we went, and soon gained a coveted position on Metamora Hill. Our artillery now came up and engaged the enemy at close range. The enemy broke and fled in confusion, leaving four pieces of artillery in our hands. About this time a heavy roar of battle reached our ears, which told us of the presence of a force of the ene-

***Opposite:* Col. Robert Kingston Scott, 68th Ohio, was promoted brigadier general in April 1865 (to rank from the previous Jan. 12) and brevetted major general in December 1865. Although considered an able, thorough and courageous soldier, Scott was characterized by historian Ezra J. Warner "as unique a mixture of hero and rogue as ever wore a United States uniform." Following the war he was appointed chief of the Freedmen's Bureau South Carolina branch, and in 1868 was elected governor of that state. Over the next four years Scott was largely responsible for the scandals, disorder and corruption that marked the introduction of Republican rule in South Carolina. Public debt tripled during his governorship, while Scott personally was "subject alike to alcoholic and female allurements" — on one occasion state officials paid a burlesque actress to induce him, while intoxicated, to sign a fraudulent issue of state bonds. In 1877 he returned to Henry County, Ohio, and resumed his former profession as real estate developer. On Christmas Day 1880 he killed a Napoleon drug clerk, whom he believed responsible for getting his son drunk. Scott claimed the homicide was accidental, and was acquitted. He died Aug. 12, 1900 and was buried in Napoleon.**

L. M. Strayer Collection

my elsewhere. A general advance was ordered, when the fighting became furious on all parts of the field, the enemy fighting from behind fences and buildings as we moved upon them. Here we fought the enemy under zouave tactics — lying down to load, then springing to our feet and making a rapid move upon the enemy, when, after delivering our fire, we would again hug mother earth. While executing one of these maneuvers we ran over one of our companion regiments, lying down, which, not to be outdone, a few moments later served us the same way.[12]

Our regiment and the 12th Mich. now dropped into a slight depression, and making a rapid move to the right, gained possession of the Hatchie bridge. The enemy's line of retreat being cut off, there was nothing less than death or surrender from which to choose, so they chose the latter, and that ended the fight on our side of the Hatchie.

In the meantime the enemy was engaged in massing his broken columns on the opposite side of the river. Before crossing the bridge our position was close to the river bank to the right of the bridge. We then moved to the left until we came to a road leading to the bridge, when we filed to the right, and with left of regiment in front, led by Maj. Welles, dashed across the bridge amidst a perfect storm of shot and shell from the rebel batteries on the high ground on the south side. Immediately upon crossing the bridge we filed to the left and took distance enough for other regiments to form on our right.[13]

Soon the whole line moved forward, rapidly firing on the enemy, and we had the satisfaction of learning that the enemy was in full retreat, leaving several heavy guns and several hundred men in our hands.[14]

Thus on Sunday, Oct. 5, our regiment assisted to finish the battle which was commenced on the previous Friday, at Corinth, in a very satisfactory manner to ourselves.

The loss our regiment sustained in the battle — which the enemy styled "Hell on the Hatchie" — was very light, considering the exposed positions we occupied from early morning till 4 o'clock in the afternoon. Gen. Hurlbut's report of the battle, in which he highly complimented our regiment, gave our loss as "eight wounded."[15]

During the engagement on the north side of the river the opposing lines were on opposite sides of an open field, and were occupying relatively the same positions along the line of fences bordering the woods on either side. The firing had become fast and furious, when a large, beautiful, dun-colored, riderless horse broke from the edge of the timber occupied by the enemy, and with head and tail up came dashing across the field in front of our regiment. On he came at full speed straight into our lines, when he was surrounded by a hundred sturdy men and captured. He was a magnificent animal, fully saddled and bridled, with a beautiful cavalry sword strapped to the saddle.

Among the first to get hold of him were Col. Scott and Maj. Welles. Scott said: "I believe I will claim this fellow by right of capture."

"You can have him," responded Welles, "but I will claim the sword." And so it was decided. Col. Scott at once took possession of the horse and rode him in all our subsequent marches and engagements until the 22nd of July 1864, when the noble horse was shot dead and Col. Scott taken prisoner.

The sword was a metal scabbard cavalry saber, ground sharp. Welles at once substituted it for his leather scabbard infantry sword, and wore it during our subsequent marches and battles to our veteran furlough, when his comrades presented him with a beautiful gold-mounted silver scabbard sword. Welles carried the Hatchie sword at the battle of Champion Hills, where a rebel ball penetrated the metal scabbard and nearly ruined its usefulness. But, during the siege of Vicksburg, Welles took it to the blacksmith of DeGolyer's Battery, who put it in good serviceable condition.

The morning after the battle we retraced our steps toward Bolivar with several hundred prisoners. They were the same fellows who confronted us at Iuka. At Bolivar we found a number of new recruits and absent comrades fresh from their Northern homes.

Oct. 9 we marched from Bolivar to Grand Junction, remained overnight, then returned to Bolivar in a cold rain, reaching camp late that night. The remainder of the month we remained in camp, preparatory to the fall and winter campaign.[16]

Oct. 20 James Harpel, Co. I, was instantly killed by the cars on the T. & O. Railroad, near our camp. Comrade Harpel is one among many who, for some reason, are reported in Ohio's Record as "unaccounted for." Harpel was born of Christian parents and was a model young man. His remains were interred in the cemetery at Bolivar.[17]

Nov. 1 we were mustered for pay. Troops came pouring into Bolivar from Corinth and Jackson until the country around Bolivar was one vast camp. Nov. 2 orders were issued to strike tents and be ready to march the following morning. The appointed hour found us

L. M. Strayer Collection

ready with three days' rations in our haversacks. The troops in our vicinity, about 20,000 strong, under the command of Maj. Gen. Grant, were put in motion. We marched out on the Grand Junction road about 10 miles, when a halt was ordered for the night.[18]

Next day we marched 15 miles and made our camp near La-Grange, Tenn. Nov. 5 our division train returned to Bolivar after supplies, accompanied by a detail from the 68th.

Nov. 12 a detail from the regiment was ordered out on a foraging expedition. While returning to camp a four-mule team broke through a bridge, severely injuring Capt. Bowen and several of his men.[19]

Nov. 23 a grand review of the army by Maj. Gen. Grant and Gen. McPherson took place. The troops were pronounced to be in excellent condition.

During the day heavy cannonading in the direction of Holly Springs was heard. Our cavalry had engaged the enemy and captured about 100 prisoners and 200 horses. The prisoners were brought in and quartered in the college building near our camp.

Thanksgiving Day, Nov. 27, we received orders to have two days' rations in our haversacks — "nary a turkey" — and be ready to march at 8 o'clock the following morning. We were ordered to turn over our Sibley tents, and in lieu of them drew shelter-tents.

Two of these tents, buttoned together and stretched over a pole supported by two stakes, constituted the bed-room and kitchen for two. In the evening, before retiring to our couch of poles, bark or anything that would keep us out of the mud, we would stand before our worldly tabernacles and devote our time in thinking of all the mean things we had ever been guilty of doing, which would cause us to feel so little that we were able to crawl into our tents with some degree of ease and soon be wrapped in the arms of Morpheus. That is, if we could brave those fellows who insisted on sleeping with us

Opposite: **Born on Independence Day in 1840, George E. Welles served as the 68th Ohio's adjutant, major and lieutenant colonel, commanding the regiment for much of the war's final two years. In June 1867 he was brevetted a brigadier general for "meritorious services" to date from March 13, 1865. A postwar grain merchant and Freemason, Welles died April 27, 1906 and was buried in Toledo's Forest Cemetery.**

— no, not sleeping with us, because those other fellows never went to sleep but kept going all the time. They went to bed with us, got up with us, marched with us, fought with us, in fact, stuck fast to us like brothers.[20]

Preparations went rapidly forward, and about 10 o'clock, Nov. 28, we formed in line, each man having strapped to his back a pup tent, and marched 10 miles in the direction of Holly Springs, Miss.

The following day we marched 12 miles, and in the evening made our camp on the banks of Coldwater River. A cold rain continued to fall all night.

Sunday, Nov. 30, found us marching toward Holly Springs, where it was reported the enemy would dispute our advance. After a march of about four miles we heard heavy firing. Our brigade was ordered to the support of our advance. The heavy firing we soon learned was our advance column engaged in dropping shot and shell into a body of timber in which the rebels were lurking. The enemy seeming to realize that a heavy body was moving upon them, quickly retired. We moved forward, and after a march of about 10 miles made our camp in the suburbs of Holly Springs, where we remained until the next day.

While marching through the city a halt was ordered, when the column retired to either side of the street, and after having fixed bayonets, stuck them in the ground. It so happened that some of our guns were stuck in the gateway fronting a beautiful dwelling-house. Our bayonets went down in the loose ground with a thump, which, of course, induced us to make an examination, when we were rewarded by finding there buried a barrel of sugar. Just about this time a wounded Confederate officer came limping down the walk from the house, and as he came near us, with a good-natured twinkle in his eyes, remarked: "I have heard it said that you Northern people can find anything, and now I believe it to be true. I buried that barrel of sugar to test the smelling qualities of you Yanks."

We were much amused over the Confederate officer's views of the matter, and at the suggestion of Maj. Welles several of the boys picked up the barrel of sugar and carried it to the house, remarking to our Confederate friend, "Try again."

We moved on through the city and made our camp in an oak grove. The weather was cold and stormy.

Monday, Dec. 1, we remained in camp until noon, when we took up our line of march for the Tallahatchie River. Night found us nine miles from Holly Springs.

Early the next morning we were in line and wading through Mississippi mud and water half knee deep. We marched 12 miles through a cold rain, and at night went into camp near an abandoned line of the enemy's works on the banks of the Tallahatchie.

We remained there in camp until about noon of Dec. 3, waiting for our pioneers to repair the bridge, which the enemy had partly destroyed, when we crossed over and toward the close of day went into camp near Abbeville. Everywhere around us were seen evidences of a hasty retreat of the enemy. They had burned the depot and other buildings containing stores to keep them from falling into our hands.

The following day we remained in camp near Abbeville waiting for our supply train to come up from the rear. The early morning of Dec. 5 found us again moving, nor did we stop until we reached Oxford, 12 miles from Abbeville, where we remained the succeeding five days. In the meantime everything remained quiet in our vicinity.

On Dec. 10 Col. R.K. Scott returned to the regiment, having been absent for some weeks on the sick-list. Late in the day we received orders to be prepared to march at 7 o'clock the following morning. The appointed hour found us in motion, and after a march of 14 miles we made our camp in a field of wild grass on the banks of a stream. The few days previous had been wet and cold, but this day was warm and pleasant. During the night fire broke out in the dry grass near our camp, and under a strong wind spread with alarming rapidity, and soon we were engaged in fighting fire away from our ammunition wagons. We suffered no injury other than the scorching of a few blankets.

Dec. 12 and 13 a portion of the regiment was engaged in building a bridge. Dec. 14 a heavy detail was made to accompany the division train back to Holly Springs.

Dec. 18 we marched four miles and made our camp near a Mississippi crossroads. The following day Lieut. L.W. Richardson and several others whose names I am unable to give started for their Ohio homes on recruiting service. Late in the afternoon we received orders to be ready to march in 20 minutes. In a short time we were in motion, and did not stop till late in the night, when we made our camp near a town named Water Valley, and well named it was, because much of the country was covered with water.

Dec. 20 everything was quiet in our vicinity; however, not so elsewhere. The rebel Gen. Van Dorn, learning that Gen. Grant had established Holly Springs as a depot of supplies from which to draw during his march southward, made a rapid move and, on the morning of Dec. 20, attacked, and after a spirited engagement captured the place, burned our supplies and sorely crippled the railroad north of us. The enemy also captured a number of our boys who were in the hospital. The boys afterward said that they never were so sick as when they signed their paroles; in fact, they were so sick that they did not know their own names, so they wrote assumed ones.[21]

Our camp at Water Valley was on a high piece of ground north of the town. Here it was that Col. Leggett, 78th Ohio, issued a strict order against all foraging. This order was fresh in the minds of several boys who were bounding rapidly through a copse of jack-oaks, close behind a long-legged razor-back pig. The pig, closely followed by its pursuers, met Col. Leggett and staff on foot, and leisurely approaching camp. The boys, seeing that they were caught, made a quick survey of the field and then renewed the chase. The pig ran close to the Colonel, who sprang at it, but failed to catch it. This effort on the part of the Colonel caused all thoughts of punishment to vanish, and soon afterward the boys captured their prize and bore it triumphantly into camp.

We remained in our camp at Water Valley until the afternoon of Dec. 21, when orders came to move. We were in the extreme front of Gen. Grant's army, and when we turned back we moved by our troops in camp along the road, each command taking up its line of march in its regular order. We moved on, passed the last campfire of our army, and off into the darkness beyond, keeping up that quick, nervous route step until midnight, when a halt was ordered until morning.

That evening the air around us was heavy with bitter imprecations on the fortunes of war that compelled a retreat, and especially a retreat over the same road that we had passed over on our outward march. Had it been left to a vote every soldier in the ranks of that army would have yelled lustily to have gone forward, as the men had great faith in their ability to live off the country. This lesson early learned by the private soldier was later accepted as possible, and put into execution on the great march to the sea.

The afternoon of Dec. 22 we arrived at Oxford, where we remained until the morning of the following day. During the night a heavy rain fell, thoroughly soaking us.

The morning of Dec. 24 our brigade was ordered out as guard for an immense wagon train. We marched on each side of and parallel with the main road. About sundown we bivouacked on the north side of the Tallahatchie River after marching or running through rain and mud 15 long miles.

That Christmas eve we were without rations. All we could find around us was corn on the ear, which we shelled and roasted for our supper. Old Santa Claus missed us entirely; not even coffee and hardtack came our way to gladden our hearts.

As Christmas morning dawned upon us we found nothing in our stockings but a pair of wet feet, and nothing in our haversacks but a vacancy. So we turned our attention to grinding corn, using for that purpose rude hand mills such as used by the colored people on Southern plantations, and then made our meal into corncakes of an approved kind. These corncakes were washed down with a cup of corn coffee.

About noon Christmas day our Commissary Sergeant, J. Dorshimer, brought us two beeves, accompanied by the owner.[22] Our happiness depended on Dorshimer's ability to withstand the pleadings of the owner for the lives of Bossy and Buckey. But while Dorshimer was parleying with the owner, one of the boys, armed with an ax, delivered a well-aimed blow and Bossy fell. The owner now grasped Buckey around the neck and made an effort to lead it away, meantime heaping all manner of vile epithets upon the heads of Northern Yankees. The flash of an ax was again seen, and a few moments later the 68th boys were busily engaged in preparing a Christmas dinner of fresh beef, broiled over our campfires on the end of our ramrods.

Christmas afternoon we moved about four miles and joined our brigade near Abbeville. Thus we spent Christmas of 1862.

About this time the Seventeenth Corps, Army of the Tennessee, was organized under General Orders of Dec. 18, 1862. Our regiment was assigned to the Second Brigade, Third Division, Seventeenth Corps, in which we remained until muster-out in July 1865.[23]

The Second Brigade, commanded by Col. [later General] M.D. Leggett, consisted of the 20th, 68th and 78th Ohio and the 30th Ill., the latter regiment taking the place of the 23d Ind., with which we were associated during the previous summer.[24]

Leggett went out as Colonel of the 78th Ohio and was numbered among the fighting generals of the army. Beloved by all, of great resolution, he seemed most at home in the wildest tumult of war. During the fierce carnage of battle on July 22, 1864, Gen. Logan dispatched to Leggett: "General, it is all-important you must

Mass. MOLLUS, USAMHI

Mortimer D. Leggett, 78th Ohio, spent most of his service as a 17th Corps brigade and division commander. Prior to the war he practiced law and was one of the founders of Ohio's graded-school system, serving successively as school superintendent in Akron, Warren and Zanesville, Ohio. In this 1865 portrait Leggett posed as a brevet major general with 17th Corps "arrow" badge pinned to his coat.

hold the hill." To which Leggett replied: "Tell Logan when the hill is given up there won't be enough of my division left to fight another battle." Leggett's words were few. Noble man, he leaves his deeds to speak for him.

For some days following Dec. 26 we remained quietly in camp, except for an occasional foraging detail. About this time five of us visited a wealthy planter's domain, and were fortunate in finding hidden away in one corner of a cellar a supply of apples and potatoes. We proceeded to fill our haversacks, and while so engaged the cellar door closed with a jam and left us in the blackness of night. At the same time a fiendish chuckle reached our ears, "There, I have you Yankee dogs caged." "Open that door or we will burn our way out," was our response, and suiting the action to the word Comrade R. of Co. A drew a match and fired a bunch of dry straw on the cellar floor. The ruse was a complete success, as the cellar was in close proximity to a large residence, and in an instant the door came open and a frightened face pleaded with us not to burn him out. We stamped out the fire and then departed from our prison. The rebel now appeared to be quite friendly, and asked us to tarry a while, but our ears caught the sound of a distant horn, and being some distance outside of our picket line, we knew that horn meant to us an invitation to visit a Jeff Davis boarding place. We walked rapidly away, then began to run, to gain the protection of a friendly copse. We made our way to camp, where we were amply repaid for our foot-race by a square meal of baked potatoes and apples.

The next day the "68th Cavalry," which consisted of about 30 of our men mounted on mules, had a brush with the enemy near this plantation, and Comrade W.H. Smith, Co. K, was wounded.[25]

Sunday, Dec. 28, we held regimental inspection, after which we butchered. Our experience in the butchering business was quaint enough, as sometimes it required two men to hold up our beeves while a third man knocked them down.

During these days of trials the cheery voice of Dave Shoemaker could be heard. Dave was a sure cure for the blues, as he used to startle other regiments in camp around us with a perfect imitation of a Mississippi rooster, which must have set our companion regiments to wondering if we were faring any better than themselves.[26]

Dec. 29 the whole regiment was ordered out on a foraging expedition, returning in the evening with about 100 head of cattle and hogs, which were turned over to the Commissary Department.[27]

The early morning of Dec. 30 we were called into line and ordered to the support of the pickets, which were warmly engaged with the enemy. But just before the order came to move a distant lusty cheer reached our ears. There was music in those cheers that told us the enemy — a body of rebel cavalrymen — was retiring as fast as their horses could carry them. Many attacks occurred along our picket line, which generally resulted in a lessening of the available force of the enemy, and often a loss on our side, too.

The following day all remained quiet, and the year 1862 passed into history.

Notes to Chapter 2

1. Confederate Maj. Gens. Sterling Price and Earl Van Dorn.

2. Col. Walter Q. Gresham, 53rd Indiana.

3. During this period a shakeup occurred among the regiment's highest ranking field officers. After Fort Donelson tense animosity apparently existed between Col. Steedman and Lt. Col. Scott, leading the latter to offer his resignation May 6. Writing Col. J.M. Thayer, Scott charged that Steedman's "only pride is the eagle on his shoulder and the amt. of money he can make out of his position. ... His commands [are] given in such a bungling manor [*sic*] that he became the Subject of ridicule to all the men. And this is not the gratest [*sic*] of his faults; an intire [*sic*] want of executive ability has reduced the Regt. from nearly a maximum Regt. to a mear [*sic*] Squad — and now I find to my regret that when an effort is being made to resusitate it if possible, that Maj Snook feels it his duty to write Governor Tod of Ohio that it is for the purpose of making me Col. and that he will never accept a commission under me. I have nothing to say against Maj Snook only that he has a very limited idea of the Regt. as he has not done a days duty since he joined the Regt. at Ft. Donelson save within the last few days he has been around a little. I did not come into the Service for the money I will receive, as I can make more at home; and do not wish longer to be associated with those who care for the pay alone." R.K. Scott Papers, OHS.

Feelings elsewhere in the 68th were mixed. From Bolivar, Tenn., Quartermaster Sergt. Jacob Bruner wrote that "Col. Steedman is a kind good hearted impulsive passionate man. If I need a favor he is just the man who would grant it. He will lend the boys money & help them all he can but he is not a military man." Bruner to Martha Bruner, June 21, 1862, OHS.

Steedman was discharged July 5, prompting Lt. Ira Kelsey, Co. I, to comment: "Col. S.H. Steedman — who stuck to us like the little old man — has been mustered out of the service, and thereby relieved the regiment of a load that has oppressed it like an incubus, and Lieut. Col. Scott has been commissioned Col., an appointment every way fitting." *The Perrysburg Journal,* Aug. 13, 1862.

Capt. Hiram Poe, Co. I, added: "Since Col. Scott has taken command, new uniforms have been issued to the men. His efficient system of discipline, and the sound judgment shown in the performance of his duties, have given the men a spirit of self reliance which soldiers never attain under any other kind of commander. He is now, as he has ever been, deservedly popular with officers and men." *The North-West,* Aug. 20, 1862.

In November 1862, John S. Snook was elevated to lieutenant colonel of the 68th Ohio, and Adjt. George E. Welles became major, their commissions backdated to July 5.

4. Brothers William and James F. Badger, farmers from Williams County, were known in the 68th as the "Badger Boys." With Pvt. William Glime, they were relegated after capture to six weeks' duty in Bolivar's hospital, then sent as paroled prisoners to St. Louis' Benton Barracks and Camp Chase, Ohio. All three returned in March 1863, when William Badger was detailed to Battery D, 1st Illinois Light Artillery. James Badger was wounded at Champion Hill, Miss., and Glime was promoted Co. G's first sergeant in January 1865. W. Badger, J.F. Badger and W. Glime CSR, RG 94, NARA.

5. Lt. Kelsey wrote Aug. 5: "We are able to compete successfully with any regiment in the Western Army, in the Battalion drill, dress parade or anything else in the line of the soldier." *The Perrysburg Journal,* Aug. 13, 1862.

6. Escaped slaves, many of whom were employed by Federal authorities as laborers, cooks, teamsters, hostlers and servants, were universally labeled "contrabands" by Union soldiers. At Bolivar on Aug. 8, Capt. Poe, Co. I, observed: "The contrabands, of which we have about 300, are doing good work, and relieving our men of many a hard day's labor. They march to and from their meals to the time of 'Old Dan Tucker,' beat on a rickety old drum, pick on a broken-backed old banjo, and shake up with any number of dry bones. Being slightly short of stars, however well provided with stripes they may be, they supply the place of both with a magnificent cotton handkerchief, under which the 'First African Tennessee' marches as proudly as our boys do beneath the old flag." *The North-West,* Aug. 20, 1862.

7. Maj. Gen. Edward O.C. Ord was in command of a "mixed force" of 5,000 troops belonging to the Army of West Tennessee. *OR,* vol. XVII, pt. 1, p. 64, 301.

8. The battle of Iuka pitted Southern forces under Sterling Price against portions of two divisions and cavalry commanded by Brig. Gen. William S. Rosecrans. Of some 7,700 combatants actually engaged, Price lost 1,516 while Rosecrans suffered 790 casualties. Price, aware that Gen. Grant with Ord's column was approaching Iuka to reinforce Rosecrans, retreated south during the night of Sept. 19. Long, p. 269.

Signing himself "S," an unidentified member of the 68th reported: "The next morning [Sept. 17], after our arrival at Corinth, we took up the line of march towards Iuka, where Price was reported in force. We arrived at Burnsville, Miss., in the afternoon. Only a few families remained in Burnsville, the others having fled some time before. We made ourselves as comfortable as we could in the store-rooms, warehouses, saloons, &c. We, a part of the 68th Ohio, took up our quarters in the Snack House Saloon, which building seemed to have done more business than any other in the town. We remained in Burnsville one night and day, when, replenishing our haversacks with two days' rations, we again pushed forward till we ran against the pickets of the enemy. We retired a short distance and waited till morning, when a flag of truce was sent in, which did not return till late in the afternoon.

"Heavy cannonading was heard in the evening to the south of us. General Rosecrans had engaged the enemy, and it was the time we should have engaged him on the west and north, which we should have been doing had it not been for the delay of the flag of truce. We advanced two miles that evening, capturing six rebel butternuts. The next morning we again advanced, throwing out skirmishers ahead, but did not advance far till word came that the rebel army had skedaddled. Gen. Rosecrans had given them 'what Paddy gave the drum.' The hotels and churches were filled with the wounded of the enemy. I had no opportunity of going over the battle-ground, neither had I any particular desire to do so." *The North-West,* Oct. 8, 1862.

9. Pvt. Nathan Lyman, a Sandusky County farmer, was hospitalized at Napoleon, Ohio, from mid-January to July 1862, and had been with the regiment only two months when killed. Those injured in the rail mishap from the 68th were Pvts. Joseph Rickey and Thomas Simmons, Co. A, Corp. John W. Kelley, Co. D, and Pvt. John Slee, Co. D. All except Slee eventually returned to duty. N. Lyman CSR, RG 94, NARA; *The North-West*, Oct. 8, 1862.

10. At the time, Maj. Gen. Stephen A. Hurlbut commanded the 4th Division, Army of West Tennessee.

11. Brig. Gen. Leonard F. Ross commanded the District of Jackson, Tenn.

12. Loop referred to the 46th Illinois, which temporarily attached itself to Scott's command after its colonel, John A. Davis, was mortally wounded. *OR,* vol. XVII, pt. 1, p. 324, 334.

13. Confederate forces at Hatchie were part of Gen. Van Dorn's command, which had been defeated Oct. 3-4 in the battle of Corinth. Those opposing the 68th Ohio's bridge crossing belonged to Brig. Gen. John C. Moore's brigade, which had been reduced to 300 men after its severe mauling at Corinth. *OR*, vol. XVII, pt. 1, p. 305, 383, 394-395.

14. Confederate Brig. Gen. Dabney H. Maury admitted the loss of four artillery pieces (12-pounder howitzers) at Hatchie Bridge. Maj. J.S. Snook reported the 68th Ohio "captured 100 stand of small-arms, with accouterments, and took a number of prisoners." *OR,* vol. XVII, pt. 1, p. 305, 335, 394.

15. Gen. Hurlbut's compliments to the 68th Ohio and 12th Michigan were published in general orders dated Oct. 8, 1862. Col. Scott reported the 68th's loss as six wounded, two of them severely. Federal casualties at Hatchie amounted to 46 killed, 493 wounded (including Gen. Ord) and 31 missing. *OR,* vol. XVII, pt. 1, p. 304, 308-309, 334.

The battle of Hatchie (also known as Davis Bridge or Metamora) was really the first in which the 68th Ohio played an active role. Consequently, its outcome generated an outpouring of correspondence back to Ohio. Excerpts from several of these letters follow:

"Semper Cresence" (unidentified): "The anxiety to 'smell powder,' which has been felt by most every member of the Regiment, has at last been gratified.

"On Friday night, the 3d of October, at 12 o'clock, orders came for our Regiment to march at 3 o'clock next morning, with three days' rations and one hundred rounds of cartridges. The men were immediately called, and preparations for moving commenced. In the morning at the proper time we reported to Gen. Hurlbut, and our Regiment, together with the 12th Michigan, the 15th Ohio Battery, and one Company of Cavalry, were placed under command of Col. Scott. Our Brigade left town at daylight, all the line officers and men being in complete ignorance of our destination. The day was warm and sultry, and the water on the route scarce; but not withstanding these difficulties we made a forced march of 26 miles.

"We bivouacked for the night within two miles of Davis' Bridge, which was destined to be the scene of a fight on the morrow. At 7 o'clock in the morning Col. Scott was ordered to move his brigade forward. We went within a mile of the bridge, where we were stopped and ordered to leave our wagon train. One of the batteries got a gun in position and shelled a house occupied by the enemy's videttes, which they literally knocked to pieces and depopulated very suddenly. The train was now put in order, and the troops moved forward to the attack. Our entire force consisted of Gen. Hurlbut's Division and our Brigade from Ross' Division, the whole being under command of Maj. Gen. Ord. We were ordered to take our position on the right of the road to the bridge, and scarcely had the line of battle been formed before one of our batteries, which was in the advance, had been engaged by the batteries of the enemy. The battery which belonged to our brigade was ordered up to the support of the other. The shells came over our way thick and fast, but all passed over our heads. Our Brigade was ordered forward to take possession of a hill on a line with the artillery, for the support of the latter. The boys started forward on a double-quick, and seemed to obey orders to forward with more alacrity than if it had been an order to 'fall in for rations.'

"When we reached the hill we found that the artillery had driven the rebels back towards the river. We were then ordered to forward and drive them from their new position. When the command was given by Major Snook to forward, not a man faltered, but all started with a will, and marched in order that would have done credit to veterans. On we went, through jungles, over fences, ditches and logs, and halted at the edge of a wood. We had scarcely halted when a most terrific volley of musketry was poured in upon us. Not a man flinched — all stood their ground. We were immediately ordered to lie down, in which position our men opened fire, and three rounds drove the rebels in confusion from their position. The 46th Illinois was now on our left with their left resting on the road to the bridge. They received the fire of the enemy at the same time with us, and suffered terribly on account of the men being massed, and not having an opportunity to take advantage of their cover. Their Colonel was borne mortally wounded from the field, and they were placed in our Brigade.

"The rebels were now formed in a lane behind a wood, and when we were again ordered to forward, the boys started on the run, cheering loudly along the whole line. The rebels, being hidden from us, and hearing the cheering, thought we were charging bayonets on them, broke and run without firing a shot. Again they formed and again we drove them. This time they filed off and crossed the bridge, of which they were still in possession. When we were ordered to forward from this position, the 46th Illinois, on our left, did not seem to obey the order with alacrity, and the 68th ran fairly over them. Their officers cheered them on and told them not to be beaten by the Buckeyes, and again they came forward and joined our line. ... We met with no more interruption until we reached the bank of the river, where fire was opened on us from the opposite side. Our position was well sheltered, and we remained there over an hour. During this time we were fighting for possession of the bridge, and it was hotly contested by both parties. As the rebels fell back from the bridge a battery was got into position that raked the road where their artillery was, and they left it literally strewn with horses, broken caissons and gun carriages.

"The rebels were finally compelled to give way, and the bridge was ours. Two regiments were ordered to cross — one an Indiana and the other an Illinois regiment. The former, while on the bridge, got panic-stricken, and the four last companies refused to go. The Illinois men, who were in their rear, charged bayonets on them and compelled them to cross." Semper Cresence, Oct. 8, 1862 to *The North-West,* Oct. 22, 1862.

Capt. Sidney S. Sprague, Co. B: "The bridge was carried, then came the order 'By the left flank, double quick march, cross the bridge at a charge.' Our regiment, the 68th O., obeyed the order most promptly, the left of our regiment being in front, I had the honor as head of Co. B to cross the bridge first; the boys bravely followed amid showers of grape and canister, shell and shot. No one faltered. We gained the steep [bank] beyond the bridge, filed to the left of the road through an open field, followed by the 12th Michigan, until we had gained a position to advance in line of battle to the hill some distance in front so as to flank the enemy's batteries on the right of the road. ... Suffice it to say the hill was carried, the battle won, victory was ours over double our number of veteran troops. ...

"The whole army envies the 68th the laurels they have won, it being the first time we were as a regiment permitted to try our hand in a fight, and most gloriously did we maintain the stars and stripes under which we fought. Sergeant Bruner, the flag-bearer, kept the noble old flag in the front rank during the whole day and the danger we passed through is well evidenced by the riddled appearance of our flag, which had been pierced during the fight by ball, shell and grape. The fight lasted from 9 o'clock A.M. until 4 o'clock P.M., during that time but few of our men tasted water, after the little they had in their canteens when the fight began, was exhausted. The heat during the action was most overpowering and the dust almost unendurable; our men were wet with sweat, from head to foot covered with dust, their faces blackened with powder, and yet they appeared as fresh as ever when the action was over, which only goes to show the great endurance of men of determined courage and energy. Gen. Ord, who commanded until we crossed the Hatchie, was wounded in rear of us when our regiment was crossing the bridge. On the field he appeared brave and energetic, yet appeared to lack coolness and system; he suffered his excitement almost to carry him into a phrenzy [*sic*]." Sprague, Oct. 14, 1862 to the *Defiance Democrat,* Nov. 1, 1862.

QM Sergt. Jacob Bruner: "I was in the battle of the Hatchie or Davis Bridge. I carried the good old Star Spangled Banner through the fight. Bullets whistled about my ears by the hundreds but I came out of seven hours battle unharmed. ... I kept the old Eagle up during the fight and felt proud of the honor. Our Color Sergeant was absent and I volunteered to go and carry the flag. ... Oh but I felt proud. If you had seen me you would have thought I was 6 feet high." Bruner to Martha Bruner, Oct. 13, 1862, OHS.

Writing Oct. 7 to a Toledo newspaper under the pseudonym "Old Zeke," Bruner added: "Through the entire engagement Col. Scott behaved with great gallantry. Passing up and down the lines cheering the men and giving orders with perfect coolness, he at once gained the admiration and confidence of his whole command. As he passed to and fro unharmed while grape and canister were flying about him thick as hail, we could not help believing that there are men who are 'born to command.' Major Snook deserves great credit. He was prompt and fearless and at every point where duty called him, counting consequences light as air, and convincing all of his ability to command. The Major at one time narrowly escaped with his life. A missile passed his head almost grazing his temple; but nothing daunted, he did his duty to the letter." *Toledo Blade,* Oct. 17, 1862.

2nd Lt. Lewis Dubbs, Co. I: "The Sixty-eighth Ohio and Twelfth Michigan were under a heavy fire during most of the battle. These two regiments did the most of their firing kneeling and lying down, which was a great protection for our men, consequently we did not suffer so great losses as the other regiments that were engaged. ...

"The field which a few short hours ago resounded with the roar of cannon and clashing of bayonets, blended with the shrieks of the wounded and dying. The pale moon which is now shining on us, shines on that battle field and the ghastly upturned faces of the dead. In the expression of the faces of the dead may be seen a type of their last thoughts and words. A calm serenity pervades the countenance of one, as if his last words were, 'Mother — home.' Another has his hands clenched fiercely, and on every lineament is plainly stamped the patriot's words, 'My country and my God,' and on the pale, resolved brow of the sleeper by his side is written, 'Victory or death.' " Dubbs, Oct. 10, 1862 to *The Perrysburg Journal,* Oct. 15, 1862.

16. Quartermaster Sergt. Jacob Bruner took notice of a relatively rare occurrence in West Tennessee — "on the 25th [of October] we had a severe snowstorm. The weather was extremely rough and disagreeable, and this part of the 'Sunny South' was covered with snow! The citizens seemed much surprised at this early appearance of winter, and say it was owing to the presence of so many Northern men, and that they must have brought the climate with them, and they are indignant at it and intend to punish us in a few days for our insolence. On the 24th it was too warm to wear socks, but on the 25th we could have worn all we could get into our boots. Some of us felt like the fellow who was drafted; we thought of *resigning* and going north to a more congenial clime." Bruner, Nov. 1, 1862 to the *Paulding Independent,* Nov. 27, 1862.

Winter's approach concerned many in the 68th, which faced a temporary shortage of some essential items. It especially needed socks, "an article of which our men are entirely destitute," wrote Co. I's Capt. Hiram Poe. "They cannot be obtained from the Government, for it has not got them." Poe appealed to northwest Ohio citizens for donations, as did Capt. Patrick H. Mooney of Co. C. A boot and shoemaker born in County Antrim, Ireland, Mooney explained that "Sutler's goods are often prohibited but anything like socks and gloves would reach the regiment. One pair of gloves (they are better than mitts) and only one pair of socks would be quite a present — two pairs would be enough for any man. ... Clothing [earlier] intended for us was burned on board boats on the Mississippi — 1800 pairs of socks for our regiment, hats, shirts — a winter supply. I have been drawing and distributing, the last few days, half-worn tents, camp kettles, mess pans, caps, knapsacks, blankets, shoes and canteens — only 50 shirts to the company, and no socks. I have 63 men in camp. I have done my best to get two to each man. I have been promised more and think I will succeed. If I do not, it will not be for want of perseverence. We are now under orders to be ready to march at a moment's notice, with three days cooked rations in our haversacks and no socks. For those having shoes, this is rather bad. I had some money (you could scarcely get $100 in the whole regiment, we are so dead broke) and I sent one of the boys up to town to buy all the knit socks he could find. He was only able to get 16 pairs at 50 cents per pair, and these were given to men having shoes and likely to march and fight." Poe, Nov. 17, 1862 in the *Paulding Independent,* Nov. 27, 1862; Mooney, Oct. 27, 1862 in the *Paulding Independent,* Nov. 20, 1862.

17. A Wood County farmer, Pvt. James Harpel, 19, was accidentally thrown to his death from a railcar upon returning to the regiment after eight months sick in hospitals at St. Louis, Mo. and Cairo, Ill. J. Harpel CSR, RG 94, NARA.

18. Before leaving Bolivar on Nov. 3, Pvt. Lyman J. Hissong, Co. I, described the town and recent activity in its environs: "Bolivar is a beautiful little town ... containing about eighteen hundred inhabitants, and judging from the appearance of the place now, it seems to have been, before the rebellion, quite a thriving town; and I have no doubt will be again, if the war closes before both town and railroad are destroyed. But the entire surrounding country is a perfect waste and ruin. Indeed, it is a desolate looking region here. The improvements are so much destroyed that great labor will be required to restore it to its former flourishing condition. There has been considerable cotton raised in Tennessee the past season, but we see a great deal going to waste by the fences being torn from around it — but more for the want of pickers. A large crop of corn was raised here, but you may bet that it is, as the darkies say, all 'done gone' ere this.

"We have here quite a large number of troops under command of Maj. Gen. McPherson, and under whose supervision there has been lately a number of additional fortifications and rifle pits constructed on the west side of the town, which completes the fortification of the place. We now have sufficient force to resist any attack of the enemy.

"On the 1st inst. we had a grand review. Our portion of the army was honored and much pleased with the presence of Maj. Gen. Grant on the occasion. The weather was pleasant; everything was conducted in the best military order and passed off pleasantly, and the troops made a fine appearance." Hissong, Nov. 3, 1862 to *The Perrysburg Journal*, Nov. 12, 1862.

19. A Florida, Ohio, merchant, Capt. Wesley W. Bowen commanded Co. F. He broke an arm in the wagon mishap. W.W. Bowen CSR, RG 94, NARA.

20. The reference is to lice, often termed "graybacks."

21. A large amount of supplies had been stockpiled at Holly Springs for Grant's intended overland advance on Vicksburg, Miss. Van Dorn seriously disrupted Federal plans by destroying Holly Springs' army stores and cotton valued at 1.5 million dollars. At least 1,500 Union soldiers were captured. Long, p. 298.

22. Jacob A. Dorshimer, a Williams County farmer, was not promoted from Co. K private to commissary sergeant until Feb. 14, 1863. He eventually rose to captain of Co. K, and in June 1865 was assigned as 3rd Division provost marshal, 17th Corps. J.A. Dorshimer CSR, RG 94, NARA.

23. Department of Tennessee General Order No. 14, dated Dec. 22, 1862, created the 13th, 15th, 16th and 17th army corps. The original commanders of each, respectively, were Maj. Gen. John A. McClernand, Maj. Gen. William T. Sherman, Maj. Gen. Stephen A. Hurlbut and Maj. Gen. James B. McPherson. *OR,* vol. XVII, pt. 2, p. 461.

24. Col. Mortimer Dormer Leggett was commissioned brigadier general in April 1863 to rank from Nov. 29, 1862. Warner, p. 278-279.

25. Pvt. William H. Smith, a Bryan, Ohio, blacksmith, was originally from Erie, Pa. He also served as a musician in the regimental band from July 1863 to June 1865. W.H. Smith CSR, RG 94, NARA.

26. Pvt. David Shoemaker, Co. B, was born in Williams County and a limeburner by occupation. He also served in the 68th Ohio's "mule cavalry," and was wounded in May 1863 at Champion Hill. D. Shoemaker CSR, RG 94, NARA.

27. "We forage sharply," wrote Quartermaster Sergt. Jacob Bruner. "We visited a plantation a few days ago and obtained corn, fodder, pork, molasses, sugar, meal, flour &c. &c. to the amount of 29 wagon loads! We are doing well and have plenty to eat. It is true the men do not have that abundance they had while lying in camp at Bolivar and consequently swear some and perhaps will write sorrowful letters home. But that is nothing. They would swear if they were fed on sweetmeats every day." Bruner to Martha Bruner, Jan. 1, 1863, OHS.

3

'Louisiana mud that stuck closer than a poor relation'

Thursday, Jan. 1, 1863, brought us continued trials. Early in the day our officers — heaven bless them — made a raid on our sutler's stock of cigars and passed them around among the men. How envious our companion regiments must have felt on that New Year's Day, as we started out on a foraging expedition enveloped in clouds of smoke.

The two succeeding days were quiet and uneventful.

Early the morning of Jan. 3 a heavy rain began to fall, which continued throughout the day and succeeding night, flooding the country round about us. Just before dark we received orders to seek higher ground. In a few moments we were in motion and marched across the Tallahatchie bottoms, a portion of the way through water knee-deep, and made our camp in the midst of a body of fallen timber. That night we were engaged in logging and burning off a piece of ground to keep ourselves warm, hoping against hope, and mad enough to whip our weight in wildcats. During the night it turned very cold so we stood around log fires, thawing on one side and freezing on the other. Thus we passed the cold, cheerless night of rain and sleet. Upon the following morning the sun came out warm and pleasant, which gave us a chance to dry our wet clothes.

The morning of Jan. 5 the welcome "fall in" was sounded. But the entire forenoon was passed in that most monotonous of all movements, marching forward a few hundred yards and then coming to a halt and waiting. During this time Capt. DeGolyer, of the 8th Mich. Battery, was engaged in a sword exercise with one of his lieutenants, when his horse fell into a ditch, breaking its neck and severely injuring the Captain.[1]

About 2 o'clock in the afternoon we were set in motion and marched back to Holly Springs, arriving there about midnight. Here it was that Wm. Swaney, Co. K, died and was buried. This comrade is reported in Ohio's Roster as "unaccounted for."[2]

The following morning we took up our line of march north toward the Tennessee line. About 4 o'clock in the afternoon we reached the Coldwater River, where a halt was ordered for the night. The next morning, Jan. 7, was an exceedingly cold one, but at an early hour we were in motion and marched 16 miles over the partly frozen ground, breaking through the thin crust of ice and mud at every step. As night began to wrap its folds of darkness about us we went into camp near Davis Mills, where we feasted on corn made up into every conceivable shape. The following day we remained in camp.

Jan. 9 we moved out of our camp and marched 14 miles. A heavy rain continued to fall the whole afternoon, but we cheerfully moved on, and toward evening tumbled over the Mississippi state line and made our camp near LaGrange. Once more we were on the soil of Tennessee, and during that cold and stormy night we rested anywhere between a roost and a perch. The southern skies and clouds were loaded down with moisture, and it almost appeared that the elements were in league with Satan and the Southern States to make us miserable.

Before daylight on the following day we were in motion, and after a march of 10 miles went into camp near Moscow, Tenn.

Sunday, Jan. 11, the regiment remained quietly in camp, except for a heavy detail doing guard duty along the line of the Memphis & Charleston Railroad.

Jan. 12 we marched nine miles and went into camp near Lafayette, where we remained till Jan. 18.

The object of the campaign just ended in my narrative has been written by able historians. How Gen. Grant and his army tried hard to force their way to Vicksburg through the swamps and mud of a Mississippi winter; how the enemy destroyed our supplies at Holly Springs, and how, being surrounded by an almost barren country and high water, Grant's army was forced to retire; how the impetuous Sherman, whom the Northern rebel papers had denounced as crazy, was repulsed upon the approaches of Vicksburg on the Yazoo.[3] Meantime, we were living on cornmeal and fresh meat and floundering through 80 miles of mud and storm on our return march to the north line of the state. After the capture and destruction of our supplies at Holly Springs we were dependent upon our own resources for the necessities of life. Consequently we let no occasion to secure food slip by, and demonstrated that our regiment could take care of itself.

The intervening time up to Jan. 18 was marked by no event other than the usual routine of camp. In my old diary I find the following: "We suffered more from the cold than at any time while in camp near Napoleon, O., yet here we are away down in the Sunny South." A chilly north wind made every day most disagreeable, and to add to our inconvenience there was no fuel with which to make a good campfire, consequently we stood around here and there or retired to our pup tents, where, wrapped in our blankets, we tried to keep warm.

Jan. 14 a heavy rain flooded our camp. Toward night the rain changed into snow, and the following morning we trod around camp in snow four inches deep.

Jan. 18 we turned our backs upon the scenes of discontent and took up a line of march in the direction of Memphis, Tenn. During the afternoon we marched along the line of the M. & C. Railroad and passed by a wreck of the previous day, in which three of our comrades who were sick and on their way to the hospital were injured. After a march of about 18 miles we reached Germantown, where we made our camp for the night. On the following day we marched 13 miles. A heavy, cold rain continued to fall, but we pushed on, and toward night camped one mile from Memphis, where we remained until Feb. 20.

On Jan. 20 we turned our attention to looking after the comforts of our camp. The next day we received two months' pay, which enabled us to buy pies, cakes and pickled pigs' feet, dealt out to us by lady hucksters from the city, who peddled their goods in camp. After settling down in camp as comfortable as circumstances would permit, many of us hastened off to the different hospitals in the city to search for our sick.

A few days after reaching Memphis we received a new stand of colors, upon which were inscribed, by orders of Department Headquarters, the battles in which we had been engaged.

The days following our arrival at Memphis were cold and stormy, and having no protection other than our shelter-tents we suffered much.

Jan. 26 we drew new clothing. The clothing was shoddy and nearly worthless, due to the rascality of Government contractors. Of course, we had to suffer the loss. But why additional suffering must be heaped upon us in monstrous misfits was something we could not understand. Some comrades would have six inches or more of shoddy rolled up about their ankles, while another would have six inches or more of arms and legs exposed to the weather. By canvassing the different companies each comrade was reasonably well fitted by making a trade.

The morning of Jan. 26 was warm and pleasant. The sun, which we had not seen for 10 days, came out. The following day the regiment held dress parade, the first time since reaching Memphis.

Jan. 28 the troops across the Mississippi River opposite the city were warmly engaged with a body of the enemy. The heavy guns in the fort on the east side promptly responded and fired several heavy shells into the enemy's ranks, after which the enemy retired, and all became quiet.[4]

Feb. 3 was one of our busy days. We were ordered to turn over our shelter-tents, and in lieu of them drew new wall tents large enough to comfortably accommodate five men each. We moved our camp about 50 rods, and were soon busily engaged in putting up our new tents and otherwise preparing for ourselves the comforts of camp. Once more we could retire for the night and not be aroused out of our best sleep to change front by reason of an approaching storm of wind and rain.

Sunday, Feb. 8, a heavy detail was ordered to report at the river landing to assist in loading the boats with commissary stores. During the day orders were received for the regiment to hold itself in readiness to march at any moment, but the order was revoked by reason of a lack of transports. The few days following we remained quietly in camp.

Feb. 15 a speech by Gen. Logan was read to us on dress parade and brought forth loud and prolonged cheers in honor of our noble commander, a man whom we afterward learned to love.[5]

Maj. Gen. John A. Logan assumed command of the Third Division, Seventeenth Corps, Army of the Tennessee, under order of Dec. 18, 1862, and led us in all our subsequent marches and battles to Nov. 13, 1863, at which time he gave a farewell address [and] took command of the Fifteenth Corps, Army of the Tennessee. Later he became a commander of the Army of the Tennessee.[6]

Among the heroes of 1861-65 stands Logan, surrounded by a halo of glory — a man who early in 1861 left the halls of Congress, shouldered his musket and fought in the ranks on the bloody field of Bull Run. A few days after the battle Logan returned to his Illinois home, and in two weeks had organized the 31st Ill. He was made its Colonel. At Fort Donelson Logan was twice wounded, but he still

Mass. MOLLUS, USAMHI

An effective orator and charismatic Illinois politician, John Alexander Logan was among the Union's most successful and popular Western-theater commanders. His genuine concern for the common soldier, during and after the war, was highlighted in 1868 when he helped institute Memorial Day as a national holiday.

continued to animate his men by his presence. "Stand firm, men!" shouted Logan, when his own blood trickled down his side.

But to return to the thread of my narrative. The morning of Friday, Feb. 20, we moved out of our camp and took up our line of march through the city of Memphis to the river, and went on board the steamer *Louisiana*. Heavy rain continued to fall all the following day, during which time we remained on the boat at Memphis and drew another two months' pay.

Early morning of Feb. 22 found our boat steaming down the muddy waters of the Mississippi. All the available space in the boat's cabin and berths was occupied, as a cold wind and rain raged with incessant fury without. During our trip the rank and file of our regiment congregated in the steamer's cabin and engaged in a contest of song and story. Our boys were good story-tellers, as well as good soldiers. In fact, it seemed more like a grand excursion party off on a tour of pleasure and recreation than a body of armed men traveling toward the jaws of death.

Early morning of Feb. 23 found us still sweeping down the raging waters of the Mississippi. About 10 o'clock our boat touched the Louisiana shore at a little river town by the name of Providence. Here we landed and went into camp about half a mile from the river and near a lake bearing the name of the village. Why the name we could not understand, as we did not believe that Providence ever had anything to do with the place — at least, not until after our arrival.

Immediately upon reaching Providence a detail of about 50 men was made and continued from day to day in the work of clearing a channel from Lake Providence through Bayou Macon to the Wachata River, the object of which was to transport the army below Vicksburg via the Wachata and Red rivers. However, this route to get below Vicksburg was abandoned by reason of an unfavorable report of Gen. McPherson.

While engaged in this work we found time to give the feathered tribes of Louisiana some little attention. On one occasion, while returning to camp, we passed Gen. Leggett's headquarters, a veritable menagerie of squealing pigs and squalling chickens. "Great Scott," remarked the General. "Orderly, go and tell the Quartermaster not to issue any meat to that command for three days."

Feb. 27 we were engaged in a general cleaning up and otherwise preparing for muster day, which took place on the last day of each month. Sunday, March 1, we were provided with light bread furnished by a regimental baker who had recently joined us. Our baker was provided with a portable oven made of sheet iron and mounted on wheels. This very acceptable change from hardtack was of short duration.

On March 4 a small-sized propeller was launched into Lake Providence and made her trial trip of about four miles. A detail from our regiment assisted in moving the boat from the river to the lake, using a system of rollers for that purpose.[7]

When not on guard or fatigue duty we lounged along the levee and engaged in watching, boy-like, the transports that passed us loaded with human freight. And thus day after day came and went until, on or about March 12, the levee at Providence was severed in an effort to turn the waters of the river into another channel.

Sunday morning following the cutting of the levee we discovered that the waters of the Mississippi would not stop in the river, but insisted upon spreading over our camp ground. Bugles were sounded and orders issued to strike tents and hasten to the levee to escape the flood of water rushing upon us. Soon we were in motion, nor did we stop until safely above the high water on board the steamer *Louisiana.*

We remained on the *Louisiana* at Providence enveloped in a dense fog until the following Tuesday, when our boat backed out into the river and started upstream, and near the close of the day we disembarked about four miles above Providence, where we again took up the usual routine of the camp, which remained unbroken until March 22, when we received orders to be prepared to march at a moment's notice. The day passed slowly, and just as the shadows of night began to fall we again embarked on the *Louisiana.* Early the following morning we reached a point about 16 miles above Vicksburg and landed on the east shore, but shortly afterward returned to the boat, where we remained during the night and succeeding day. During the day a terrific storm of rain, accompanied by a violent wind, burst upon us. The smokestacks of the *Louisiana* were torn from their fastenings and hurled across the deck, causing no little excitement and injuring two comrades.

The morning of March 25 we were set in motion, the object being a united attack upon the enemy's stronghold at Haynes' Bluff. After a march of about three miles we came to a halt on the banks of Steele's Bayou, there to hold ourselves in readiness to reinforce Gen. Sherman. However, the gunboats under Admiral Porter being unable to cooperate with the land forces, the attack was abandoned and we were ordered to retrace our steps. We went on board the boats and returned to our camp.[8]

The day following our return to camp a large cotton-gin took fire and burned to the ground.

Sunday, March 29, another terrific storm of wind and rain burst upon us with wildest fury, tearing and blowing some of our tents away.

On April 1 Lieut. L.W. Richardson, H.J. Hunter and others who had been absent on recruiting service since the previous December, joined us, accompanied by a number of new recruits.[9]

During the intervening time to April 16 we remained quietly in camp, storing up our strength for the coming campaign, the object of which was the reduction of the rebel Gibraltar of the Mississippi, Vicksburg.

April 8 we were honored by the presence of Adjt. Gen. Thomas, U.S.A., who made us a speech on the subject of organizing colored troops.[10] The General came among us robed with full power to commission anyone, officer or private, who desired to take up that branch of the United States service. After having considered his remarks, L.J. Hissong and B.F. Perrin, Co. I, and Jacob Bruner, regimental quartermaster sergeant, offered their services and were commissioned to enter upon the work of organizing a regiment of colored troops, which, on June 7 following, made a noble fight at the battle of Milliken's Bend, in which Perrin and Bruner were killed.[11]

Gen. Thomas was followed by Maj. Gen. James B. McPherson, who gave us a short talk. But the speech of the day was by the silver-tongued orator, Maj. Gen. John A. Logan. We well remember the avalanche of words that flowed like a torrent, Logan's countenance lighting up with the wildest enthusiasm, which spread like contagion to everyone with whom he came in contact, as he engaged in a grand panegyric of his command on former fields. At length Gen. Logan came to his conclusion, and in a manner about as follows, said, "Comrades and representatives of the Third Division: Our President down at Washington has heard from you, and when the port-holes of Vicksburg are opened he will hear from you again. Then joyful words may reach you. Brave boys, representatives of the Third Division, come to the arms of Father Abraham."

These words contained two meanings. Logan knew too well that the frowning bluffs of Vicksburg meant a shadow across the threshold of many, many Northern homes.

While in camp Logan mingled with his men, talking with them and shaking hands. He was the idol of his soldiers. But when the boom of artillery and roar of musketry aroused him, his fierce black eyes, heavy black mustache and dark complexion gave him a look terrible to behold, during which time his restless spirit and flashing eye showed a patriotism which knew no bounds. Such was Logan, our dearly-beloved commander.

April 17 we moved to the landing and went on board transports which were to take us farther down the river. During the succeeding night our boat landed at Milliken's Bend, a few miles above Vicksburg, where the morning of April 18 found us. Early in the day we disembarked, and toward the close of day went into camp in a large cornfield one mile from the river. Here we remained until the morning of April 21. Was it muddy? No; the ground was solid. However, there was a foot or more of Louisiana mud spread over the top of the solid ground — a sort of mud that stuck closer than a poor relation, as every time a foot was raised several pounds of mud would rise with it. Some of the boys who wore the army brogans took them off in order to give their organs of locomotion a rest. Those who wore boots had to observe the greatest caution, lest the mud serve them in the capacity of a Louisiana bootjack.

The morning of April 20 we heard very heavy cannonading in the direction of Vicksburg. Late in the day we received orders to be prepared, with three days' rations, and be ready to march at 6 o'clock the following morning. The appointed hour found us in motion, and after a march of about six miles we were engaged in constructing a military road in the direction of Richmond, La.[12] For several days Logan's men built roads through swamps and fields, using for this purpose fence rails and lumber from barns and other buildings along our line of march. About noon of April 23 our brigade was ordered to return to Milliken's Bend, 10 miles away. The following day we remained quietly in camp and drew four months' pay.

About April 25 a call was made for volunteers to run the transports past the Vicksburg batteries. This was a perilous undertaking. Among the men from our regiment who offered their services were Lieut. J[edediah] C. Banks, W[illiam] Barnhart, J[oshua] Dicus and J[oseph] Longberry of Co. C, and J[ohn] Snyder of Co. A. These men safely landed their charge a few miles below the heavy guns of the enemy, where a few days later we found them in fairly good condition, considering the storm of iron hail through which they had passed.[13]

Gen. Logan fully realized how hazardous was the undertaking. It was said that the men who volunteered their services waited upon the General and asked: "Will it be required to report with equipments?" "No, no," replied Logan. "To furnish the men is enough; we can't afford to lose both."

In an old memorandum I find the following:

> "About the hour of midnight the gunboats moved from their fastenings and dropped silently down the river, and in their wake followed six transports. The night was intensely dark, which greatly favored us. Our fires were banked, and not a light was visible on any part of our boat. Not a sound broke the stillness of the night, saved the muffled breathings of the engines. In a short time we discerned in the darkness of the night a flashing of lights on the high bluffs above Vicksburg, which informed us that we were approaching the rebel batteries, which were to belch forth their rain of iron hail, and a moment later the stillness of the night was broken by a terrific crash almost in our faces, followed

> by peal upon peal of heavy thunder tones from the enemy's heavy works and our gunboats. We now hugged the west shore of the river, and under a full head of steam swept past the upper batteries, during which time our gunboats were giving the enemy their whole attention.
>
> "Just at this time immense bonfires sprang up all along the river bluffs, which, reflected by the river, changed the gloom of night to the glare of midday. We now glanced around from behind our barricade of cotton-bales, and were pleased to find our companion boats still safely outriding the rebel storm of iron hail. Here and there along the bluffs could be plainly seen crowds of the enemy standing, spellbound in utter amazement, and watching our frail wooden boats safely passing their boasted Gibraltar of the Mississippi. Under a full head of steam we fairly flew through the water. The engines labored and groaned in a mighty struggle to get away, beyond and out of range of those fiery-throated demons on the bluffs above us.
>
> "The upper river batteries were safely passed, and we left the lights of Vicksburg behind us. At the lower batteries the scenes were again repeated, but in due time we tied up on the Louisiana shore, where we found the advance of Gen. Grant's army awaiting us. Five of the transports sustained more or less injury, but the sixth received a heavy shot near the water-line, and went down a short distance below the heavy guns of the enemy, the crew escaping to the west shore."[14]

Saturday, April 25, orders were received to hold ourselves in readiness to march at any moment, our camp equipage and sick to be left at Milliken's Bend. After the usual delay of an hour or more the regiment was called into line, the advance was sounded and away we went. The first day out we marched about 10 miles, and went into camp near the little town of Richmond. The following day we marched 12 miles through mud and storm, going into camp on a rich planter's domain.[15] Being without tents, and a heavy rain continuing to fall, many of the men sought the protection of the plantation buildings. The writer, with a number of others, ascended one at a time to the loft of one of the buildings, when the upper joist gave way and we all came down together. Fortunately we escaped with only a few bruises.

April 27, during a heavy rain, we began our third day's mud march. We found the roads almost impassable for men, much less for our teams, which made our progress unusually slow. Still, with unfaltering ranks, we pressed forward and after a march of eight miles a halt was ordered for the night.

The following day we marched 12 miles, going into camp about two miles from the big river. About midnight we were aroused from our camp slumbers by an earnest voice of command, "Battalion, fall in!" after which we hastily moved one mile and remained on picket guard until the dawn of another day.

April 29 we took up our line of march around Lake St. Joseph to Hard Times, La., which place we reached at nightfall after a tramp of 16 miles. Late in the evening the gunboats moved to the attack of the rebel works at Grand Gulf, Miss., which was only intended as a ruse to enable our transports to run the rebel batteries. Being unable to cross the Mississippi at this point, we plunged into the Louisiana forest again and, after marching a short distance, bivouacked for the night.

While marching along the west shore of Lake St. Joseph an alligator suddenly emerged from the dense, swampy marsh on our right and made a mad rush for the lake on our left. Fifty or more rifles gave tongue, and Mr. Gator stopped right there. Gen. Logan, hearing the firing, hastily dispatched an orderly to learn the cause, when he was told to inform the General that "we decidedly objected to being run over by any Louisiana alligator."

Before dawn on April 30 we were in motion down the west bank of the river, and about 10 o'clock came to a halt a short distance above and opposite Bruinsburg, Miss., where we remained until the following day. Meantime our advance columns were transported to the opposite shore, Gen. Grant being among the first to set foot on Mississippi soil.

Early Friday, May 1, a collision took place between two transports while crossing the river, sinking one of the boats, one battery of artillery and a number of horses, which delayed our crossing over until midday.[16]

Immediately upon landing we pushed on with all speed in the direction of Thompson's Hill, where our advance columns had encountered the enemy. The rebel firing in our front quickened our steps and we joined our advance, ready to take a hand in the contest. Shortly after reaching the front the rebels were driven from their strong position on Thompson's Hill, and began a precipitate retreat toward Port Gibson. A pursuit was ordered, when we sprang to the front and rapidly marched on the heels of the retreating foe in a go-as-you-please gait so well remembered by the boys. At dark we lay down on our arms in line of battle two miles from Port Gibson. The following morning we marched into the town, the enemy having evacuated the place during the night.

Words are wanting to express the agony and despair among the inhabitants, lest the Northern army would apply the torch and spread desolation in their homes. Here and there a retreating form was seen hastening around some friendly corner; women and children with blanched faces peered through partly closed doors and curtained windows, and the colored people shouted with delight: "Bress de Lord, de day ob jubilee am come."

Upon reaching what once had been the business part of the town a short halt was ordered, during which time some of the boys made a visit to a large bank building and paid themselves off in Confederate States money, Bank of Port Gibson — bright, crisp, flat money of large and small denominations, made payable 10 years after a treaty of peace between the Confederate and the United States of America.

There was never a time during our service when we were so lavish with money as during the few days following, as what we considered worthless paper was eagerly accepted by some of the citizens in payment for chickens. They appeared to be satisfied, even if they could not change a $500 note, and of course we were satisfied with the deal, because $500 chickens made us an excellent bill of fare.

The enemy thought to check our further progress by burning a fine suspension bridge spanning Bayou Pierre, whereupon our pioneers were brought forward and were soon engaged in constructing a new crossing.

In the meantime a portion of Logan's command was ordered down the bayou to engage the attention of the enemy, who was said to be strongly posted on the north side. During this time the Second Brigade was hastily moving up the bayou about two miles to a ford, where we crossed, after which we moved down on the north side in a northeasterly direction, until we came to the Raymond road, where the rest of our division soon joined us.[17]

These maneuvers seemed to bewilder the enemy, who evacuated their works and retired in confusion. We now made a rapid move to the east branch of Bayou Pierre, reaching there just after the enemy's rear guard had crossed over, firing the bridge behind them. One of our companion regiments dashed across the burning bridge and succeeded in extinguishing the fire, after which it returned to the south side. Night now coming on, we went into bivouac to wait for the dawn of another day.

Notes to Chapter 3

1. Capt. Samuel DeGolyer died Aug. 8, 1863 of wounds received during the siege of Vicksburg. The 8th Michigan Battery's official designation was Battery H, 1st Michigan Light Artillery. *Official Army Register of the Volunteer Force of the United States Army* (Gaithersburg, Md.: Olde Soldier Books, Inc.), vol. V, p. 281.

2. Born in Columbiana County, Ohio, Pvt. William Swaney farmed in Williams County prior to enlisting Aug. 23, 1862 at Bryan, Ohio. He died of disease in Holly Springs' general hospital on Christmas Day 1862. W. Swaney CSR, RG 94, NARA.

3. In late December 1862, a 31,000-man expedition under Sherman's command traveled down the Mississippi River from Memphis, landing on the Yazoo River near Steele's Bayou Dec. 26. While approaching the northern bluffs protecting Vicksburg, his progress was bloodily halted three days later in the battle of Chickasaw Bayou. Sherman suffered 1,776 casualties before withdrawing. Long, p. 300, 301.

4. The heaviest Union guns in Memphis' Fort Pickering were 8-inch Columbiads, 8-inch siege howitzers, 32-pounder smoothbores and rifles, and 20-pounder Parrott rifles. *The Official Atlas of the Civil War* (New York: Thomas Yoseloff, Inc., 1958), plate 114.

5. The text of Logan's address was published Feb. 28, 1863 in the *Toledo Commercial.* Col. Scott urged its publication, writing to the *Commercial* on Feb. 15: "Gen. Logan is a sound war man and the 68th is with him. I have no anti-war men in my regiment. Not a man has deserted, and such a cheer as went up when this address was read on dress parade was cheering."

6. John A. Logan, a native of Jackson County, Ill., was commissioned major general March 13, 1863 to rank from the preceding Nov. 29. He commanded the Army of the Tennessee for five days in July 1864, and was nicknamed "Black Jack" due to his dark eyes, mustache and hair. Warner, p. 281-283.

7. This small, propeller-driven craft was named the *Rawlins,* about "the size of a canal boat," wrote Quartermaster Sergt. Jacob Bruner. "They are cutting the canal ... from the river to the lake for the passage of steam-boats. They are also cutting at the other end of the lake to connect it with Bayou Macon. The work is still progressing. I think it will flood a great part of the southern part of the state." Bruner to Martha Bruner, March 4, 1863, OHS.

8. At the time, acting Rear Admiral David D. Porter commanded the Federal Mississippi Squadron.

9. Co. K Sergt. Henderson J. Hunter, a house painter from Williams County, was promoted April 14, 1863 to second lieutenant of Co. E, then transferred to Co. I. H.J. Hunter CSR, RG 94, NARA.

10. Brig. Gen. Lorenzo Thomas was the U.S. Army's adjutant general from 1861 to 1869. In March 1863 the War Department authorized Thomas to begin organizing regiments of former slaves in the Mississippi Valley. White officers for these regiments were drawn mostly from personnel already serving in the field. Warner, p. 502-503; William A. Gladstone, *Men of Color* (Gettysburg: Thomas Publications, 1993), p. 25.

11. Hissong, Perrin and Bruner, after April 1863 discharges from the 68th Ohio, were commissioned line officers in the 9th Louisiana Volunteers of African Descent (later designated the 63rd U.S. Colored Troops). On June 7, 1863 some 1,500 Confederates attacked the Union post at Milliken's Bend, La., forcing its defenders, including the 9th Louisiana A.D., to the Mississippi riverbank. Friendly gunboat fire helped rally the Federals, who then drove off their attackers. Of 652 Union casualties, Bruner and Benjamin Franklin Perrin were killed. Perrin, a native of Nova Scotia, Canada, had been a Bowling Green mechanic prior to December 1861 enlistment in the 68th Ohio. Long, p. 363; L.J. Hissong, B.F. Perrin and J. Bruner CSR, RG 94, OHS.

12. According to a member of Co. K, on April 22 the 68th "made about 3/4 of a mile of causeway and dirted it one foot deep." Before noon the following day it laid down an additional half mile of roadway. Simeon Gillis diary, CAC.

13. This riverine expedition occurred the night of April 22. All those mentioned by Loop ran Vicksburg's batteries aboard the steamer *Empire City.* J.C. Banks, W. Barnhart, J. Dicus, J. Longberry and J. Snyder CSR, RG 94, NARA.

14. The author of this account is not identified.

15. The diary of Pvt. Simeon Gillis, Co. K, states the 68th camped April 26 on the Holmes' plantation, midway between Richmond and New Carthage, La.

16. The steamboats *Horizon* and *Moderator* collided at 3 a.m. May 1, with the loss of the former boat and all guns, vehicles and most of the horses belonging to Battery G, 2nd Illinois Light Artillery. Two soldiers also drowned. *OR*, vol. XXIV, pt. 1, p. 643.

17. Brig. Gen. Elias S. Dennis temporarily led the 2nd Brigade while Gen. Leggett was absent on leave. Leggett resumed command May 16. *OR,* vol. XXIV, pt. 1, p. 647.

4

'How varied are the charms of military glory'

Before daylight on Sunday, May 3, we crossed the west branch of Bayou Pierre and started in the direction of Hankinson's Ferry on the Big Black River. Early in the day the enemy appeared in our front and tried to check our onward course, but we continued to press them back until about noon, when we found the main body advantageously posted on a high, commanding ridge.

The Second Brigade was ordered to move west on the Grand Gulf road while the rest of our division was engaged in developing the enemy's position. We moved a short distance on the Grand Gulf road, and then made an abrupt turn to the north. Our march was noiseless and all orders were given in a low tone. Off to our right the sound of heavy skirmishing was heard, which became more distinct as we hastened along through swamp and thicket, when suddenly, late in the afternoon, we fell upon the enemy's right flank, crushing it with a single blow, which caused the rebels to rush pell-mell toward Hankinson's Ferry, four miles away.

The face of the country was broken and hilly, and was partly covered with a dense undergrowth of timber, which afforded the enemy a chance to cover his retreat. We, however, quickly took up the pursuit and followed close upon the heels of the panic-stricken foe, capturing about 200 prisoners who had hidden in the canebrake and swamps along the line of march; also a lot of wagons. We reached the ferry just as the enemy's rear guard was crossing over, capturing a lot of pioneer tools and preventing the destruction of the bridge. It now being night the chase was discontinued, and we went into camp where we remained the three succeeding days.[1]

A heavy guard was put out in the best defensive position, and those off duty hoped to be able to get a good night's rest, but about 10 o'clock we were called to repel a supposed attack. A bright moon was shining, making the night nearly as light as day, volleys of musketry meanwhile breaking the stillness of a Sabbath evening on the Big Black. At last a battery of artillery responded and awoke the echoes across the Black by hurling a storm of shot and shell into the enemy's lines, which caused a general stampede. We were then permitted to rest in peace until morning.

The following morning everything appeared quiet on the opposite side of the Black, so we went to the river and procured water to make our coffee. In the meantime a number of officers and men repaired to the river to take a quiet bath. We closely examined the opposite shore, but could see no signs of an enemy; yet our picket guards were confident that the bushes over there were full of Johnnies. Lieut. Richardson and several others thought differently. We had removed our clothes and were engaged in removing an accumulation of Southern mud, when suddenly from the opposite side of the river came a terrific crash of musketry, followed by the bellowing of artillery. Quickly the bathers rushed out of the water and hurriedly they dressed, in all fantastic ways. Some, with shirts on inside out, with bosoms behind, and grabbing coats and vests, made a hasty retreat.

While Lieut. Richardson was hastily engaged in executing a series of hops, skips and jumps, a 12-pound shot from a rebel gun struck a tree about 10 feet away. The tree came down, and for a moment the Lieutenant's form was hidden from view in a mist of falling boughs. He soon after appeared, minus his hat, and as he joined us remarked: "How varied are the charms of military glory!"

Soon afterward the regiment moved into position on the top of an elevation about 60 rods away. Two batteries also rolled into position and opened with solid shot and canister, which soon caused the enemy to retire from our front.

May 5 we remained in camp in the timber half a mile from the river. Late in the day the pickets on either side of the Black had a lively engagement. Then all would become quiet, only to be broken a few moments later by the bang! bang! of muskets of the blue and the gray. Thus the next two days rolled around.[2]

Our division train was ordered to return to Grand Gulf — recently evacuated by the enemy — after supplies, and on May 7 we marched up the south side of the Big Black to Rocky Springs, where we remained until the morning of May 9. The utmost vigilance was maintained to guard against an attack by the enemy, and for this purpose heavy detachments were sent far out on the flank to ascertain, if possible, the presence of any hostile force.

L. M. Strayer Collection

A lifelong resident of northwest Ohio, Lay Whitney Richardson assisted raising the 68th Ohio's Company G and was promoted its second lieutenant in January 1863 (to date from Sept. 29, 1862). Following his January 1865 muster-out at Savannah, Ga., Richardson visited Washington. "Before leaving the capital," he later wrote, "I took advantage of my first and only opportunity to call at the White House, and was introduced to Mr. Lincoln, and was cordially welcomed by a shake of his big hand. This was only a few weeks prior to his assassination."

Sherman's men, dirty and way-worn, but with a wild fire of delight and pride in their eyes, were now swiftly approaching us from Grand Gulf. The early morning of May 9 found us once more in motion. After a march of about 10 miles we went into camp near the little village of Utica.

Early the following morning, Sunday, our brigade was ordered out to lead the advance. However, the order was revoked and we remained in camp until late in the afternoon, when we formed into line as Third Division train guard, marched 10 miles, and toward the hour of midnight went into bivouac.

On May 11 we took up our line of march in the direction of Raymond. We moved rapidly over the ground, now in bright sunshine and now in a torrent of rain, until late in the day, when we came to a halt and stacked arms on Roache's plantation, where we remained until the next morning.

The morning of Tuesday, May 12, we silently moved out of camp. Soon the enemy showed up in our front, when a heavy line of flankers was deployed on each side, and all moved forward in line of battle until about 10 o'clock, when we found the enemy strongly posted about two miles from Raymond.

Gen. Logan ordered an advance against the enemy's position. Our regiment deployed and moved across an open field on the double-quick to a rail fence bordering the timber, when we quickly moved by the left flank and crossed to the opposite side of the Raymond road, then moved by the front and dashed into the timber. At this moment a loud shout reached our ears, coming from our companion regiments, "Go in, boys, we are with you!" We hastily moved forward to the opposite side of a narrow belt of timber and soon gained a position near an open field, where we were ordered to stand to arms and watch our front.[3]

Hardly had we reached our position when the battle opened in its wildest fury on our right, where, under cover of the timber, a heavy force of the enemy was massed under the command of Gen. Gregg.[4] As our regiment was in position on the extreme left of our division, and the heavy fighting took place on the right and center, we were not so warmly engaged as were our companion regiments. It was trying to us to remain quiet, listening to the terrific roar of battle which deepened every minute only a short distance away, and yet know little or nothing of how goes the battle.[5] But there we were in company with our companion regiments, and there to stay. Such was the fortune of war; in battle some regiments' losses were appalling, while others in close proximity escaped with a few slight wounds.

We were, however, suddenly awakened to the fact that a heavy body of the enemy was moving in our front. In an instant the rattling click of gunlocks ran down the line of our brigade, and a terrible volley flashed from that wall of steel that carried death in its train. We were too earnestly engaged in watching our front and listening to the answering roar of the enemy to have noticed DeGolyer's battery, which had taken a position close to our left, and opened upon the enemy with shot and shell.

About this time what appeared to have been a move of the enemy for the purpose of charging DeGolyer's battery was met by such a terrific fire that the enemy halted, then turned and fled.[6]

Logan, in the meantime, with a portion of his command, was moving to the extreme right, where they fell upon the enemy's left flank, causing the enemy to flee from all parts of the field, leaving Logan's proud command master of the situation.

The battle of Raymond, which Gen. Grant said was one of the hardest-fought battles of the Vicksburg campaign, was fought and won by Logan's Third Division alone and unaided. The battle raged with wildest fury about four hours, during which time Logan's loss in killed and wounded was very heavy. Our regiment, however, was fortunate to escape with a few slight wounds. The enemy's loss was much greater than Logan's.[7]

A captured rebel officer, in speaking of the battle, said: "We saw your men coming in on our left, and held our fire until you were in close range, and then poured a volley right into your faces. We supposed that when the smoke lifted your line would be gone, but imagine our surprise to find you coming right along, and had not my men got out of your way you would have walked right over them."

After the battle, while waiting for orders to move, the writer walked down the line to the right where once had been a living wall of gray. At one place I could have walked for some distance over the bodies of the dead, the result of an enfilade fire by Logan's men.[8]

As the sun was nearing the western horizon we went into camp in the suburbs of the town of Raymond. Early the next morning we marched out on the Clinton road, our regiment acting as rear guard of the entire division. During the afternoon the heavens wept great billows of moisture, but we tramped on through mud and storm, and about sundown stacked our arms in the streets of Clinton. The leading brigade of our division entered Clinton early in the afternoon, and when we came up we found the boys busily engaged in celebrating the event by making bonfires of the inflammable part of the [Vicksburg & Jackson] Railroad.

May 14 we were set in motion toward Jackson, the capital of the state. Logan's men followed close upon the heels of Quinby's Division, which was leading the advance.[9] No resistance was encountered by Quinby's men until they had reached a point about two miles from Jackson, where the enemy was found advantageously posted. The Third Division (Logan's) was ordered to the front and, in company with other commands belonging to Gen. Grant's invincibles, engaged the enemy. The attack was successful, and our boys ate their supper in the city. Meantime our regiment remained about two miles west of the city as Third Division train guard, where the stormy night of Thursday, May 14, found us.

The campaign, the object of which was the reduction of Vicksburg, thus far had succeeded admirably, and Gen. Grant was well pleased, as he had planted his army between Pemberton's and Johnston's armies. Meanwhile Gen. McClernand's command in our rear was making noisy demonstrations to deceive Pemberton, in Vicksburg, as to Grant's real intentions until Johnston's force could be disposed of. This program was carried out to the letter. Johnston's army was badly whipped and driven from the field, the city of Jackson captured and wholly destroyed as a military depot, and our noble chieftain was now ready to cultivate the acquaintance of Pemberton.[10]

For 14 long days we had kept our backs to the Mississippi River, but on the morning of May 15 all was hurry and bustle in making ready for a rapid march toward Vicksburg, 40 miles away. The day after the battle of Jackson rain came down in torrents, until every gully and ravine was a raging flood. The country was broken and the soil a sticky clay that clung to the feet of the men, making it hard marching. Still, we pressed forward, and late in the day came up in the rear of Gen. Hovey's Division of the Thirteenth Corps, and went into camp in the woods about three miles east of what afterward became known in history as Champion Hills.[11]

A short distance from our camp was a large farmhouse, which the writer, armed with a camp-kettle, visited for the purpose of getting water to make coffee. Back of the house was the well where a number of my comrades were busily engaged in drawing water. But being of an inquisitive turn, and anxious to learn more of my surroundings, I soon found my way into the house, which to all appearances had been abandoned upon the approach of the Yankees. The rooms were bare save for a lone covered wash-tub, which of course must bear investigation, when my curiosity was rewarded by finding it nearly full of honey, a portion of which was hastily conveyed to my camp-kettle. I then started for camp, when my attention was called to a number of boys who were sampling the contents of a barrel containing an elixir that makes a fellow forget his trials and remember his misery no more. My kettle, half full of honey, I filled with the liquor and hastened away to join my comrades, whom I found in a much-disturbed state of mind because of my being gone so long. After the facts were made known coffee was dispensed with in our mess, as my preparation of "aqua vitae" and honey answered all purposes.[12]

Early on May 16 we formed in line and rushed to the relief of Gen. Hovey's command, which had engaged the enemy at Champion Hills.

By way of digression I will say Champion Hills were so called because they were part of a plantation owned by John Champion. The first hill had an elevation of about 60 feet, but on the west side of this was another hill with an elevation of about 80 feet, which was considered quite a prominent elevation for that otherwise flat section of country. On the top of this second hill was planted the enemy's artillery, commanding the approaches from all directions, and making the position a remarkably strong one. West of the second hill were spurs or foot-hills, etc.

Our enemy's hearts must have sunk with fear as they saw from the heights above us that solid phalanx, with our grand old flags proudly floating in the early morning breeze.

Logan's Division rapidly moved to the right of the Jackson road and crossed a wide field of bottom land, gaining a position near the edge of timber skirting the high grounds in our front. We were hardly in position on the right of Gen. Hovey's command before the enemy made a furious assault, uttering their wild rebel yell.

DeGolyer's battery had gone into position near our regiment, and from the moment the enemy came from cover hurled shot and shell, to which was added a storm of leaden hail from the 68th and its companion regiments. Great gaps were made in the enemy's ranks, yet on came the living toward the position we held. We saw that compact mass of gray come out of the timber; saw them as they reached a rail fence in our front; saw the rails fly as they threw it down. Volley followed volley in quick succession.

One of Logan's staff at this moment galloped up and shouted: "Logan commands you to hold your position and we will bag the whole of Pemberton's army," which command was answered by a withering volley from the muskets of Leggett's men that threw the enemy into confusion and drove them to cover. Gen. Grant had dispatched an aide-de-camp to inquire of Logan, "How goes the battle?" To which Logan replied: "Tell the General that my division can't be whipped by all the rebels this side of hell. We are going ahead, and won't stop till we get orders."

We were still holding our position with a death-like grip, momentarily expecting a renewed assault by the enemy. "Hold your fire," shouted Maj. Welles, "until you are sure of your man." Directly in our front was observed a rebel flag. "Hand me your gun," said Lieut. Col. Snook. "I believe I can stop the bearer of that rebel rag." But the next moment our Lieutenant Colonel was struggling in the agony of death. In his death the flag of our country lost a gallant defender, and the 68th Ohio an officer who was like a father to his boys. Many brave men fell on that fateful day, whose loss was just as much felt by comrades and friends, but who were not as widely known as was Lieut. Col. John S. Snook of Antwerp, Ohio.[13]

But, hark! a terrific cheer followed by another and still another assailed our ears as coming from our right, accompanied by volley upon volley of musketry and the groaning and thundering of heavy guns. What did it mean? Had a heavy force of the enemy assaulted our flank and were they sweeping on with irresistible fury? We looked at each other and grasped our muskets more firmly. Again that wild confusion reached our ears. There was no mistaking the long drawn-out Union cheer from the rebel yell, "Wah-hoo." The intrepid Logan had hurled one brigade of his division upon the enemy's left flank, crushing it with a single blow and capturing a battery of artillery. Co. F, 32d Ohio, afterward manned this battery.

This charge by a portion of Logan's division started the enemy on the run, and the battle of Champion Hills was over. A great victory was won; the road to Vicksburg was now open. We took up the pursuit and rapidly moved over the western spur of the hills and joined the rest of our division near where it had made the charge and captured the battery.

About this time DeGolyer's boys came up, and as the battery was moving into line to give the enemy a parting shot, Thos. Lang, formerly a member of our regiment, was violently thrown from a caisson and fatally injured.[14]

The battle of Champion Hills began about 9 a.m. and raged with fury until about 3 o'clock in the afternoon, when the enemy broke in the wildest confusion, leaving cannons, wagons and guns in our hands, besides the killed and wounded. Our regiment suffered a loss of 11 killed and 47 were wounded. A large percent of our wounded comrades remained with the regiment.[15]

Notes to Chapter 4

1. Gen. Logan reported 154 Confederates were captured the afternoon of May 3. The Hankinson's Ferry bridge was secured by 2nd Brigade skirmishers and advance guards commanded by Col. Manning F. Force, 20th Ohio. *OR,* vol. XXIV, pt. 1, p. 645.

2. Co. K's second lieutenant, James F. Cosgro, related that the Confederates "shelled us yesterday morning [May 6] as we were in line of battle and they came very near giving us 'some sore heads.' One shell bursted right over company K, but, 'as we all belong to the church' we escaped and nary [a] man in the regiment was hurt. We took quite a number of prisoners, and they keep coming in all the time. I was on picket last night and three came up like men and gave themselves up. I ought to have shot them, but the 'poor seeds' said they never had shot at us and never would, so I sent them up to Headquarters and let Gen. Logan dispose of them. There are two more in camp now within forty feet of me; one of them is a Mississippian and the other is an Irishman, the 'dirty blackguard;' to fight against as good a government as this he ought to hang." Cosgro to "Friend Hank," May 7, 1863 in *The Weekly Bryan Democrat,* May 28, 1863.

3. According to 2nd Lt. Samuel R. Adams of Co. A, "On the 12th ... Our brigade had the advance and opened the fight, the 68th Ohio on the extreme left of the line. Col. Scott, however, upon examination of the ground, ascertained that by throwing the left of his regiment forward so as to form an acute angle with the balance of the line, he could place his men under cover of a creek bank and get an enfilading fire on the rebel position. This was scarcely done when the battle opened on the right and centre with terrible vigor." Adams, June 17, 1863 to the *Toledo Commercial,* July 1, 1863.

4. Brig. Gen. John Gregg commanded Confederate forces at Raymond, which consisted principally of 2,500 Tennesseans and Texans belonging to his infantry brigade. *OR,* vol. XXIV, pt. 1, p. 739.

5. To the 68th Ohio's right, the 20th Ohio was heavily engaged, as described by its adjutant, 1st Lt. Henry O. Dwight: "When we rushed through [a] brook we found the enemy upon us, but we found also that the bank of the brook sloped off a bit, with a kind of bench at its further edge, which made a first-rate shelter. So we dropped on the ground right there, and gave those Texans all the bullets we could cram into our Enfields until our guns were hot enough to sizzle. The gray line paused, staggered back like a ship in collision which trembled in every timber from the shock. Then they too gave us volley after volley, always working up toward us, breasting our fire until they had come within twenty, or even fifteen paces. In one part of the line some of them came nearer than that, and had to be poked back with the bayonet. It was the 7th Texas which had struck us, a regiment which had never been beaten in any fight. We soon found that they didn't scare worth a cent. They kept trying to pass through our fire, jumping up, pushing forward a step, and then falling back into the same place, just as you may see a lot of dead leaves in a gale of wind, eddying to and fro under a bank, often rising up as if to fly away, but never able to advance a peg. It was a question of life or death with us to hold them ...." Dwight, "A Soldier's Story. The Affair on the Raymond Road," *New York Daily Tribune,* Nov. 21, 1886.

Another 20th Ohioan, Sergt. Osborn H. Oldroyd of Co. E, wrote that "For two hours the contest raged furiously" on the 2nd Brigade's center and right. A bullet crashed into the head of Oldroyd's bunkmate, mortally wounding him. "One by one the boys were dropping out of my company. The second lieutenant in command was wounded; the orderly sergeant dropped dead, and I find myself (fifth sergeant) in command of the handful remaining. In front of us was a reb in a red shirt, when one of our boys, raising his gun, remarked, "see me bring that red shirt down," while another cried out, "hold on, that is my man." Both fired, and the red shirt fell — it may be riddled by more than those two shots. A red shirt is, of course, rather too conspicuous on a battle field. Into another part of the line the enemy charged, fighting hand to hand, being too close to fire, and using the butts of their guns. But they were all forced to give way at last, and we followed them up for a short distance, when we were passed by our own reinforcements coming up just as we had whipped thc enemy. I took the roll-book from the pocket of our dead [orderly] sergeant, and found that while we had gone in with thirty-two men, we came out with but sixteen — one-half of the brave little band, but a few hours before so full of hope and patriotism, either killed or wounded. Nearly all the survivors could show bullet marks in clothing or flesh, but no man left the field on account of wounds. When I told Colonel Force of our loss, I saw tears course down his cheeks, and so intent were his thoughts upon his fallen men that he failed to note the bursting of a shell above him, scattering the powder over his person, as he sat at the foot of a tree." Oldroyd, *A Soldier's Story of the Siege of Vicksburg* (Springfield, Ill.: H.W. Rokker, 1885), p. 17-18.

6. "The rebels moved to the charge with wild yells," recorded the 68th Ohio's Samuel Adams, Co. A. "The fight became desperate and lasted with unabated fury for two hours, when the rebels were driven back with great loss. During this time, DeGolyer's 8th Michigan Battery was ordered to take position on the left of the 68th Ohio, and opened on the rebels with great precision. A few minutes after, a line of rebels, probably two regiments, seemed to rise out of the ground immediately in front of us, and with fixed bayonets prepared to charge our battery. They moved up splendidly, but their advance was checked by a withering fire from our men behind the creek bank, sending them back in confusion, thereby saving the battery and preventing the flanking of our entire line." Adams, June 17, 1863 to the *Toledo Commercial,* July 1, 1863.

7. Federal losses at Raymond totaled 66 killed, 339 wounded and 37 captured or missing. *OR,* vol. XXIV, pt. 2, p. 167. Confederate casualties as reported by Gen. Gregg were 73 killed, 251 wounded and 190 captured or missing. The 3rd Tennessee and 7th Texas sustained 67 percent of these losses. *OR,* vol. XXIV, pt. 1, p. 739.

8. When the firing ceased, recalled Adjutant Henry Dwight, 20th Ohio, "we could stand up and stretch our legs and rinse the charcoal and saltpetre out of our mouths at the muddy brook. I looked at my watch. We had been at work on those Texans near two hours and a half, although I must say that after it was over it did not seem more than an hour. We were a hardlooking lot. The smoke had blackened our faces, our lips and our throats so far down that it took a week to get the last of it out. The most dandified officer in the regiment looked like a coalheaver." Dwight, "A Soldier's Story. The Affair on the Raymond Road," *New York Daily Tribune,* Nov. 21, 1886.

9. At the time, Brig. Gen. Isaac F. Quinby commanded the 7th Division, 17th Corps.

10. Ordered May 9 to take command of all Southern troops in Mississippi, Gen. Joseph E. Johnston attempted unsuccessfully to reinforce Vicksburg's bastion with 12,000 men. Cut off by Grant, he left two brigades at Jackson in vain hope of delaying the Federals before withdrawing to the north. Lt. Gen. John C. Pemberton defended Vicksburg as commander of the Department of Mississippi and Eastern Louisiana. Long, p. 351, 353; Ezra J. Warner, *Generals in Gray: Lives of the Confederate Commanders* (Baton Rouge: Louisiana State University Press, 1959), p. 161-162, 232-233.

11. At the time, Brig. Gen. Alvin P. Hovey commanded the 12th Division, 13th Corps.

12. In Mississippi, wrote 1st Lt. George W. Kniss of Co. C, "We soon found ... that our line of supplies was too long and difficult and we must of necessity do some heavy foraging, *and we did.* It seemed rough to take the meat, molasses, sugar and corn meal from farmers along the road ... and the women and children would ask us to leave it, as *their men,* the rebels, had taken most all they had before we came. ..." Kniss, June 13, 1863 in the *Defiance Democrat,* Aug. 1, 1863.

13. Three weeks after Snook's death at Champion Hill, Maj. George Welles of the 68th informed his widow: "The Regiment became engaged about 11 1/2 A.M. in this terrible battle; owing to the broken and hilly nature of the ground, all the field officers dismounted early in the engagement and our horses were sent to the rear. We soon moved forward through an open field into the edge of a thick wood and formed in a small ravine where we remained until the battle closed. From the moment we first arrived at this position the battle raged all around us fiercely, and for two long hours Lieut. Col. Snook gallantly and cooly stood at his post, encouraging the men by his words and actions. About one o'clock P.M. his attention was called to a Rebel Flag, which could be seen a few hundred yards ahead of us. He had no sooner stepped up on the bank and had taken five or six steps to the front, when the fatal ball struck him. He immediately turned round and walked slowly back over the hill and fell into the arms of one of the men, which was the first notice we had that he was hurt. He was immediately carried back to the hospital, but expired before he reached there. He never uttered a groan or spoke a word after he was struck — the ball entered his right breast and passed diagonally through and probably lodged in his heart.

"... having been constantly on the march ... and neither officers or men having their baggage or any facilities for writing, must be my apology for the seeming delay in notifying you of this great bereavement. The fact of our being in the heart of the enemies [*sic*] country, and all our communications *via* Grand Gulf being cut off by the enemy in our rear, and not yet having opened communications to the Yazoo [River], we were unable to send his body north, and were obliged to inter him on the Field. This sad duty was performed by Lieut. Chas. Bates, Co. 'B,' and privates [Daniel A.] Covert [who was himself wounded at Champion Hill], and [Seymour] Carpenter, of Co.

Ohio Historical Society

1st Lt. George W. Kniss, Co. C. After the 68th Ohio entered Jackson, Miss. on May 14, 1863, the Defiance, Ohio native observed that Mississippi's capital was a "gay and festive burg," possessing "some of the finest residences imaginable. Oh! how it did hurt the ladies to see the Yankee promenading the streets of the sacred city." Promoted captain of Co. H in June 1865, Kniss temporarily commanded Battery D, 1st Missouri Light Artillery, for several months late in the war.

'C,' who took every pains that love and friendship could dictate to bury him properly and to mark his grave in such manner that it may be found at any future time if desired by his friends." Welles to Mrs. J.S. Snook, June 5, 1863 in the *Paulding Independent,* June 25, 1863.

Snook's remains later were disinterred and buried in Vicksburg National Cemetery, Section O, Grave 61. *Ohio Roster,* vol. V, p. 802.

14. Loop was partially in error. Pvt. Thomas Lang, a stonecutter born in Glasgow, Scotland and formerly of Co. B, 68th Ohio, had been detailed since April 10, 1863 to Battery D, 1st Illinois Light Artillery, not DeGolyer's battery. T. Lang CSR, RG 94, NARA.

15. Lt. George Kniss, Co. C, tallied the regiment's loss at Champion Hill as 74 killed and wounded. Kniss, June 13, 1863 in the *Defiance Democrat,* Aug. 1, 1863.

Among the injured was Pvt. Simeon Gillis, Co. K, who scribbled in his diary May 16: "I got wounded early in the engagement, layed on the battle field until sundown. I was then carried to the hospt. Shortly afterward my [left] leg was amputated." The procedure was performed by 68th Ohio surgeon Eugene Beauharnais Harrison, a 31-year-old native of Dover, England, and 1857 graduate of Philadelphia's Jefferson Medical College. Harrison noted in his own diary: "Worked very hard. Operated until 2 o'c A.M. Never worked harder. Ampt leg for Gillis 68th below knee. May 17. Rose at 5 o'c A.M. and operated until 9 o'c P.M. Had not the least idea that it was Sunday. Got through with all operations for 3d Div and started for Vicksburg." S. Gillis diary, CAC; E.B. Harrison diary, Civil War Miscellaneous Collection, USAMHI; *Henry County Signal,* April 19, 1906.

Gillis' younger brother, 19-year-old James F. Gillis, spent the fighting May 16 with the 3rd Division's ammunition wagons. That night he was detached to assist in the division hospital, caring for his brother and other wounded. A diarist himself, James recorded the deaths of three men in his ward during the following week, and on May 26 wrote: "The Secesh came here [today]. Took us prisoners and paroled both wounded and nurses and then schadaddled takeing nothing from us but a bottle of brandy." Three more patients died in James' ward before month's end. On June 1, "The Secesh came back and took the names of all they paroled on the 26th of May, which they neglected to do before." Over the next three weeks he noted 10 additional deaths, including those of Co. K comrades Jacob Wiseman (June 1), William H. Beard (June 7) and Henry C. Kime (June 22), who "left $3.40 in my care to be sent to his wife."

The 17th Corps' 3rd Division hospital at Champion Hill closed June 24 with all remaining sick and wounded transported by ambulances and wagons to the Yazoo River. Simeon Gillis was placed aboard the hospital boat *City of Memphis,* on which he found "very good acomidations, good nurses, good grub and good cots to lay on." James Gillis, after reporting to the division provost marshal, was sent June 27 with 26 others to Chickasaw Landing north of Vicksburg. He traveled via the steamer *Jacob Strader* to St. Louis, spent several days at Schofield Barracks, then was ordered to Camp Chase, Ohio, to await exchange. While there his health, damaged by exposure in Louisiana and Mississippi, deteriorated to the point that he was discharged from service Sept. 23 for consumption and "colliquative diarrhoea." Four days later he succumbed to these illnesses at the Gillis farm in Spring Lake, Williams County, Ohio. Simeon Gillis survived his brother by almost 56 years. Discharged for disability Nov. 29, 1863, he eventually became business manager, editor and publisher of the *Bryan Press* (1877-1889), was elected Williams County auditor, and served a number of terms as secretary and president of the 68th Ohio veterans' association. He died March 15, 1919. J.F. and S. Gillis diaries, Gillis Family Papers, CAC; J.F. and S. Gillis CSR, RG 94, NARA; Charles A. Bowersox, editor, *A Standard History of Williams County, Ohio,* vol. I (Chicago: The Lewis Publishing Company, 1920), p. 284.

5

'A liberal sprinkling of rebel shot and shell'

The evening after the battle of Champion Hills we lay on our arms a short distance west of the battlefield, near Baker's Creek. At dawn on Sunday, May 17, we were up and moving on. After a rapid march of about 10 miles we reached the Big Black, where our advance columns were warmly engaged with the enemy; but Sherman's men, having crossed the river above us, caused the enemy in our front to melt away like snow under a warm sun.[1]

Pontoons were thrown across the Black, and our advance columns were soon climbing the bluffs on the west side. It now being dark, we went into bivouac till morning. About 10 o'clock the following morning the silvery notes of Mort's bugle once more called us into line.[2] We turned our faces in the direction of Vicksburg and that night went into camp four miles from the city. By 6 o'clock the morning of May 19 we were again in motion. The thundering of heavy guns in our front seemed to infuse new life into our bodies as we hastened to the support of our comrades. Upon reaching the front we were ordered in line on the reserve, where we remained through the day and succeeding night.[3]

Being anxious to learn more of our surroundings, a number of us ascended a slight elevation in our front, when behold! There before us stretched away a long line of rebel works. We had been there but a short time when a rebel battery threw several solid shot in our vicinity. We hastily retired behind the hill.

The following day we remained in reserve, but were ordered to hold ourselves in readiness to move at a moment's notice. Heavy cannonading occurred at intervals throughout the day, but no infantry firing, save by the sharpshooters of friend and foe.

Early May 21 our regiment moved forward along the Jackson road and went into position in a bushy ravine directly in front of the enemy's heavy works. At short distance away was a large fort [the

3rd Louisiana Redan]. DeGolyer's boys were on hand and hurled a terrific storm of iron over our heads and into the enemy's works, which we imagined caused the unfriendly heads watching us to turn back-somersaults into their works and grant us a little more respect.

The enemy's batteries responded and we were treated to the grandest display of iron hail we had ever witnessed. Unfortunately, one of DeGolyer's guns threatened to do us injury, as some of the shells had an unpleasant habit of exploding just as they left the muzzle, and there was no way of telling just where the pieces would strike. Col. R.K. Scott sent back word to Capt. DeGolyer "to give that slobbering gun a rest."

I think I am safe in saying that up to this time our position on the Jackson road was nearer to the enemy's works than was that of any other regiment in Logan's Division. Late in the day orders were issued by Gen. Grant for a simultaneous assault by the three corps investing the enemy's lines, to take place at 10 o'clock the following morning. The day closed with heavy cannonading all along the lines of the blue and the gray.

Heavy firing continued throughout the night, and at daylight, May 22, grew more rapid and furious. Then the artillery ceased and all remained quiet except the incessant firing of the pickets.

Promptly at the appointed hour the signal gun was fired and the assault commenced. The assaulting columns moved forward under a furious fire from the enemy's artillery and infantry, which was responded to by nearly 100 guns along McPherson's front. The three points of attack were the enemy's works in our front, the city by the mortars opposite, and the river batteries by the gunboats.

Heavy cannonading and a steady roll of musketry, mingled with the howling of shot and shell and whistling of musket balls, made the day one long to be remembered. At the designated hour our regiment made a rapid forward movement and a demonstration against the enemy's main fort, just north of the Jackson road,

Opposite: **Close-quarters combat during the unsuccessful Federal assaults at Vicksburg May 22, 1863, as dramatically depicted in a wartime issue of *Frank Leslie's Illustrated* newspaper. That day Grant's Army of the Tennessee suffered 3,199 casualties — 359 of them in the 17th Corps' 3rd Division, to which the 68th Ohio belonged.**

and gained a new position about 200 yards in front of the enemy's heavy works, where we remained till nightfall, when we returned to our first position. Our regiment's loss during the day was "eight wounded."

The assault on the enemy's lines was extremely gallant on the part of the men engaged. But in vain did they try to breast a storm of shot and shell that rained in one ceaseless, raging torrent upon them. At last the bugles sounded a recall, and the bleeding columns fell sullenly back, beaten for the first time since crossing the Mississippi. The enemy's works were too strong to be taken that way, although some regiments succeeded in planting their flags close up under the enemy's works. They were not able to maintain their position, therefore very reluctantly retired from a too-close proximity to a line of powerful earthworks, which vomited forth death and destruction.[4]

May 23 we began to settle down to a new life. The assault on the previous day had been a failure, and we now entered upon a regular and determined siege, which progressed satisfactorily for 40 long days and nights.

We started the construction of roads around the hills or over them to the Yazoo River, in the rear of our army, and soon supplies of food began to reach us, which we needed very badly. We had left our tents, knapsacks and cooking utensils at Milliken's Bend, and many of these articles we never saw again. In fact, we were hard up for cooking utensils and shelter from a boiling hot southern sun. However, our canteens served us well in our dilemma. One half of the canteen was used for a frying-pan, and our tin cups for coffee pots.

May 24 to 27 we occupied our first position, in front of DeGolyer's battery. All this time there was more or less artillery-firing, and not a little musketry. We soon became accustomed to the roar of heavy guns and the whiz of minies.[5]

May 26 an armistice of some hours' duration was observed to permit friend and foe to remove and bury those who fell on the 22d. The field presented a sickening sight. During the cessation of hostilities a number of the enemy deserted their colors and came into our lines; but after the armistice was ended the ball again opened. We were friends one moment, enemies the next, and seeking to destroy each other.

Heavy cannonading lasted all night. A number of the enemy's shells struck in the hollow near us, wounding several of our regiment. One large shell struck in the camp of the 30th Ill., killing and wounding a number of men.

Early the morning of the 27th we were taken out of the line investing Vicksburg — one brigade from each division — and marched out on the Ridge road toward Yazoo City for the purpose of holding and engaging Gen. Johnston, it being reported that he had assembled a large force to attack our rear. We marched about 40 miles into the country, but Johnston's "heavy force" only developed into a small body of guerrilla cavalry, which hastily retired upon our approach.

The evening of the second day out we arrived in the vicinity of the little village of Mechanics[burg], and went into bivouac on the south side of a deep, swampy and wooded ravine. Several of the boys crossed the ravine. In our front were several buildings belonging to some rich planter. While we were engaged in discussing the project of making the place a visit there appeared near the buildings a number of the enemy. We now remained quiet and counted heads before opening the battle, which, however, was never inscribed on our regiment's flag. Joe Harpel of my company ordered the boys in low tones to scatter out, and at a given signal to charge the rebels, who were seemingly ignorant of our presence.[6] We scattered, as Joe ordered, and then waited his further pleasure, which soon rang out, "Battalion, run, shoot and yell — March!" And away we went after those Johnnies, firing our guns and yelling. The enemy must have thought that the whole of Gen. Grant's army was after them, as they left the vicinity too badly frightened to even think of their guns. In the house we found a table loaded with the necessaries of life, which we stuffed in our haversacks. The house was found to be occupied by some old folks, who, of course, were Union people; but under a feather bed was discovered a small arsenal of muskets, carbines, etc. The writer captured a revolver and a Sharps carbine. The carbine I soon after sold to Sergt. Spurgeon, then First Sergeant of Co. A.[7] We shortly afterwards recrossed the swamp and joined our regiment, with fat haversacks and a whole arsenal of firearms.

The morning of May 31 we took up our line of march down the Yazoo River, destroying everything that might be of use to the enemy as we moved forward, and late in the afternoon went into camp near Haynes' Bluff, where June 1 found us.

One evening about this time a man called Bunker, dubbed by the boys "Capt. Bunker," who was engaged in the dangerous calling of scout and spy, suddenly appeared before the pickets of one of our companion regiments, and was taken prisoner as being a "genuine" rebel. The supposed rebel demanded to be immediately taken to the General's headquarters, which request was granted. The guard, in passing to the rear with Bunker in charge, passed close to a 68th Ohio camp-fire, around which a group of officers was standing drying their clothes, as a heavy rain had fallen, when someone called out: "Hello, Bunk; have they got you?" The officer in charge of the guard, overhearing the remark, called a halt and ordered the guard to "About face — To your posts — March." Bunker now went on his way rejoicing, while the officer felt sold that he had captured Gen. Grant's trusted scout.

Bunker did some fine work for Gen. Grant during the Vicksburg campaign, entering Vicksburg several times and securing reliable information as to the enemy's earthworks, number of men, etc. To everyone who tried to quiz him as to where he had been and what he had seen, he would tell of his desperate encounters and hair-breadth escapes, until his listeners were convinced that he was the biggest liar on earth, to everyone except his General.

We remained in camp near Haynes' Bluff until the morning of June 3, when we were relieved by a division of troops that had come to Gen. Grant's assistance from the North.[8] Our command then started for the trenches at Vicksburg. The day was blistering hot, but we moved forward through clouds of dust until about noon, when, reaching a beautiful stream of water, a halt was ordered to make coffee.

On the opposite side of the road from our watering place was a body of troops in camp, who had a guard on duty along a rail fence. No sooner had we stacked arms than the boys made a rush for some of the rails to start a camp-fire, when they were stopped by the men on guard, causing some little excitement. An officer rode up and ordered the guard to arrest every man who touched one of those rails.

Gen. Blair, who had observed the difficulty, rode forward and inquired of the officer in command of the men guarding the rails, "Colonel, where is your regiment?" To which the officer replied, with a wave of his hand, "Over there."

"Very well," said Gen. Blair, "and I have the honor of commanding the men over here." Then, turning to his men, he said, "Boys, take those rails and make your coffee," adding, "don't you take anything but the top rails." Being accustomed to obeying orders we complied, but when we removed the top rail the next one would be

Mass. MOLLUS, USAMHI

Commanding the Haynes' Bluff-Mechanicsburg expedition, Maj. Gen. Frank P. Blair Jr. reported his forces burned or destroyed grist mills as well as "immense quantities" of corn, bacon and cotton, and seized nearly 1,300 cattle, horses and mules. "Joe Johnston," he wrote, "will find very little for his army in the country between the Black River and Yazoo, for 45 miles north of Vicksburg." Later in the war Blair commanded, at different times, the 15th and 17th corps.

the top, etc., as long as a rail remained.[9]

After the above little colloquy, Blair rode off with a merry twinkle in his eyes. The Colonel now inquired, "Who was that officer?" when one of the boys replied, "Gen. Grant?" "Oh, thunder!" the officer was heard to say as he rode away. Thereafter we never had our right to build a camp-fire disputed.

In the afternoon we resumed our march. While tramping down the Yazoo bottoms a terrific thunder storm burst upon us. A halt was ordered, and our regiment broke ranks. We had taken refuge under the spreading branches of some large trees near the road, when a terrible crashing, grinding report of heaven's artillery rendered us speechless. A tree under which some of the boys were standing had been struck by lightning, but fortunately no one was seriously injured, although some of our guns that were propped against the side of the tree were rendered worthless. After the storm passed over we marched about three miles, when a halt was ordered for the coming night.

Early June 4 we were again set in motion, but as we were getting accustomed to walking we soon covered the distance to our camp, then located in a hollow a half mile from the trenches of Vicksburg. Shortly after reaching our camp a voice was heard calling, "68th Ohio, here's your mail." No more the thought of being tired or hungry, as that most welcome voice brought every comrade to his feet. Bunches of letters and packages were handed over to the Orderly-Sergeant of each company. The Orderly would then mount a log or a stump and call out the names on the envelopes, passing out each one as its owner answered, "Here." When the last name was called and the last letter delivered the men would retire to some quiet place to read and meditate upon what they contained of joy or sorrow, love or friendship.

June 5 we were assigned to duty in the line investing Vicksburg, where we remained until June 22. During the siege covering the intervening time we occupied a position on the Jackson road. Nearby was a battery of siege guns that had been brought forward from the Yazoo River landing during our absence.

The enemy's formidable works once more loomed up in our front. These to all appearances were deserted. But upon closely observing the top of that long line of earthworks, we could now and then see a head, when a leaden ball would whisper a word of caution for the owner to take it down. The same whispers were heard on our side, and we were not long in line before the besieged city before we learned that those leaden messengers carried death with them, as well as words of caution. If the enemy's heads were not visible to us, we would fire at the upper part of their works, well knowing that many heads were in that vicinity.

We felt able to maintain our position and that the end would be all right. However, we needed shovels and picks that we might be able to more thoroughly intrench ourselves. In due time these came, after which a detail was made from each regiment to dig rifle-pits and zigzag trenches in the direction of the enemy. This work, well remembered by us, may not be so plain to others. When in range of the enemy's guns, trained upon us from different directions, we were compelled to guard ourselves against them all. If we dug a trench straight toward the enemy, either infantry or artillery would get in a position to shoot through the whole length of it. But if we

Jerry B. Everts Collection

Corp. Henry Clay Williams, Co. A, was shot June 11 in the Vicksburg trenches. While recuperating from the wound at Cairo, Ill., he contracted "bilious fever and diarrhoea," dying Sept. 3, 1863.

dug the trench crooked and threw the dirt up high on the side next to the enemy, we increased our chances of living a while longer, which most of us preferred to do. We never dug our trench far enough in one direction to make it possible for the enemy to rake it with his deadly fire, but made frequent turns, when chug! The enemy's leaden and iron balls would go into the piled-up dirt. Most of this dangerous though important work was done under cover of darkness.

Where there was special danger we dug the trench quite deep, and threw up the dirt for defense, and by so doing the enemy could not hit us until he first shot a hole through the piled-up dirt. We never dug our trench so deep that we required long ladders to climb out. And right here I am reminded of a plate in Headley's life of Gen. Grant, where in the siege of Vicksburg the soldiers are represented carrying ladders to scale the enemy's works. In reply I ask: How many of the heroes of Vicksburg ever saw one of those ladders?[10]

Generally, when digging in the trench, the head or end men would be compelled to prosecute their work under the protection of a sap-roller, which consisted of a round basket eight or 10 feet long and from four to six feet in diameter. These rollers were made of woven wire and willow brush, the center firmly packed with cotton, and as we moved forward were rolled over and over straight toward the enemy, and in front of those working in the trench, thus protecting them from the fire of sharpshooters. Under these friendly protections we worked our way toward the enemy's lines, notwithstanding the ceaseless volleys of musketry and a blazing sun.

In the meantime there was more noise around us than that made by the muskets of both armies, as back behind us were planted our batteries, which at intervals would send shot and shell over our heads and into the enemy's works. Our guns were sure to get a response from the enemy, and there was nothing that would flatten us out in the trenches so quickly as the roar of the enemy's heavy siege gun, named Whistling Dixie, as its ponderous shell came shrieking and squalling through the air in our direction and exploded in our lines. On one occasion one of these big shells failed to explode, when some of the boys went and dug it out of the ground. The rebel measured 11 inches.

Our colored boy, Dick, used to explain to us the language of those ponderous rebel shells, or as he styled them, "Yankee hunters." "What is you? What is you? Here you is — bung!" Shells from different guns made different noises when passing through the air, but our Dick was equal to the occasion and translated the voice of another as “I'se a comin, whar's dat nigger? I'se a comin, whar's dat nigger?”

In the trenches the danger from stray balls was not very great, so long as we kept our bodies behind our works. On one occasion a man of Co. D raised himself above the works and shouted to the enemy, only a few yards away: “Oh, you fools, you can't hit anybody.” Immediately following his assertion was a thump. The shot had struck our comrade's head. The wound did not prove fatal.

A day spent in the trenches was anything but agreeable, as the scorching rays of Old Sol poured down without any regard to our comfort. We would stand in mud and water for hours where not a breath of air was stirring, with a mid-summer's sun beating down upon us until we felt a sense of smothering suffocation. Special attention would always be given us when moving past any exposed position, and a liberal sprinkling of rebel shot and shell would generally increase our desire to gain the protection of some friendly shelter. If we could not readily reach shelter we would lie down and flatten out as thin as possible, then turn ourselves edgeways to the enemy until the firing ceased, when we were up and away like a shot. Occasionally when on duty in the trenches we would elevate our caps on ramrods so they would show above the works, in order to test the marksmanship of the enemy. Sometimes the enemy hit the mark, which fact taught us to be careful of our heads when they were inside of our caps.

As a rule we went on duty every other morning; that is, about half of the regiment would be ordered out each morning to relieve those who were on duty the previous day. Oftentimes when in camp we were engaged in writing letters to our Northern homes, many of which cast a shadow over a home circle. The tidings they brought to many an aching heart were “killed, wounded or missing.”

As previously stated, our camp was located on low ground a half mile in the rear, but not far enough away to escape the mewing and shrieking of balls and shells from the enemy's guns. Therefore, we remained quiet, as there was no particular pleasure in rambling about the hills and ravines where balls and shells were falling. Many were the daily incidents of the long and trying siege, which, should I try to enumerate, would fill a volume. We used to go on duty directly in front of the formidable fort to the left of the Jackson road, where we made ourselves as comfortable as possible, never failing to bserve all precautions and, with good head protection, do the watching and shooting while our comrades did the resting. Our trenches or rifle-pits were provided with head logs, which were propped up a few inches, leaving a space large enough to poke our guns through as often as occasion required. Should we depart from this rule of warfare and expose any portion of our body above the head log, we were almost sure to be rewarded by hearing the whiz of a rebel ball. Once, the head log was hurled into the trench upon Co. I by a solid shot from the enemy. Co. F immediately came to the rescue and helped to extricate the boys from a not very desirable situation. Strange as it may appear, no one was seriously injured.

Some writers contend that there was no heavy gun called Whistling Dick in position anywhere along Grant's line. I claim, however, that a 10-inch gun was brought up from the Yazoo landing, and on June 10 was placed in position on McPherson's line. I also claim that it was this gun, Whistling Dick, that silenced the enemy's gun named Whistling Dixie, which was in position some distance in the rear of the enemy's main line. Dick played an important part on McPherson's front and succeeded in silencing a number of the enemy's guns.

June 14 a number of the rebels' heavy guns gave Dick their attention. Dick, however, stood the racket without injury and at regular intervals growled out his response. Early the next morning the enemy made another effort to silence Dick, but without success. Dick continued to hurl shells to the close of the siege.

Night after night we were entertained by a display of fireworks from Admiral Porter's fleet of mortar boats anchored in the river above the besieged city. Burning fuses of the large shells from the contending guns were a grand sight, and from our position in the trenches we would watch them as they described a half circle through the air, accompanied by an unearthly screeching noise that would strike terror to the hearts of those not used to them. When one of the enemy's heavy guns gave us its attention and sent a 100-pound shell in our direction, it was not quite so entertaining.

One day during a terrific artillery engagement, Gen. Logan joined us in the trenches. To see Logan in the trenches was nothing unusual, but upon this occasion he observed some of his men standing in an exposed position, earnestly engaged in watching the puffs of smoke from the enemy's works, and apparently oblivious of the fact that they were a target for the enemy's sharpshooters. In commanding tones, Logan ordered the men down, saying: "Men, don't unnecessarily expose yourselves." The men complied, while Logan walked along the trench to a point which seemed fitted for his purpose, when, raising himself up high enough to get a good view of the enemy's works, he drew his field-glass and was intently studying the enemy's line of battle when one of the men in the trench addressed him: "General, please get down; don't unnecessarily expose yourself." To this sally, which was only to remind the General of his own words of caution to the boys, Logan, in his usual happy vein, replied: "Boys, never mind me. It takes men to make good soldiers. We can find a General almost anywhere."

The enemy had a hand grenade or shell. These were about six inches long by three inches in diameter, with a short fuse attached. After lighting this fuse the shell was thrown over into our trench, only a few yards away. Sometimes it burst, but often it was seized by willing hands and thrown back to those that sent it, there to play mischief among its friends.

Such incidents remind me that there were men in my regiment who were first and foremost in putting into practice any scheme to molest the enemy. Of Hanson Barr, a member of Co. C, I will make special mention. Comrade Barr served on detached duty with the Third Division engineers, and to him was given the credit of devising and constructing two mortars made from a sweet-gum log. These wooden guns were placed in convenient locations in the trenches, and proved to be of service in tossing shells over the enemy's breastworks at short range, which must have created consternation in the enemy's ranks.[11]

There was another character who was known to the officers and men of Logan's Division by the sobriquet of "Coonskin," so called because he wore a peculiar headdress made of coonskin. He was a noted sharpshooter named Foster, a member of the 23d Ind. Others, however, give his name as Pennock, 32d Ohio.[12] Coonskin erected, near a battery of 32-pounder guns, an observatory made of railroad ties, where from his elevated position he could plainly see into the enemy's breastworks and report anything of importance to Gen. Grant's headquarters. He was afterward captured while on the Atlanta campaign, and was in prison with Col. Scott, Capt. Poe and Lieut. Urquhart of our regiment, and was exchanged with them.

I have said that in front of Logan's Division, and close to the Jackson road, was the enemy's [3rd Louisiana Redan]. It was decided by our engineer officer, Hickenlooper, of McPherson's staff, to undermine this fort and blow it up.[13] Accordingly, on June 19, a portion of our regiment was engaged in digging a deep diagonal trench which led directly under the rebel fort. In some manner the enemy learned what was being done, and made an effort to head our miners off by digging counter trenches, so that the explosion would break out at the sides and save the fort. During the progress of this work the miners of both sides were at times so close together that they could hear the thumps of each other's picks. A turn would then be made in some other direction, and thus they avoided coming together.

In due time the mine was completed, whereupon a large quantity of powder was carried in, a fuse was then attached, and on June 25 the match was applied, lifting an immense body of dirt and in a measure leveling the enemy's works. Simultaneous with the explosion a charge was ordered to take the works, but without success, though a fierce struggle ensued for possession.[14]

It was said that when the mine was fired a number of the enemy were hoisted in an informal manner over into our trenches, and among the number was a rather intelligent colored man, who, when asked his views upon the situation, and what he thought of the shake-up, replied: "I, sah, didn't had time to think, fur de fust ting I knowd de groun' begin to shake and dis nigger begin to go up." A comrade asked him how high he went. "Dun don't know, sah, for sure," was his reply. "Guess t'was 'bout half a mile. When I'se a comin' down I dun met a white feller goin' up. Never stop to ax him, 'whar's you gwang?' "[15]

The night of June 22 our regiment was taken out of the works confronting Vicksburg and, with many other regiments, was assigned to the army of observation on the Big Black.[16] All sorts of rumors were in circulation. One was that Joe Johnston, in command of an army, was advancing from Jackson for the purpose of

***Opposite:* Attired in gauntlets and a jacket decorated with Russian shoulder knots, Capt. Andrew Hickenlooper (left) posed shortly after the battle of Shiloh with his good friend Capt. William E. Strong. At Vicksburg, both officers served on Gen. J.B. McPherson's 17th Corps staff, and by war's end both received brigadier general brevets. Hickenlooper, a native Buckeye, was Ohio's lieutenant governor from 1880-1882.**

Abraham Lincoln Presidential Library

raising the siege of Vicksburg.

The days following in succession from June 20 were filled with earnest words directed to Gen. Grant's lieutenants. To McPherson: "There is every indication that the enemy under Johnston will attack within 30 hours. Notify Logan to be ready to move at a moment's notice. The greatest vigilance must be observed all along our front, as the Vicksburg garrison may also make an attack." To Ord: "The utmost vigilance must be observed in watching the crossings of the Big Black. Keep your command under arms ready for an engagement at any moment. Hold your command in readiness to keep the enemy from massing on McPherson."[17]

The early morning of June 23 found us 10 miles from Vicksburg, where we remained until June 27, when we marched to Bovina on the railroad one mile from the Big Black. We stayed there until Sunday, July 12.

On July 1 a paymaster came down from Haynes' Bluff and our regiment received two months' pay. This circumstance made us feel happy; yet there was very little use we could find for money, unless to engage in a game of "chuck-a-luck." Col. Scott called the paymaster's attention to the fact that 67 of the regiment, sick and wounded, were in camp near Vicksburg and unable to be present. Arrangements were made by which our absent comrades could be paid, and they were vouched for by the company officers. Lieut. L.W. Richardson, Co. G, was selected to carry the money to our comrades at Vicksburg.

I will now leave our regiment in the woods near the Big Black and follow Lieut. Richardson to Vicksburg. When the morning of July 3 began to dawn over the hills of the city a scene was revealed long to be remembered by those who were present and participated in the long and trying siege. The whole Confederate line was alive. White flags were floating all along the enemy's works. It soon began to be whispered that a meeting was to be held between Gen. Grant and Gen. Pemberton, the object of which was the surrender of Vicksburg.

The place of the meeting was midway between the lines and under the shadow of an oak tree, which stood just opposite where Logan's Division, of which our regiment was a part, held the line during the siege. A number of comrades made an effort to get as near to the two chiefs as the rules of military etiquet would permit. They were not close enough to hear the conversation, but had a fair view of all who were present at the conference, which lasted less than half an hour. But in that short period terms were agreed upon by which the formal surrender would take place on the following day, the day of our Nation's birth.

At 10 o'clock the morning of July 4 Gen. Grant and staff, escorted by the bulk of Logan's Division, rode into the city.[18] This occasion gave the men an opportunity to view the situation as it existed at the time of the surrender, and to converse with the men who occupied the works immediately in our front. These men expressed themselves as glad that the struggle for Vicksburg was at an end, saying that they had enough of the siege, and the war generally, and were ready to quit and shake hands over the bloody chasm. The noon hour coming on, we divided the contents of our well-filled haversacks with those who were entertaining us with a description of their side of the line during the long siege. They showed us about their camp and quarters where we espied what remained of half a mule, which proved what we had heard but were reluctant to believe, that they were living on rations of mule meat.

After dinner a number of the boys took a stroll down into the city, one mile distant, and visited the Court House, which had been a target for our heavy guns during the entire siege. In the dome of the Court House was a large clock which was plainly visible from different parts of our lines. One pillar supporting it had been shot away, but the clock remained untouched and showed the hour of the surrender. There were also many other places of interest. The high hill above the city had been honey-combed and converted into residence properties. Here it was the non-combatants, women and children sought protection.

The Vicksburg *Citizen,* a daily paper, in the issue of the morning of July 3, which was printed on wall paper, had noticed our boast that we would eat our dinner in Vicksburg on July 4, and declared that the best recipe for cooking a rabbit was "first catch your rabbit." Our wideawake, enterprising boys, sure enough, were in the city on the 4th and issued the next number of the paper, and, after quoting the advice of the previous day, responded, "We have got our rabbit."

About 29,000 troops surrendered to Gen. Grant, together with 170 pieces of artillery, munitions and arms for 60,000 men.[19]

After the surrender Gen. Grant ordered Logan's Division into the city to do garrison duty. In the meantime the Second Brigade of Logan's Division remained in camp in the woods near the Big Black, where I will again join it.

Maj. Gen. Ulysses S. Grant, commander of the Army of the Tennessee at Vicksburg, posed for this portrait at Swymmer's Gallery in New Orleans.

Mark Warren Collection

The few days following, our camp on the Big Black was increased by the arrival of troops from Vicksburg, which made it evident another move was about to begin.

July 10 a large number of the paroled prisoners from Pemberton's army passed us on their way east.

Monday, July 13, we were ordered to prepare two days' rations and be ready to march at a moment's notice. In due time the assembly was sounded, when we again crossed the Black and hurried off in the direction of Jackson, where Sherman's boys had met with serious opposition by a heavy force of the enemy under Johnston. Shortly after we crossed the Black the sun passed behind a dark cloud and a low rumble of thunder told us of the approach of a storm. And come it did; nevertheless, we hastened on through the rain and mud. Toward the close of the day we made our camp a short distance east of Champion Hills. The following day we marched to Clinton, reaching the place about noon, where we remained until the next morning.

Early July 15 our brigade — except the 78th Ohio, which remained at Clinton — moved out of camp and marched off toward Jackson, about 10 miles away. The roar of heavy guns in our front hastened our steps and soon we reached our advance columns in line of battle two miles from Jackson.

Early the following morning a large detail was ordered from our brigade to construct earthworks. But just before going on duty we received orders to march with all speed back to Clinton, where our comrades of the 78th Ohio were having a red-hot time with a force of the enemy's cavalry. The rebels, however, having become alarmed because of the marksmanship of the 78th Ohio boys, left before we came up. That same morning Jackson was found to be evacuated by the enemy, so our regiment remained in camp at Clinton until July 21.[20]

July 17 the 30th Ill. of our brigade was ordered out to guard a supply train to Vicksburg. July 20 Gen. Grant issued orders from his headquarters to furlough 5 percent of his army to their homes.

July 21 we received orders to march back toward Vicksburg, having in our charge 357 prisoners. That evening we went into camp near the little village of Bolton. The afternoon of the following day we marched over the recent battlefield of Champion Hills and went into camp at Baker's Creek.

Our return march to Vicksburg was slow and uneventful. The Jackson campaign coming as it did close upon the hard work of the siege of Vicksburg, and being at a time when the blistering rays of a mid-summer's sun beat with relentless fury upon us, left us worn out. We gladly welcomed a rest that we felt sure was awaiting us.

The afternoon of July 24 our regiment marched into Vicksburg and turned the prisoners over to the Provost-Marshal. The men utterly refused to accept a parole and requested to be sent north, as they were tired of the war.[21] The next day we went into camp a half mile from the city, where we remained until Aug. 22.

On July 27 we received two months' pay. Many of our officers and men were now given a furlough for 30 days to visit with loved ones in Ohio homes.

Our camp life at Vicksburg was quiet and uneventful. The time when off duty was spent in reading such books and newspapers as came our way, writing letters or strolling along the silent earthworks of both sides. A few would engage in a friendly game of euchre or seven-up to while away dull hours.

Aug. 1 a terrific thunder storm, accompanied by strong winds, burst upon us, ripping and tearing our tents. Such a thorough soaking as we got put all previous storms in the shade.

Aug. 8 Col. Scott, along with a number of officers and men, started for their Northern homes, the men on furlough and the officers on recruiting service.[22]

Notes to Chapter 5

1. Before pulling back to Vicksburg's defenses, half of Pemberton's Confederates entrenched on the east side of Big Black River. Portions of Grant's forces attacked their fortified opponents who, in danger of being cut off from crossing the river, retired west in disorder, burning a bridge behind them. As many as 1,700 Confederates were captured, while Federal losses amounted to 279 killed, wounded and missing. Long, p. 354.

2. The reference was to Gen. Mortimer D. Leggett's brigade bugler.

3. By midday May 19, Grant's army was arrayed at Vicksburg with Sherman's 15th Corps on the right (north of the city), McPherson's 17th Corps in the center and McClernand's 13th Corps on the left. An assault along Sherman's lines later that day was repulsed, resulting in almost 1,000 Union casualties. Long, p. 355.

4. Surgeon Eugene Harrison, 68th Ohio, recorded in his diary that the unsuccessful May 22 assaults cost Logan's 3rd Division alone 225 men wounded. "Very busy operating," he wrote May 23. "The patients bear the operations well. The Board performed amp[utations], resections, excessions &c." The next day "Patients [were] still being brought in from [the] field. Could not get to them before. Some dreadfully fly blown when brought in." Harrison diary, USAMHI.

5. "I hope that these fiew lines may finde you in [good] health but not so many bullets a whistling around your head as there is about mine," wrote Pvt. Andrew Altman, Co. D, to his father in Napoleon, Ohio. "We are a firing at the rebbels in the fort at vixburg all the time and kill many of them. ... the rebs threw their whisky bottle out of the fort on our men and our men threw it back. They are that close to one an other and neither one dare sho his head or he will get it shot." Altman to John Altman, May 26, 1863, CAC.

Convalescing from a leg wound suffered at Champion Hill, Capt. Edwin J. Evans of Co. K viewed the shooting partly from an ambulatory vantage point, explaining on May 25: "We are now within three miles of Vicksburg, and have been fighting three days. Lieut. [Abram C.] Urquhart of Co. [A] and myself are laying behind the regiment about a mile, and as they advance we move up. We have a good mule and a fine covered buggy, that we travel in. He is shot in the big toe. ... The fighting here is principally with artillery, as their fortifications are very strong; yet there has at times been some very heavy infantry fighting. ... The gunboats and siege guns are just more than pouring it into the Rebels now." Although he recovered from his leg injury, feeble health forced Evans to resign Aug. 9, 1863. Evans, May 25, 1863 in *The Weekly Bryan Democrat,* June 4, 1863; *Ohio Roster*, vol. V, p. 664.

6. A Wood County mechanic, Corp. Joseph A. Harpel, Co. I, was detached to the 3rd Division pioneers from April 1863 to his muster-out Oct. 29, 1864. J.A. Harpel CSR, RG 94, NARA.

7. 1st Sergt. Upton Spurgeon, a Henry County farmer, was promoted first lieutenant of Co. A on Nov. 26, 1864, and temporarily commanded Cos. D and F in 1865. U. Spurgeon CSR, RG 94, NARA.

8. Grant was reinforced between June 3 and 14 by troops from the 9th and 16th corps, and the Department of the Missouri. E.B. Long, editor, *Personal Memoirs of U.S. Grant* (Cleveland: The World Publishing Company, 1952), p. 284-285.

9. At the time a 15th Corps division commander, Maj. Gen. Francis P. Blair Jr. led the Haynes' Bluff - Mechanicsburg expedition. *OR,* vol. XXIV, pt. 2, p. 435.

10. Loop referred to Joel Tyler Headley's *The Life of Ulysses S. Grant,* first published in 1868 by E.B. Treat & Co. of New York.

11. Pvt. Hanson Barr, Co. C, was a Paulding County farmer originally from Trumbull County, Ohio. His detached duty as a mechanic in the 3rd Division pioneers lasted from March 1, 1863 to January 1865. H. Barr CSR, RG 94, NARA.

12. "Coonskin" was 2nd Lt. Henry C. Foster, Co. B, 23rd Indiana. A resident of Jeffersonville, Ind., he was promoted first lieutenant to date from July 4, 1863. R.U. Johnson & C.C. Buel, editors, *Battles and Leaders of the Civil War,* vol. III (New York: The Century Company, 1888), p. 541; W.H.H. Terrell, *Report of the Adjutant General of the State of Indiana 1861-1865,* vol. II (Indianapolis: W.R. Holloway, 1865), p. 222.

No one with the surname Pennock served in the 32nd Ohio.

13. Capt. Andrew Hickenlooper, a Hudson, Ohio native and former commander of the 5th Ohio Battery, was the 17th Corps' chief engineer. His journal of Vicksburg engineering operations (April 17 - July 4, 1863) can be found in *OR,* vol. XXIV, pt. 2, p. 197-203.

14. Hickenlooper's mine under the so-called 3rd Louisiana Redan was packed with 2,200 pounds of black powder and fired at 3:30 p.m. June 25. The 1st Brigade (commanded by Gen. M.D. Leggett since June 4) charged the resulting crater, spearheaded by the 45th Illinois. For three successive days six different regiments rotated to hold the crater before the last one was withdrawn June 28. Leggett reported that "Hand-grenades were ... freely used by the enemy, which made sad havoc amongst my men, for, being in the crater of the exploded mine, the sides of which were covered by the men, scarcely a grenade was thrown without doing damage, and in most instances horribly mangling those they happened to strike." *OR,* vol. XXIV, pt. 2, p. 202, 294.

15. Gen. Grant recalled the man "was not much hurt, but terribly frightened. ... General Logan commanded at this point and took this colored man to his quarters, where he did service to the end of the siege." *Personal Memoirs of U.S. Grant,* p. 288.

16. The Big Black forces (40,000 troops), including three 17th Corps brigades, were commanded by Maj. Gen. William T. Sherman. *OR,* vol. XXIV, pt. 3, p. 428.

17. The exact wording of Grant's orders to McPherson and Ord can be found in *OR,* vol. XXIV, pt. 3, p. 427-428. Ord succeeded McClernand as 13th Corps commander on June 18.

18. Led by the 45th Illinois, Leggett's 1st Brigade of Logan's 3rd Division was the first to enter Vicksburg. *OR,* vol. XXIV, pt. 2, p. 294.

19. Officially, 29,491 Confederates were captured at Vicksburg, with another 1,147 taken at Jackson, Natchez and Yazoo City, Miss. *OR,* vol. XXIV, pt. 1, p. 62.

20. Pvt. William R. Snook, Co. C, claimed the 68th Ohio marched eight miles in just one hour and fifty minutes to reach the 78th Ohio on July 16, "then [was] ordered out on a foraging expedition, four miles out in the country, which we made and loaded the wagons with corn and returned" by 7:30 p.m. Snook, Sept. 15, 1863 to the *Paulding Independent,* Oct. 8, 1863.

21. Pvt. Snook wrote of these prisoners who had been captured at Jackson: "A more happy body of men you never saw, as they were all very glad that they had fallen in the hands of the Yanks. ... all agreed that the Southern Confederacy was a used institution, or in their words, 'done gone up,' and some went so far as to say that they believed the southern leaders, if they should succeed, they was going to establish a Monarchal form of Government. They were much pleased with the manner in which they were treated by us, as they said the treatment they received from us was better than they received from their own 'Government,' and at parting with us they said they would ever remember the ol' 68th, with the kindest gratitude, and all along the line of the Regt. you could see them shaking hands with their several guards, and bidding officers and men farewell, as though they had always been old friends. To the Col. and Major they expressed themselves in terms of warmest gratitude for the manner in which they attended to their comforts while on the march." Snook, Sept. 15, 1863 to the *Paulding Independent,* Oct. 8, 1863.

22. The editor of Napoleon's *North-West* observed: "We noticed, last week, the return of Col. Scott and several other officers of the 68th Regiment, to their homes in this vicinity, on furloughs, which expire about the last of this month. This is the first visit home of many of these officers since their Regiment left the State, now over eighteen months ago. They look considerably bronzed and war-worn, but are generally, we are glad to say, rugged and healthy." *North-West,* Aug. 19, 1863.

6

'Adopting their old rule of skedaddling'

The morning of Aug. 10 it was reported in our camp that the Third Division (Logan's) was to be ordered up the river to Memphis. This rumor, however, failed to materialize and we remained in camp. About this time several businessmen, post sutlers, etc., began to open up their wares in Vicksburg, which gave us an opportunity to provide ourselves with something more palatable than army rations.

Aug. 16, during a heavy thunder storm, an electric bolt struck a wagon to which five of our regiment's mules were standing, knocking all down and killing two. The following day a steamboat laden with munitions of war was being unloaded at the wharf, when, through carelessness, a box of percussion shells dropped into the hold and caused an explosion, blowing up the boat, and killing or injuring a number of men. A detail from our regiment was on the way to the landing after supplies, but fortunately did not reach there until after the explosion.

Early Aug. 21 we received orders to be ready to march at any moment, but it was nearly night before we were in motion, when, going on board a transport, we were soon on our way up the river. The next morning found us tied up at Goodrich Landing, 60 miles from Vicksburg, where we disembarked on the soil of Louisiana.[1] After landing we marched about four miles up the levee, where we stayed through the day and succeeding night.

By dawn of another day we formed into line in answer to the bugle call and marched back down the levee to the landing, where we remained until night. During the day a force of the enemy came out to the levee on the opposite shore and fired across the river at us. A command of colored troops crossed the river and routed the enemy. All honor to our colored comrades.

About the close of the day we formed in line as rear guard of our division and marched at a rapid gait until daylight the next morning, when a halt was ordered to make coffee.

Sunrise found us again in motion. We marched about 10 miles through a Louisiana canebrake, our road being a narrow defile, on each side of which was a dense growth of cane from 20 to 50 feet in height. Many of our comrades fell by the wayside wholly overcome by the poisonous vapors of an alligator swamp, with a hot August sun pouring its blistering rays upon us and not a breath of air moving to revive us from an almost sinking condition. Late in the afternoon we reached Bayou Macon, and went into camp for the coming night on a wealthy old planter's domain. A beautiful country, with all kinds of fruit in abundance, surrounded us.

Early Aug. 25 we were again moving and after a march of 15 miles through a heavily wooded country a halt was ordered for the day. A strong picket guard was put out in the best defensive position, and the greatest vigilance was observed, as the enemy was said to be all around us and threatening an attack. The night, however, passed quietly.

We moved at an early hour the following morning and, after a march of 10 miles, reached a little village called Oak Hill, near which we forded a stream called Bayou Boeuf, and went into camp for the night. In the bed of the bayou were found freshwater clams in abundance, some of which the boys tried to prepare for their supper. But the clams did not prove to be a very appetizing bill of fare.

The next day we marched 15 miles in the direction of Monroe, where it was reported that a large force would dispute our advance. Just at the close of day we crossed a low, swampy stream and went into camp eight miles from Monroe. Early the morning of the 28th we started toward Monroe, but it was thought we would have to fight before we got there. The enemy showed a bold front, but upon being pressed adopted their old rule of skedaddling, so we went into camp in the suburbs of the city to wait for another day.[2]

Monroe was situated on the Washita [Ouachita] River about 80 miles by rail west from Vicksburg, and why we were led out there was a mystery to us.[3]

About 4 o'clock the morning of Aug. 29 we left Monroe on our return march to Vicksburg. We marched 24 miles that day, reaching Oak Hill at 4 o'clock and going into camp. At sunrise the following morning, Sunday, we again moved forward. Early in the afternoon we went into camp on Boeuf River, 10 miles from Oak Hill. We remained here until 2 o'clock on the following morning, when we de-

L. M. Strayer Collection

camped, and at 3 o'clock in the afternoon, after a march of 18 miles, went into camp on the banks of Bayou Macon. The next day we remained in camp, as nearly one-third of our regiment were sick and unable to march. C. Delong, Co. A, and S. Morris, Co. G, died and were buried there. Their remains were afterward removed to the National Cemetery at Vicksburg.[4]

Leaving this camp about 1 o'clock the morning of Sept. 2 we again took up our line of march, our sick comrades in the wagons, and about 9 o'clock stacked arms on the banks of the Mississippi. After enjoying a cup of coffee we went on board of a transport in waiting, and were soon on our way to Vicksburg, reaching there just at the close of day, when we disembarked and proceeded to our old camp.

Sept. 8 we moved our camp close to the city and were assigned to duty as provost-guard. Our camp was in a beautiful grove overlooking the city, where we remained till Oct. 14.[5]

Sept. 14 a number of our comrades who had been home on thirty days' furlough joined us, bringing with them many recruits who had in their care boxes and packages of good things for us. Could our dear friends at home have seen us open these parcels they would have been amply rewarded for sending them. Long would we gaze upon the intricate knots, tied by the hands of a dear mother, sister, wife or sweetheart, until tears of joy would roll down our weather-beaten cheeks. But whatever the packages were found to contain in the way of cakes, candies, etc., our messmates came in for a share.

Oct. 6 there took place a grand review of the troops around Vicksburg, but on account of a very strong wind the march through the city was anything but pleasant.

Oct. 13 our State election was held, and many of my comrades cast their first vote for a Governor of our own Buckeye State. I am

Opposite: **1st Lt. William F. Williams, Co. A. Writing to the Napoleon *North-West* in mid-September 1863, he noted the recent deaths by disease of five regimental comrades, including his younger brother Henry (see Page 101). "All were with us during the campaign and siege of Vicksburg," he eulogized, "and acquitted themselves honorably. We admired their bravery, and mourn their loss." Williams, a farmer born in Seneca County, Ohio, was promoted captain of Co. D in May 1864 and mustered out July 10, 1865.**

here reminded of remarks made by those who were not our friends, that on election day in the army the men were marched up to the polls and compelled to vote thus and so. In reply I fearlessly declare that a more absurd falsehood never had its birth in the mind of man. The facts are, the men were at perfect liberty to vote for whom they wished, and no one questioned them.[6]

Late the afternoon of Oct. 14 we received orders to be ready to march at 6 o'clock the following morning. At the appointed hour we were ready with our war harness all on. The bugles sounded the advance, and away we went in company with our companion regiments in the direction of Jackson, Miss. The first day we marched 18 miles when a halt was ordered for the night. At 6 o'clock the morning of the 15th we were up and moving. We marched about 20 miles, and late in the day reached a little village called Brownsville, near which our cavalry had met with spirited opposition.

Early the next morning we moved forward in line of battle, but met with no opposition until we had advanced about four miles, when the enemy in some force suddenly appeared in our front. Skirmishing then began and continued all day, the enemy stubbornly retiring as our boys moved on them. Thus the day drew on till near night, when we found the main body of the enemy advantageously posted on high ground east of Bayou Chitta Creek.[7] Our regiment, being in the advance, moved quickly across a bridge spanning the creek, and under fire of a rebel battery deployed and advanced on the foe. In the meantime our companion regiments were hastening forward to our support.

Surgeon Wm. Massie of our regiment and his efficient assistants were on hand, and were awaiting the bloody work which we all felt was sure to take place.[8] But night dropping her mantle of darkness about us, a halt was ordered and we lay on our guns to wait the dawn of another day.

Early morning of Oct. 17 found us where we had bivouacked under a low growth of trees, which protected us from the cold damp of the night. Soon musket shots, accompanied by the roar of artillery, began to disturb the morning quiet as we moved up the incline toward the enemy, who upon being closely pressed fled from our immediate front. With a Union cheer Logan's men swept up the slope and gained the hill's summit in time to give the enemy a parting salute as they passed out of sight in the wood beyond. Soon after we were ordered in pursuit and about night, without further mishap, we went into camp on Pearl River some distance north of Jackson.

The object of the march now being accomplished, we, the following morning, turned our faces toward Vicksburg and after a march of about 22 miles, late in the day went into camp near Clinton. A body of guerrilla cavalry followed us the whole day, keeping up a lively skirmish with our rear guard. Occasionally one of our batteries would respond, keeping the enemy at a respectful distance.

Oct. 19 we marched over the Champion Hill's battlefield, and that evening reached our old camp in the woods on the Big Black. We took up our line of march at the usual hour the following day, and in the afternoon came to a halt in our camp at Vicksburg.

For some days the weather was as pleasant as we could wish, but Oct. 23 rain began to come down in true Northern style and seemed in no hurry to stop, which fact kept us pretty well housed up in our tents. We remained in camp on the high ground a short distance from the city until Monday, Oct. 26, when we were ordered to move our camp back to our brigade, which was about one mile from the city on what was called the "Graveyard road."

While our regiment was in camp near the cemetery an incident took place which still remains fresh in the memory of the writer. A company of actors had come down the river from the North and had pitched its tent in the city. A performance was given afternoon and evening, and always to a good-sized audience, as the boys patronized the company pretty liberally.

Late one evening four boys were returning to camp after attending the show, and had reached a point opposite the cemetery when a heavy thunder storm burst upon them. In the cemetery were a number of vaults containing the embalmed bodies of the dead. The door of one vault was standing ajar, and there the four boys sought protection from the elements.

Hardly had they reached their refuge when the voices of other comrades, who also were returning to camp, were heard far above the roaring of the storm: "Come this way."

"Back into the vault, boys," whispered one of the first party, "and we will have some fun."

Suiting the action to the word, the four boys stepped into and behind the door of the vault, just as several comrades rushed in under the protection of the covered way leading to it. One of the boys in the vault now commenced a series of such long-drawn-out, blood-curdling and terrifying shrieks and groans as never before came from an abode of the dead, which were heard above the wild fury of the storm. The boys who had sought the protection of the covered way rushed out into the blinding storm. The door was now thrown open and the first flash of lightning disclosed to those in the vault that the covered way was vacant. The boys could lead a forlorn hope or charge an enemy's line up to the cannon's mouth, but the groans and shrieks that emanated from that vault they could not stand.

I have said previously my comrades were great letter-writers, even in response to ads found in Northern papers mailed us, viz., "Inclose 10 cents, color of hair and eyes, and receive a beautiful picture of your future wife." We, of course, were anxious to learn what the future had in store, so we invested 10 cents. But, oh, how kindly disposed was the future to us, as the reply to those letters of inquiry brought to our hands photos of the biggest, fattest and ugliest of females. The boys, however, were too bashful to press their suit.

Friday, Nov. 13, a grand review of the army took place in camp around Vicksburg. After the review Maj. Gen. Logan delivered a farewell address to the men of his old Third Division, he being assigned to command of the Fifteenth Corps, Army of the Tennessee.[9]

About Nov. 18 the 30th Ill., with which we had been associated since the summer of 1862, was taken out of our brigade and the 32d Ohio put in its place, Col. Potts, 32d Ohio, commanding the brigade.[10] Our brigade now was composed wholly of Ohio regiments, which military composition we maintained until about July 10, 1864, when the 32d Ohio was transferred to the Fourth Division, Seventeenth Corps.

Referring to my diary, I find that a U.S. paymaster paid us a visit the previous September, and on Nov. 23 we were again made happy by his presence. In the meantime the comings and goings of the boys on furlough and the occasional arrival of new recruits was all that occurred to break the dull monotony of the camp.

Dec. 5, with fuel getting scarce about us, we were ordered to move camp to near the old Confederate lines in order to be better prepared for the rigors of a Mississippi winter. The weather was very cold, with now and then rain and sleet, that added not a little to our general discomfort.

About this time Uncle Sam began to think it a wise plan to get as many as possible of his good nephews to enlist for another term of service. He knew that the boys who had already served two years would make much better soldiers than those fresh from civil life. He also realized that the time spent in drilling new regiments would be saved if the old ones could be induced to remain in the service. Accordingly, Uncle Sam agreed to pay a bounty of $402 to each one who would re-enlist for three years or during the war. Besides this bounty we would be given a furlough for 30 days, and if three-fourths of the regiment would re-enlist we could go home together.

Upon this question Lieut. Col. Welles gave us a short talk, about as follows: "Comrades of the 68th Ohio: Taking into earnest consideration all the trials and sufferings you have undergone, and without a single murmur of complaint, yet I am unable to speak for you, but whatever course you may pursue in this matter your Colonel will go with you. And now, in order to get an expression upon this question, I ask that all who have given the question of re-enlisting a favorable thought to step three paces in front."

We had become pretty familiar with the hardships of a soldier's life in war time, and whatever the novelty of being a soldier that occupied our thoughts while in Camp Latty, there was none of it on the bluffs of Vicksburg. However, here and there along the line a comrade stepped to the front. Soon the line in front swelled to nearly half the regiment. Men were there who had seen brothers go down at the cannon's mouth. With the terrible carnage of the Vicksburg campaign still fresh in their memories, yet they were willing to longer bare their bosoms in defense of the old flag.

Those who re-enlisted brought their influence to bear upon the rest of us, which caused us to feel that our country's call to them to stay by the old flag was no stronger than for us, and so the re-enlistments began to increase. The question, to enlist or not to enlist, became the same as in 1861 — the foremost one in our minds.

We seriously discussed the matter among ourselves and decided upon our course of action. Those who felt that they ought to enlist did so, and those who felt it was their duty, coupled with their declining strength, to return home to their families and friends at the end of their first term, declined to give their names for a second enlistment. Every day, however, the veteran roll increased in numbers, and every day the roll of non-vets grew less, but still we lacked the requisite three-fourths.[11]

Christmas Day our veteran roll had increased to nearly 300,

and each was engaged in recruiting service.[12]

Friday, Jan. 1, 1864, a day known throughout the North as a frigid New Year's, we were lying quietly in camp on the bluffs of Vicksburg, breasting a piercing cold wind from the river.

The time for becoming veterans would expire on Jan. 6, and as the date drew near all possible persuasion was brought to bear upon those who still held out. Comrades who had again re-enlisted were anxious to get the required quota in order that we might be able to return as an organization to our homes on a 30-day furlough.

The morning of Jan. 6 Col. Welles called the regiment into line and made a speech. He began: "Comrades, the 68th Ohio needs just 68 more men on its veteran rolls to enable us to go home on 30 days' furlough as a regiment." He then devoted a few moments in exhorting us to stand by the flag, even if it should take three more long years to vindicate its honor, and succeeded in arousing fresh enthusiasm. Enlistments in the veteran service now went on with renewed vigor, and before the sun went down the regiment had more than its required quota.

The best figures that I have been able to obtain of those who marched out of Camp Latty and again enlisted in the veteran service were as follows: Co. A, 44; Co. B, 40; Co. C, 42; Co. D, 30; Co. E, 26; Co. F, 43; Co. G, 28; Co. H, 27; Co. I, 25; Co. K, 36. The total strength of the regiment on Jan. 1, 1864, was about 640. These figures may not be exact, but they are not far off.

From May 1, 1863, to Jan. 1, 1864, a period of eight months, our total loss in killed, died of wounds and disease was about 82. Up to May 1, 1864, at which time our non-vets left Vicksburg, we suffered a further loss of about 20, making a total of 102 — 47 of whom sleep in the cemetery at Vicksburg.

Jan. 7 the excitement of enlisting in the veteran service had passed and everything assumed its usual quiet. The officers, however, had planned to give the boys a grand treat in recognition of their patriotism. Beer — a barrel to each company — was secured, and soon the bluffs of Vicksburg rang with the glad shouts of a genuine Union jubilee. Each veteran, non-veteran, officer and private was ordered to fall in and help himself.

Monday, Jan. 11, a Vicksburg landmark met its demise. Much has been said and written concerning the famous tree known by us as the "Pemberton Oak." This oak stood midway between the lines during the siege, and nearly in front of the position held by our

Originally sketched by H.L. Stephens and engraved by Augustus Robin of New York, the famous Vicksburg oak tree shaded discussion of surrender terms between Gens. Grant (left) and Pemberton, July 3, 1863.

Mass. MOLLUS, USAMHI

regiment, and under it was held the conference between Gen. Grant and Gen. Pemberton for the capitulation of Vicksburg and its garrison.[13] More than six months after the surrender this tree was cut down by some of the boys of Co. C and hauled away by one of our mule teams to the Third Division repair shop. There it was sawed up and made into canes. The work of making these canes was done largely by S.C. Carpenter, Co. C, 68th Ohio.[14]

The tree, standing as it did midway between the lines, contained many leaden balls, and in the manufacture of the canes Comrade Carpenter observed the utmost care so as to have one of the balls retained in the wood. Canes so made readily sold to the boys at $2 and $3 each, while other canes not containing a ball sold at 50 cents. Many comrades obtained chips from the tree, which they whittled into all conceivable forms, some of which, I doubt not, are still held as keepsakes.[15]

Notes to Chapter 6

1. Commanded by Brig. Gen. John D. Stevenson, the so-called Louisiana Expedition (Aug. 20 - Sept. 2, 1863) was composed of the 3rd Division, 17th Corps; 3rd Brigade of the 6th Division, 17th Corps; Battery D, 1st Illinois Light Artillery; Battery L, 2nd Illinois Light Artillery; and a battalion of the 4th Illinois Cavalry. *OR,* vol. XXVI, pt. 1, p. 248.

2. With an effective strength of 1,000, mostly cavalrymen, Brig. Gen. Paul O. Hébert commanded Confederate forces in the area. *OR,* vol. XXVI, pt. 1, p. 249.

3. Gen. Stevenson reported that the expedition's military results included breaking up Confederate camps at five Louisiana towns, "and the precipitate flight of the enemy beyond the Washita [*sic*] River, in the direction of Shreveport." *OR,* vol. XXVI, pt. 1, p. 248.

Pvt. Gilbert L. Myers, Co. C, surmised the expedition's purpose was to allow "the Union people [of Monroe, La.] a chance to express their sentiments" and "to rid the country of the Guerrillas. All the citizens whom we found at home were loyal, the disloyal ones having all deserted. The negroes at Monroe all tell a horrible tale of the death of two of our officers who had held commissions in a negro Reg't, and been taken prisoners. They (the negroes) say they were both chained together and thrown off [a] bridge ... and drowned. I can not say how true this is, but I have heard the same statement corroborated by a dozen negroes. ... The expedition, aside from bearing in view the relief of Union men from guerrillas, was to be a trip for the health of the troops. So all who were able to walk were compelled to go along. I scarcely need say we brought back more sick than we started with, besides burying quite a number on the route. In the 68th, only one man died, but we had a great many very sick men." Myers to S.R. Brown, Sept. 4, 1863 in the *Paulding Independent,* Oct. 1, 1863.

4. Pvt. Charles Delong, Co. A, died Sept. 5, 1863 of "acute dysentery" and "sinking chills." He was a Henry County farmer from Damascus Township, married and the father of a small child. Co. G Pvt. Solon Morris, a farmer from Pioneer, Williams County, Ohio, died at Bayou Macon Aug. 31, 1863 of typhoid fever. C. Delong and S. Morris CSR, RG 94, NARA.

5. Using the pen name "Quince," an unidentified member of the 68th wrote from Vicksburg early in September: "The *ennui* of camp life is one of the soldier's worst enemies. A soldier gets up in the morning, eats his breakfast, and then, if he is not the lucky one for picket, lassitude sets in. He knows not what to do, unless he has a letter to write or a *Union* newspaper to read. If this be the case, he then employs the time in reading or writing, as I am now doing, and for the very same purpose. Reading matter in camp is scarce, and anything to relieve the monotony of camp life is eagerly grasped after by the soldier. Some read newspapers and tracts, who would not look at them at home. ...

"Bathing in the Mississippi is considerable sport for the boys. Evening is the time for bathing, and the banks of the Mississippi are lined with soldiers *without uniform,* ready to jump into the tempting waters at their feet. The river at present is very low; boats can run only in the day time. ...

"The citizens of Vicksburg, under the genial influence of 'hard tack' and bacon, are becoming very intimate. They can be seen every morning, with their basket on their arm, going to Uncle Sam's Commissary to draw their daily rations; they seem as contented as if going to the merchant's shop, as in years gone by. Even the aristocracy have to 'stoop so low' as to have hard tack and bacon on their tables. The citizens term us their deliverers, instead of their enemies, as they have in conquered cities heretofore. Officers and Vicksburg ladies can be seen parading the streets together, or sitting on balconies talking about something that might result in something serious after the war is over. I have no right to criticize, but Northern ladies look out if your *intended* is an officer. ..." Quince, Sept. 7, 1863 in the *Toledo Commercial,* Oct. 2, 1863.

6. Union ticket candidate John Brough handily defeated Peace Democrat Clement L. Vallandigham in Ohio's gubernatorial election. The state's eligible soldiers voted overwhelmingly for Brough — 41,467 to 2,288. Reid, vol. I, p. 169.

7. Bogue Chitto River, about 10 miles north of Clinton, Miss.

8. William Massie was appointed the 68th Ohio's assistant surgeon July 20, 1863. He joined the regiment Aug. 11 at Vicksburg. W. Massie CSR, RG 94, NARA.

9. Following Logan's promotion, Brig. Gen. M.D. Leggett was given command of the 3rd Division, 17th Corps.

10. Benjamin Franklin Potts, a native of Carroll County, Ohio, finished the war a brevet major general. From 1870 to 1883 he served as governor of Montana Territory. Warner, *Generals in Blue,* p. 383-384.

11. On Dec. 10, Welles wrote Col. Scott: "The Veteran recruiting service is all the rage in the Regt now. Twenty four (24) of 'B' Co. have already enlisted and twenty eight (28) of 'G' Co. are already to go providing they be given a furlough within a month, and most of the other companies will go in I think." R.K. Scott Papers, OHS.

Myron Loop was among the 68th's re-enlistees, signing his paperwork Dec. 16, 1863. He officially was mustered into the veteran volunteer service on Jan. 20, 1864. M. Loop CSR, RG 94, NARA.

12. Back in northwest Ohio, by contrast, 68th Ohio recruiting officers found it extremely difficult to procure new enlistees, as they informed Col. Scott from the towns of Maumee, Franklin, Pioneer and Bryan:

"Recruiting so far has been poor business ... yet I think that I am in a pretty fair way to get men although there is all kind of opposition." — Sergt. Thomas H. Kellogg, Co. I, Dec. 3, 1863.

"I have been running all of the time since I got home and have not got any one yet. ..." — Lt. Robert Masters, Co. G, Dec. 4, 1863.

"I have been traveling all over Williams Co. and Fulton and have got only one Soldier for certain and have got the Promis of three more but they have not enlisted as yet." — Lt. Masters, Dec. 12, 1863.

"I am sorry to inform you that recruiting is very slow." — Capt. James H. Long, Co. K, Feb. 8, 1864. R.K. Scott Papers, MSS 176, Box 1, Folder 2, OHS.

At least one of those recruited inflated his age by four years. Enlisting Feb. 29, 1864 at Toledo, Jacob Winfield Scott Parmer stated he was an 18-

year-old farmer from Henry County's Harrison Township. In reality, Parmer was born June 6, 1849, making him just 14 upon enlistment in Co. F. He later served with the 3rd Division pioneers and forage train. J.W.S. Parmer CSR, RG 94, NARA.

13. At 3 p.m. July 3, 1863, Grant and Pemberton had met on the 17th Corps' front to discuss surrender terms.

14. Pvt. Seymour Carpenter, Co. C, whose surname mirrored his civilian occupation in Antwerp, Ohio, spent his entire three-year enlistment as regimental and division blacksmith. S. Carpenter CSR, RG 94, NARA.

15. Years later, Gen. Grant reflected that his meeting with Pemberton occurred "on a hill-side within a few hundred feet of the rebel lines. Near by stood a stunted oak-tree, which was made historical by the event. It was but a short time before the last vestige of its body, root, and limb had disappeared, the fragments being taken as trophies. Since then the same tree has furnished as many cords of wood, in the shape of trophies, as 'The True Cross.' " Grant, "The Vicksburg Campaign," *Battles and Leaders of the Civil War,* vol. III, p. 531.

7

'Legitimate plunder for our hungry boys'

Monday, Feb. 1, 1864, large bodies of troops landed at Vicksburg from up the river, which fact convinced us that Gen. Sherman was planning an expedition of some importance.[1] The Mississippi River was in the possession of our forces from Cairo, Ill., to the Gulf of Mexico, but the enemy was in control of the railroads east of us, which proved to be a continual menace. This compelled Gen. Sherman to keep large formations of troops stationed at different points along the river ready for any emergency.

Sherman fitted out an expedition consisting of four divisions, whose object it was to destroy the railroads east of us. On the morning of Feb. 2 we began the Meridian raid.[2]

The evening of the first day we went into camp on the bank of the Big Black. About noon of the following we again took up our line of march and at the close of day made our camp near Edwards Station, west of Champion Hills.

Early Feb. 4 our brigade took the lead. We had proceeded about two miles when the enemy, from the high grounds of Champion Hills, called us to a halt. A heavy line of skirmishers was thrown out, and when all was ready we briskly moved forward, driving the enemy from the hills and sending them in precipitate retreat toward Jackson. Soon after we were following in pursuit, and late in the day discovered the enemy in line of battle on the north side of Baker's Creek near Bolton.

At dawn the following day we could see the enemy's line of battle on the opposite side of the creek, and soon they began to throw solid shot into our lines. The Third Division, of which our regiment was a part, was ordered forward across the creek. Over the creek we went in one wild torrent, and deployed to the right of a road along the low grounds fronting the enemy's lines. Hardly had we reached the position assigned us when an advance was ordered. About this time a battery of 24-pounder guns came up and gave the enemy their attention. These heavy guns must have created consternation in the enemy's ranks, as they hastily limbered up their little six-pounder guns and the whole shooting-match moved off toward Jackson in a cloud of dust.

Leggett's men now took up the chase, and pushed the enemy with such persistence that the march of the main column was not checked. We swept on through the town of Clinton close upon the heels of a rapidly retreating foe, until dark, when our bugles called a halt.

About noon of the 6th we marched into Jackson, meeting with no resistance. We crossed Pearl River on a pontoon bridge that the enemy did not have time to take away with them. After crossing the river we pressed forward toward Brandon, which we reached the evening of the following day.

Feb. 9 we reached a place called Morton and, as our rations began to run low, it became necessary to order out a foraging party. It was while out on one of these foraging expeditions near Morton [Feb. 10] that five of our comrades — Chas. Reynolds, Thos. Burrows, Remus Howard, Rob't Mayman and Joe Lewis — ran plump into a nest of Johnnies and were taken prisoners.[3]

The morning of Feb. 11 we left Morton and turned northward, marching through Hillsboro and Decatur, reaching the latter place on the 13th. On the 14th our brigade was ordered to move eight miles south to destroy bridges and trestlework at Chunky's Station, on the railroad west of Meridian, Miss. Before reaching the station we encountered the enemy, which the Second Brigade drove in confusion through the town, capturing a number of prisoners. After completing our mission at Chunky's Station we rejoined our division, in camp about four miles from Meridian.

Feb. 15, after 12 days of marching and skirmishing with the enemy, we reached Meridian, 140 miles by rail east of Vicksburg. We camped near the city four days, devoting our time to the destruction of Confederate storehouses and rail track for miles each way from the city. All along our route from Jackson railroads, bridges, machine-shops and everything in the way of public property were completely destroyed.

Feb. 20 we turned our faces westward and marched toward Canton, 24 miles north of Mississippi's capital. On the 26th we reached Canton, where we remained until the morning of March 1.

I will relate an incident that took place on the Meridian raid.

Lieut. L.W. Richardson had the reputation of being a little sharp in driving a bargain. One evening as we were moving by the headquarters train on our way to camp, one of the boys picked up an empty ham sack, and partly concealing it under his blanket, lumbered along seemingly as happy as could be. Lieut. Richardson, then in command of Co. F, saw the sack, which he supposed contained a sugar-cured ham. He approached the soldier and said: "Shaffer, what will you take for it?"

"Oh, I don't know," replied Shaffer. "What will you give?"

"I will give you a dollar for it," said Richardson.

"All right," said Shaffer, "fork it over."

Immediately a dollar and an empty canvas sack changed hands. The boys fairly roared. Richardson, however, said that he was 50 cents ahead on the trade, because it was worth $1.50 to any man to fondle that empty ham sack.[4]

Soon after reaching Canton we were met by our division train that had come out from Vicksburg with provisions. For several days previous we had been forced to look to the country through which we were passing for rations. Of course, all chickens, hogs and cattle along our route were legitimate plunder for our hungry boys, and very little escaped the army. In the meantime the enemy's cavalry kept hanging on our flank and rear, but doing us little or no harm. In one of their attacks on our rear guard they lost about 100 men taken prisoners, which made the rest a little more careful how they bumped up against us.

The morning of March 1 we began a march for our camp at Vicksburg, which we reached March 4. Our regiment's loss on the Meridian raid was two killed, seven wounded and five taken prisoners.[5]

During our absence about 100 recruits for the regiment arrived from the North. Most were old friends, in some cases relatives of the old members, and many were the glad greetings.

I should add that upon our return to Vicksburg we were accompanied by an army of colored people, who seemed to think that to go with us meant to be free. There were bright, young darky boys, bashful girls and middle-aged men and women. These poor people were going with Massa Linkum's soldiers to be free. They left the old plantation to go with us, with little thought as to how they would live. They, however, had an abiding faith that somehow everything would be made right. A great many found employment as cooks, but most of them shifted for themselves, and followed us from day to day, with only the desire to be free beings to urge them on. No fear of Massa's dogs or lash while with us; and if we should ask one of the new recruits to our army of contrabands, "Where is you gwine, Sambo?" an answer was ready, "I'se gwine to be free, ya-ya-ya!"

I have heard it said that the colored people in the South were satisfied with their former condition of servitude, but I am prepared to say that they cheerfully accepted a chance to exchange it for anything else, even death. Large numbers of the men enlisted in the colored regiments raised at Vicksburg, and not a few of them were brutally murdered at Fort Pillow.[6]

For some days following the Meridian raid we remained idle in camp. We were rejoiced to get back to Vicksburg after a 350-mile tramp, and we now commenced to speculate concerning our veteran furlough.

The raid had prevented our going home as soon as we otherwise would have done, but Thursday, March 17, orders were received to be in readiness to move at any moment. It is not necessary to say that we were ready, and to our unlimited joy the assembly was sounded. We bade adieu to the scenes of many days of trials and pleasure and marched to the landing, where we embarked on board a steamboat for our far-away Ohio homes. Our non-vets and new men, except two comrades from each company, remained in camp at Vicksburg. We crossed the gangplank, the bell rang, the great wheels began to revolve, and we were moving. It was about 10 o'clock at night under a bright full moon when Vicksburg faded from our sight. We never saw the city again.

Our boat was crowded, there being besides our regiment, the 45th Ill. and 16th Iowa, also going home on furlough.

Nothing occurred to mar the pleasure of our trip. About 9 o'clock the morning of the 21st we reached Memphis, where we remained until about 4 o'clock in the afternoon. In the meantime a number of the boys hastened away to the hospitals in the city in search for an absent friend or relative.

Our boat made much better time the succeeding night and following day, owing to the coal taken on at Memphis. The afternoon of the 22d we met a boat of veterans who were returning from a visit to their Northern homes.

At 9 o'clock in the morning of the 23d we passed Columbus, Ky., and about 2 o'clock in the afternoon landed at Cairo, Ill., six days from Vicksburg. Just after our arrival at Cairo a fire broke out and raged in a block of frame buildings fronting the Ohio River levee. Here it was that our grand old regiment showed its mettle and the material of which it was composed.

We were cold and hungry, not having eaten a good meal since leaving Vicksburg. Instead of standing idly by, watching the fire, we cheerfully furnished relays of men to work the hand fire engines, as the firemen were nearly exhausted, and by our timely help much was done toward checking the fire. A Cairo paper, in speaking of the fire, made mention of a boat-load of troops that had opportunely arrived from below, who proved to be ready and willing to face danger in defense of Northern homes.

After the fire was under control a train was made up, and during the night of the 23d we were moving through Illinois via Centralia and Effingham. The morning of the 24th found us at Indianapolis, Ind., where we remained until nearly noon.

Upon reaching Indianapolis we were escorted to the "Soldiers' Home," a large edifice of circular form, and when once inside we shouted, "Glory!" Oh, what a sight met our eyes. There were long tables groaning under all the good things that heart could wish, and there was room at the tables for the whole regiment. Then came the crowning glory of the scene. Ladies in pink and blue swarmed around us with pitchers, and with their beautiful hands filled our cups with coffee and our hearts with joy, then passed the cream and sugar, and served us in every way they could, in the meantime actually talking and chatting with us until we hardly knew whether we were in Indianapolis or in Paradise.

Too soon Col. Welles shouted, "Battalion, fall in." We returned to our train and were soon speeding on our way. About 3 o'clock in the afternoon we reached Muncie, Ind. Here it was that we met with another grand reception from a dear people whose hearts were full and running over with patriotism. No sooner had our train come to a stop than we were surrounded and captured by the good citizens. There was nothing during our long service that exceeded the kindness showered upon us by the good people of Indiana, who seemed to vie with each other in some expression of friendship toward us.

After the wants of the inner man were supplied we were right royally entertained by a glee club of many voices, which rendered several patriotic songs, one of which was "Babylon Has Fallen." The music and words being new to us, they nearly lifted us off our feet and brought forth loud and prolonged applause. Our martial band, of which the Army of the Tennessee could furnish no superior, was now heard from and gave our friends several favorite selections. The evening shadows began to lengthen when, with many a sigh of regret, we parted with those who were so kind to us.

March 25 found us on the soil of our own loved Buckeye State. We passed through Bellefontaine and Marion, and about 2 o'clock in the afternoon arrived at Cleveland. Soon after our arrival we formed in line and marched out to Camp Taylor, two miles south of the city, where we remained until April 6.

The morning after reaching Camp Taylor a heavy guard was placed around us, composed of a slick-looking lot of fellows with the letters S.S. on their hats. What the letters signified we were unable to say, so we dubbed them "sap suckers."[7] This action by the camp's commander aroused indignation among us, which found vent in a notification to the camp commander that we had been engaged the past two years in battling for our country's honor; that we had not forgotten our duty to God, our country, our flag or our manhood, and we considered to be placed under guard a shameful insult. Therefore we demanded that the guard be immediately removed. It was asserted in those days that soldiers in active service had become so accustomed to a harsh life that upon returning home it would be found that all their sensitive natures were destroyed, and they would be dangerous people. The camp commander complied with our demand — the guard was taken away.

April 5 we received our pay and also the first installment of veteran bounty. The following morning we left Cleveland, and at 3 o'clock in the afternoon reached Toledo. There we were met by a large, enthusiastic delegation of citizens headed by the Mayor, and were escorted to the "Island House," where we were royally feasted and petted by a host of admiring friends.[8] Special trains were made up on the different roads, and that night we reached the town or village nearest our homes. As the train comes to a stop we look out the car windows. One glance is sufficient. We hasten, we fly to the depot platform and into the arms of fathers, mothers, sisters, brothers or wives, with the happy voices of the little ones ringing in our ears as they shout with delight, "Oh, mama, papa has come." The imprint of a kiss upon each cheek; a dear wife weeping for joy as the soldier-husband supports her quivering form.

But many family circles had been sundered by the ruthless hand of war. Some fathers, husbands or brothers never returned.

Notes to Chapter 7

1. In February 1864, Maj. Gen. William T. Sherman was commander of the Department and Army of the Tennessee. On March 12 he was promoted to command the Military Division of the Mississippi.

2. Sherman's effective strength for the Meridian Expedition was 23,519 officers and men drawn principally from the 16th and 17th corps. The raid's purpose, Sherman reported, "was to break up the enemy's railroads at and about Meridian, and to do the enemy as much damage as possible in the month of February, and to be prepared by the 1st of March to assist General [Nathaniel P.] Banks in a similar dash at the Red River country, especially Shreveport, the whole to result in widening our domain along the Mississippi River, and thereby set the troops hitherto necessary to guard the river free for other military purposes." *OR,* vol. XXXII, pt. 1, p.172, 174.

3. Pvts. Thomas Burrows (Co. A), Remus Howard (Co. F), Robert Mayman (Co. D), and Joseph J. Lewis (Co. F). Mayman died Dec. 10, 1864 in prison at Andersonville, Ga. Quartermaster Sergt. Charles E. Reynolds endured a year confined in Andersonville before he was paroled in March 1865. He also was captured in May 1863 and spent one week in a Richmond, Va. prison. C.E. Reynolds CSR, RG 94, NARA; *Ohio Roster,* vol. V, p. 635, 647, 651, 653.

4. 2nd Lt. Lay W. Richardson, in temporary command of Co. F, belonged to Co. G, which contained five men named Shaffer.

5. The 68th Ohio's two fatal casualties were Pvts. John Maul, Co. D, and Frederick Waggoner, Co. H. *Ohio Roster,* vol. V, p. 647, 661.

6. Confederate cavalry under Maj. Gen. Nathan Bedford Forrest attacked Union-held Fort Pillow, Tenn., on April 12, 1864. The garrison of 557 troops, including 262 Negro soldiers, was overwhelmed, suffering 231 killed, 100 wounded and 226 captured or missing. Federal testimony claimed most of those killed and wounded, especially the black troops, were "massacred" by being shot down after they surrendered. Confederate authorities vehemently denied the charge, which "echoed infamously" across the country for many years afterward. Long, p. 484.

7. The guards likely belonged to the 9th or 10th Independent Companies of Sharpshooters. At Cleveland they mustered in Feb. 26 and April 1, 1864, respectively, and eventually were assigned to the 60th Ohio as Cos. G and H. Frederick H. Dyer, *A Compendium of the War of the Rebellion,* vol. II (Dayton, Ohio: Press of Morningside Bookshop, 1979), p. 1495-1496.

8. Mayor Charles M. Dorr. Toledo's Island House was erected in 1854 on a spit of land known locally as the "Middle Grounds" between the Maumee River and Swan Creek. For more than three decades it served as a railroad passenger terminal and one of the city's leading hotels. John M. Killits, editor, *Toledo and Lucas County, Ohio 1623-1923* (Chicago: The S.J. Clarke Publishing Company, 1923), p. 303, 547.

8

'Hastening on to the end of their earthly existence'

All things must come to an end, and so did our veteran furlough. The good-bys were once more said, and perhaps with deeper feeling than in 1861 because we knew this time just what was the meaning of war.

Friday, May 6, 1864, 30 days after we had made a grand charge on the hearts and homes of friends and relatives in northwestern Ohio, and had captured everything in sight, we were speeding eastward over the Lake Shore Railway to Cleveland, the still unconquered old 68th. We reached Cleveland in the evening and again took up our soldier life where we had dropped it.

Early in the morning of May 7 we boarded the cars at Cleveland and were soon whirling southward. At 4 o'clock in the afternoon we arrived at Columbus, where we were joined by the 78th Ohio of our brigade, who, like ourselves, were returning from furlough. We left Columbus that same evening, and at 5 o'clock the next morning, Sunday, we were at Cincinnati. Soon after our arrival we marched through the quiet city to the western depot and boarded a cattle train for Cairo, Ill.

All day Sunday we rolled over the beautiful prairies of Indiana and Illinois. It seemed that the people along our route had been notified of our coming, as at every town and village a great many had assembled to see us pass. Early in the day we set ourselves to work to establish a line of communication with every vision of beauty we chanced to see, using for that purpose pieces of cardboard, upon which we wrote our names and regiment with the request, "Please write to us." These were dropped at the feet or handed to the owner of a pair of laughing eyes, and in many cases a correspondence thus brought about was kept up to the close of our service.

Early May 9 we rolled into Cairo and went into camp on the north side of the city. Here we were joined by our non-vets and recruits, whom we had left in camp at Vicksburg when we started on our veteran furlough.

Before going on with my narrative I will briefly speak of the campaign mapped out by two men, whose very names made the enemies of our country quake with fear.

After Gen. Grant had opened the Father of Waters to the Gulf, he was sent to take command of the army of the Union around Chattanooga.[1] This army had met with sore defeat in the battle of Chickamauga, a few miles to the south. The Confederates had taken strong positions on Lookout Mountain and Mission Ridge, and were holding Union forces at Chattanooga in a virtual state of siege. But Grant, the hero of Vicksburg, instilled new life and energy into the hearts of the almost-discouraged troops. Shortly after his arrival he ordered a combined assault upon the enemy and sent their broken and routed columns whirling southward.[2] Not long afterward Gen. Grant was appointed commander of all the armies of the Union, and his place in the West was assumed by Gen. Sherman.[3]

Grant and Sherman now set themselves to work, planning a great double campaign that was to continue, rain or shine, until the last armed rebel ceased to exist. Carrying out this double campaign could not have been intrusted to abler men. Sherman knew that if Grant got a good hold, all the powers on earth could not make him let go, and Grant knew that Billy Sherman's men would go anywhere that their commander might think best to lead them. Accordingly, about the 5th of May, Gen. Grant touched the button and the two great Union armies were put in motion.[4]

I now return to Cairo, Ill., where on the morning of May 10 we turned over our Enfield muskets and drew new Springfield rifles. Late in the day we embarked on the steamer *Illinois* and started up the Ohio. The next morning our boat tied up on the Illinois side of the river opposite Paducah, Ky., where we landed and drew ammunition and provisions. We remained here until the evening of the 12th, when we started up the Tennessee River on our way to join Sherman's army.

The next day we passed Fort Henry, and about 4 o'clock the morning of the 14th reached Clifton, a little Tennessee river town about 30 miles below the scenes of our sore trials of two years previous. Thirteen transports convoyed by two gunboats accompanied us to this point, bearing the Third and Fourth Divisions, Seventeenth Corps, commanded by Maj. Gen. F.P. Blair. Soon after our

When the Atlanta Campaign began, wrote Maj. Gen. William T. Sherman, "I wanted to set the example, and gradually to convert all parts of [the] army into a mobile machine, willing and able to start at a minute's notice, and to subsist on the scantiest food." Here Sherman wears the badge of the Military Division of the Mississippi.

National Archives

arrival at Clifton we received orders to disembark, and as the shadows grew longer we went into camp about half a mile from the landing, where we remained over Sunday.

Monday, May 16, we moved out of camp with three days' rations in our haversacks. The first day out we marched 16 miles. The following day we took up our line of march in the rear of our division, and reached camp late in the night after a tiresome tramp of 18 miles.

Early the morning of May 18 we were again in motion. We marched 17 miles over a hilly country, fording the same stream four times in as many hours. In the evening we passed through a little village named Lawrenceburg, when a halt was ordered for the night.

The next day we marched 16 miles, and as daylight began to wane we went into camp near Pulaski, Tenn., a pretty town on the railroad running from Nashville to Huntsville, Ala.

May 20 we remained in camp at Pulaski. A detail was called for to assist in unloading rations from the division train, after which we were ordered to load our knapsacks on the wagons. We shouted "Glory" upon this agreeable change, as our organs of locomotion were beginning to feel pretty sore. Late in the afternoon we received orders to be ready to march at 4 o'clock the next morning. At the appointed hour, May 21, we started in the direction of Huntsville. About the middle of the afternoon we went into camp on the banks of a wide stream named Elk River, 20 miles from Pulaski. Early next morning we were moving on. After a march of 16 miles a halt was ordered to allow the rear of the column to close up.

May 22 our regiment was rear guard of the entire division. We remained in camp until noon, when we formed in line in rear of the division train, and after a march of 10 miles went into camp at Huntsville. Here we found the 32d Ohio of our brigade, they having been in camp at Huntsville for some days waiting for our arrival.

We remained here one day, washing and otherwise preparing ourselves for a long march into Georgia. Huntsville was a beautiful city, hid away in a grove of forest trees; but what we admired most was a large spring of pure water, sufficient in volume to furnish the power to operate a large flour mill. The country round about us was enchanting, and I doubt not many of my comrades have thought they would like to live in northern Alabama.

The following day we marched 16 miles, and about 2 o'clock in the afternoon went into camp.

It might be well for me here to explain to my readers why we went into camp at such an hour in the day. Six o'clock in the morning was the usual hour for the advance column to take up its line of march, and when a large body of men, artillery and wagon trains were moving over the same road the advance column would be miles on the way before the rear of the line could get in motion. Therefore, it would often be late into the night before the rear columns, which were marching behind a heavily-loaded wagon train, could reach camp. The following day the order of march would be reversed, and those late into camp the previous evening would be among the first to move in the morning.

May 26 we again marched in the rear of the whole division, and after a tramp of 12 miles went into camp on the banks of the Tennessee River opposite the town of Decatur, Ala.

The afternoon of the following day we crossed the Tennessee on a pontoon bridge and moved off in a southeasterly direction. The shadows of night had enveloped us before the glad notes of the bugle called us to a halt 10 miles from Decatur.

May 28 we marched about 14 miles, and early in the evening made our camp near the little village of Somerville.

May 29 we marched 16 miles over hilly country, fording a number of streams that lay in our path, and late in the day encamped near the foot of a mountain range. Great, gloomy rocks that had never worn a cheerier look than a frown, lifted their heads to the skies; rugged trees, struggling to thrust their life-giving roots into narrow crevices, and a beautiful stream rushing onward until lost in a cave in the mountain side — all lent enchantment to those of us enjoying our first view of mountain scenery.

Next morning we began to climb a spur of the Appalachian range, a rough and rocky path, making it hard marching. Near the close of day, after a march of 18 miles, we descended the mountain and went into camp for the night near the town of Guntersville, Ala.

May 31 we marched 16 miles over another mountain range, reaching camp just at dark, weary and footsore.

June 1 we were in the rear of the whole command. We moved very slowly until dark, when we went forward at a rapid pace until midnight. We marched 18 miles and camped near the little village of Van Buren.

The bright sunlight of joy filled our hearts the next morning when Col. Welles said: "Boys, we have orders to remain here today." Few words could have been more pleasing. Our war harness was quickly thrown aside, and we were soon lounging on the green-carpeted earth, nursing a pair of sore feet or bathing our weary bodies in the clear waters of a mountain stream near our camp.[5]

June 3 we marched about 18 miles over mountain roads and along winding mountain streams. At midday a strong storm of wind and rain burst upon us, making our march a trying one; but we pressed on, defying the elements, and about dark went into camp on the soil of Georgia.

At 4 o'clock the following morning we were moving, our brigade leading the advance. How monotonous to repeat the story of this long, dull, uneventful march, a march in which many of our comrades were hastening on to the end of their earthly existence.

Sunday, June 5, our regiment was the rear guard. We marched 16 miles and late in the day went into camp on the bank of the Oostanaula River, near Rome, Ga. Next day we crossed the Oostanaula and marched along a branch railroad running to Kingston, 18 miles away, which place we reached late in the evening.

June 7 we marched 12 miles, and as the shadows began to lengthen we went into camp beside the Etowah River near Cartersville. On the following morning we left the Etowah behind, marched 10 miles, and about 5 o'clock in the evening came up to the advance of Sherman's army near Acworth. Our long march of more than 300 miles from Clifton was ended.

Soon after going into camp Maj. Gens. McPherson and Logan paid us a visit, and with hats in hand rode slowly along the line, bowing acknowledgments here and there amid a cyclone of wild and vociferous cheering, the men flinging their hats high in the air as our beloved old commanders passed.[6]

We remained near Acworth until the morning of June 10, when that portion of the army in camp about us moved forward to Big Shanty, near which place our regiment took its first position and entered upon the historical Atlanta campaign.

The enemy was intrenched on two mountains in our front, Kennesaw and Brush. Beside these mountains was Marietta, while farther on flowed the Chattahoochee River, and 10 miles beyond was Atlanta.

Our first work upon reaching the front was to assist in constructing a heavy line of earthworks. Our line of battle was so close to the enemy's works on towering Kennesaw that we could not with safety to ourselves do any work during the day; therefore we were divided into two reliefs for night work. The first relief, going on duty at dark, was in turn relieved by the second at midnight. The work was wearisome, but coming as we had, the recently feasted and petted soldier-boy guests of our Northern homes, we felt equal to any emergency, and cheerfully answered the call of duty without grumbling or complaining.

Directly in front of our regiment was a large, open field, and across this field, partly hidden in a grove, was a large cotton-gin, from which Confederate sharpshooters sent bullets disagreeably near.

A German chief of artillery had observed this building and ordered one section of guns to open fire upon it. The effect not being very satisfactory to the chief, he ordered up the entire battery, and when the lanyards were pulled six guns gave tongue. A moment later the chief, with a loud guffaw, shouted: "Goot! Goot! Dem tam rebels can todge vun schot, bud tay cannit todge a volley." In a moment the building was wrapped in flames, and as the enemy fled from that vicinity our regiment's rifles bade them hurry.[7]

Soon after reaching the front the following colloquy was said to have taken place on the picket line:

"Hullo, Yank; we'uns are goin' to make yo'uns run before long!"

"Yaas, yo'uns have been making we'uns run all the way down from the Tennessee River."

"But Yank, we'uns have got yo'uns where we'uns want yo'uns, and now 'twill be yo'uns turn to run."

"Naw, Reb; what's up now?"

"Why, Yank, haven't yo'uns heard that the Seventeenth Corps has just joined us from Vicksburg, and when Billy Sherman tells them to move, we'uns will move too. See?"

Early in the morning of June 11 we moved about half a mile in the direction of Brush Mountain, and went into an intrenched position, where we could look across the field and see the enemy on the opposite side, and presently we could hear them, as they appeared to be angry and persisted in shooting at us, contrary to any feelings of love or friendship.

Constant firing was kept up by the opposing lines, and now and then somebody would get hit. Sometimes the enemy would turn a battery loose upon us, which immediately would be responded to by a battery of our guns, when for a time matters would get interesting, as each battery would do its best to silence the other's guns. During the time these duels with big guns were taking place we were earnestly engaged in watching our front, where now and then a good shot from one of our guns would land, causing a scattering of the enemy. A good shot by the enemy would have the same effect on our side.

When we first joined Sherman's army a few days previous, the carpenters were engaged in rebuilding the railroad bridge across the Etowah River at Cartersville. That being completed, the track was repaired up to our advance lines. One of the engineers now concluded to come up to the front and greet the enemy. We heard the engine coming, and the noise it made while running over the rough track was pleasant music. The engine came thundering on, and at last came to a stop close to the enemy. There it began to sound a saucy defiance to the rebels on Kennesaw in a succession of long and short toots. The enemy on towering Kennesaw thought to silence the bellowing of that iron horse by turning a battery upon it. But the engineer stood his ground and responded to the enemy's fire by a succession of little toots and big toots, straight toots and crooked toots, until the country around us rang with the echo. This caused a good bit of merriment, as the tooting of the engine's whistle spread like contagion to all parts of the line, from which there rolled and re-echoed an accompaniment of all kinds of Union toots, cheers and yells, until the enemy became disgusted and kept quiet.

June 15 a furious cannonade took place all along the lines, during which Gen. Polk of the rebel army was killed.[8]

During the firing of artillery we would get a little too enthusiastic for our own good and expose ourselves above our works, watching the results of a duel between the big guns, when Mr. Reb would observe us and send a solid shot humming our way instead of at the battery with which he was engaged. Of course, we needed no second admonition to get down into the trench.

Our line of works lay parallel to a large field, on the opposite side of which the enemy was strongly intrenched. To the left of our regiment was a cluster of young trees and blackberry bushes, at which point the opposing lines were only a short distance apart. Here it was our regiment met with its first losses on the Atlanta campaign.

In the early part of the day, June 15, our pickets opened fire upon the pickets opposed to us. The enemy responded, when a warm engagement took place, resulting in a number of our regiment being killed or wounded. The Clippinger brothers of Co. K were among those killed.[9]

Meantime, [Garrard's] cavalry on our left made a charge and crushed the enemy's right, intrenched on Noonday Creek, which caused them to evacuate the works in our front and establish a new line.[10] Therefore our next move was to follow them up and construct another line of earthworks. As usual, we were forced to do our digging under cover of night. The ground being soft and the digging easy, we soon had a new line of works completed.

June 17 Co. I's Capt. Poe, picket officer on the brigade staff of Col. R.K. Scott, in command of a heavy detail, advanced across the field in our front to attack a rebel picket post near the edge of the timber opposite. The men cleared our front with a bound, and soon disappeared from sight in a rank growth of wild grass on the low intervening space. They reached the opposite side of the field and entered the thicket with a mad rush. The surprised Johnnies beat a hasty retreat, and then occurred a footrace with the rebels just a little ways in the lead. From our side of the field we could see the race, and we cheered our comrades to renewed exertions. But the pleasures of following in pursuit were brought to a sudden close by our boys bumping up against a strong line of the enemy, who opened fire upon them at short range.[11]

The boys succeeded in getting out of this tight place with a few slight wounds, as the enemy fired too high to do them serious injury. Capt. Poe, however, while engaged in reconnoitering the enemy's position, was taken prisoner.[12]

The night of June 18 the enemy abandoned his line of works along our front and retired to the frowning defenses of Kennesaw. Early Sunday, June 19, the bugles sounded "Forward," and soon after we were in motion. We moved about two miles, meeting with no opposition from the enemy, and about noon went into position on Brush Mountain. Here we found an immense line of earthworks which the enemy had abandoned the previous evening.

Brush Mountain was about one mile northeast of Kennesaw. A deep valley separated it from the latter, and along this valley was the railroad running southward to Atlanta. The country around us was one vast fort, and as we pressed the enemy back from one position, they had another all ready for us.

Towering Kennesaw, an elevation of about 700 feet, stood before us and threatened us with total annihilation. But it was only a question of time when Sherman would execute another flank movement, and Kennesaw would pass into history.

Notes to Chapter 8

1. On Oct. 16, 1863, Grant was placed in command of the newly created Military Division of the Mississippi, combining the Departments of the Ohio, the Cumberland and the Tennessee. At Chattanooga, Army of the Cumberland commander William S. Rosecrans was replaced by Maj. Gen. George H. Thomas. Long, p. 423.

2. The battle of Chickamauga, Ga., was fought Sept. 18 - 20, 1863 between the Army of the Cumberland and the Confederate Army of Tennessee, reinforced by five brigades from the Army of Northern Virginia. Confederate investment of Chattanooga ended Nov. 24 - 25, 1863 when Union troops successfully stormed Lookout Mountain and Missionary Ridge, forcing their opponents south to Dalton, Ga.

3. Grant was promoted lieutenant general March 9, 1864 and assigned to command all the armies of the United States. He chose to accompany the Army of the Potomac in Virginia while Sherman remained in the west. Long, p. 473, 474.

4. In the east, Grant began his Overland Campaign in Virginia's Wilderness, while Sherman launched the Atlanta Campaign from the environs of Chattanooga.

5. Probably Will's Creek, which flows in the narrow valley separating Raccoon and Lookout mountains.

6. When the Atlanta Campaign opened, Logan commanded the 15th Corps of McPherson's Army of the Tennessee.

7. Loop probably referred to Maj. Clemens Landgräber, the German-born artillery chief of the 1st Division, 15th Corps. The two batteries he commanded at the time (F, 2nd Missouri Light and 4th Ohio) were composed mostly of Germans or men of German descent.

8. A shot from the 5th Indiana Battery struck and instantly killed Lt. Gen. Leonidas Polk, an Army of Tennessee corps commander, while he observed Union troop movements from atop Pine Mountain. Richard A. Baumgartner, *Kennesaw Mountain June 1864* (Huntington, W.Va.: Blue Acorn Press, 1998), p. 30-32.

9. Three Clippinger brothers and a cousin with the same surname, all farmers from Williams County, Ohio, served in Co. K. The oldest, John H. Clippinger, had enlisted in October 1861, while George, Peter and John W. Clippinger enlisted in January 1864. John H. and John W. were killed June 15, 1864, and later buried in Marietta National Cemetery. Clippinger CSR, RG 94, NARA; *Ohio Roster*, vol. V, p. 797.

10. Brig. Gen. Kenner Garrard commanded the 2nd Division of the Army of the Cumberland's Cavalry Corps.

11. The Confederates Poe's men encountered belonged to Lt. Gen. John Bell Hood's corps, Army of Tennessee.

12. At the time of his capture, Capt. Hiram Poe, Co. I, also was acting assistant inspector general on Scott's 2nd Brigade staff. Poe spent nearly two months confined at Macon, Ga. before transfer in August 1864 to City Work House Military Prison in Charleston, S.C. On Aug. 14 he informed his wife: "We came here a few days ago, most of us think for the purpose of being exchanged. Had a fine ride from Macon, Ga., here, and luxuriated on melons, fruit, &c., all the way. This was a good thing for me, for I have been living so exclusively on other diet that I have been afraid of scurvy. I sold my watch on the way here and so made a raise of a little money, but at the prices we have to pay for fruit, &c., it won't last long. We think we will be able to get boxes of eatables that they can't furnish us (sugar, coffee, &c.) from home, if we are not exchanged soon.

"[Three other captains] and myself have a small room which is clean and comfortable. The prison officials treat us well and have done so ever since we have been here. Our room, which fronts on a street, is well ventilated, having three large windows. These are finely furnished with a good strong lattice work which is so arranged as to furnish an admirable chance for a game of *checkers* with our noses."

Poe was paroled Sept. 28, 1864 and mustered out of service one month later. H.H. Poe CSR, RG 94, NARA; *The Perrysburg Journal,* Sept. 14, 1864.

9

'Behind those works was a saucy enemy'

Late in the evening of June 21 we received orders to be ready to march at 4 o'clock the next morning. The appointed hour found us in motion and silently moving off to the left. We moved about one mile, and came to a halt directly in front of a very strong line of earthworks that fairly bristled with guns. Just at that time came an order for us to "lie down." Down we went, feeling thankful that the command came at such an opportune moment, as little leaden messengers of death were singing the lullaby of eternity around us. Heavy skirmishing continued through the whole day, our regiment suffering a loss of two killed.[1]

The following morning Gen. Leggett, under instructions from Gen. McPherson, made a reconnaissance with the Third Division some distance to the left. We made a wide detour and moved to a point nearly east of the city of Marietta, and up to within about 500 yards of a line of the enemy's works. The works were opened upon by a battery of artillery, but drew forth no response.

Dispositions were now being made to move upon the works, when we were surprised to hear a long, scattering fire in our rear, which soon developed into the roar of battle. We were ordered to "about face" and started off on the double-quick through tangled brush and over logs in the direction of the sound of battle, the cause of which was soon made known to us.

A part of [Garrard's] cavalry command, having been ordered forward to cover Gen. Leggett's left had been fiercely assaulted. Our brave troopers, however, withstood the onset and in turn fell like a thunderbolt upon the enemy, sending his broken and bleeding columns reeling backward into their intrenchments, and as they were too powerful to attack with our small force, we returned to our position on Brush Mountain. This was only one of many demonstrations made on different parts of the line while a more important move was being made elsewhere.

The few days spent on Brush Mountain were not disagreeable, as the weather was pleasant, our elevated camp healthy, and our duties not so trying as when in the valley below. We were a little below and in plain sight of the enemy on Kennesaw, who never tired night or day in hurling iron and lead at us.

In the evening their band music came floating across the intervening space, mellowed by the distance, and appeared to me to be unusually sweet for Confederate music. Our bands would play the "Red, White and Blue," and the enemy would respond with "The Bonny Blue Flag," and so on, different pieces of music following in succession from each side, which seemed to lend an air of friendship, as during these courtesies no firing was done on either side.

Sunday, June 26, our regiment was ordered out on the left almost two miles, where, just at dark, the rest of our brigade joined us. In our front was an open field about 400 yards wide, which we contented ourselves in watching throughout the night, to penetrate the designs of the enemy said to be moving on our left flank. The night, however, passed quietly, and in the early morning we returned to our camp on Brush Mountain.

In the meantime, Gen. Sherman had issued orders for a grand assault upon the enemy's lines to take place on Monday, June 27. Accordingly, early on the 27th the signal was given and the charge sounded to attack the enemy intrenched upon and around Kennesaw. No sooner were the assaulting columns in motion than from behind rifle-pits, from rocky ledges, and down from the top of towering Kennesaw rained shot and shell in one ceaseless, fiery torrent. Still onward pressed our comrades through the storm of death, right up to the rebel intrenchments, when a halt was sounded, as over the bristling works they could not go. Being on the extreme left, our regiment was not brought into action, yet we were under orders to be ready to move to the support of our comrades at any moment.

From our elevated position on Brush Mountain we could look across the bloody field, and as we turned our eyes toward lofty Kennesaw the thought of charging its gloomy sides was not a pleasant one, as the whole mountain-top and side seemed to be wrapped in billows of smoke and flame.

Our comrades were struggling against fearful odds, and as the shadows of night fell around them most retired from several advance positions to their intrenchments. Once, and only once, did the wily Johnston score a victory over Sherman.[2]

The few days following we remained in camp. Everything, meanwhile, remained unusually quiet on our part of the line, except for an occasional lively exchange of compliments by the artillery. Thus matters progressed until the evening of July 2, when we were ordered to quietly buckle on our war harness and form in line. About 8 o'clock we moved silently down a winding mountain road to the valley below, and, clothed with the stillness of death, marched close along the enemy's lines toward the southwest.

During the dark night a number of boys of the 3d Ohio Cav., which followed us down through the dense brush on the mountain side, lost their hats. But upon reaching level country each one replenished his loss at the expense of some line infantryman. These troopers would ride up beside the shadowy form of a walking comrade, and with the sweep of a long arm grab a hat and then dash off into the night.

Morning found us on the right flank of Sherman's army, when the fact was revealed to us that the rebels were on the retreat from Kennesaw and Sherman's boys were after them. At sunrise a short halt was ordered to make coffee, after which we again moved forward, marching all day, and about 7 o'clock in the evening came to a halt on the Sandtown Road, about three miles from the Chattahoochee River.

On Independence Day we remained in camp until late afternoon, enjoying a rest after 24 hours of marching. We then moved down the Sandtown Road about two miles, driving the enemy's skirmishers into a strong line of earthworks, from which they opened upon us with artillery. We retired a short distance, and as night was coming on a halt was ordered.

About 9 o'clock the following morning we were put in rapid motion toward the right, but had moved only a short distance when we encountered the enemy heavily intrenched near the mouth of Nickajack Creek.

On the opposite side of the Nickajack was an open field, and beyond that, on high ground, was heavy timber. We soon learned that there was something else on those high bluffs besides timber. There was a fort with strong earthworks extending out on each side, and behind those works was a saucy enemy, for as we looked across the creek we could see little puffs of white smoke, and then larger puffs, followed by the screaming of shot and shell all around us. We then turned our faces to the south and found some fellows on the opposite side of the Chattahoochee to be engaged in the same unfriendly actions, which caused us to retire to a place of safety. Night coming on, we soon were busy throwing up a line of earthworks fronting east and south along the Nickajack and Chattahoochee. The next morning we were safely ensconced behind an equally strong line of earthworks, which made us feel reasonably contented in spite of the enemy's incessant firing.[3]

Close to our regiment was a battery which engaged in daily duels with the enemy. We would watch their works until we saw a flash or a puff of smoke, when down we would dive to hug the ground behind our works, there to remain until the shell had exploded or had passed by. Occasionally one of our batteries would turn its attention to some rebel picket post on the opposite side of the Nickajack, causing the fence rails and sand to fly and the enemy to seek places of safety.

Thus day after day were the scenes repeated until the morning of July 10, when the fact was made known to us that the enemy had evacuated his works on our front, and had fallen back to the south side of the Chattahoochee River. Early in the day an advance was ordered along the whole line, and soon after the rebels' abandoned works were occupied by Union troops, and our skirmish line pushed to the river bank.

Immediately upon the order to advance our regiment was ordered forward to the support of the skirmish line, which was having a warm engagement with the enemy's rear guard, capturing a number of prisoners and trying to outrun the rest; but were unable to do so, as in cases of emergency those other fellows knew how to keep grass from growing under their feet, and hastily crossing the river they hid themselves away among the hills on the south side.

What an agreeable change the morning of July 11 brought to us, which, however, made us almost feel that a cog in the master-wheel of Billy Sherman's thrashing-machine had been broken. The screeching of shot and shell and the cracking of rifles along our front had died away, and everything assumed an unusual quiet.[4]

The rapid and brilliant movements of Sherman's army seemed to bewilder the enemy. He was discouraged, as he felt the importance of holding the country north of the Chattahoochee; and, to further add to his discomfiture, when Johnston retreated to the south side of the river, he was relieved from command of the Confederate army, and Hood was put in his place. The reason for this change, we surmised, was that Johnston had not been able to keep Sherman's Yankees out of Georgia.[5]

A country with better natural advantages for defense would be hard to find. Every hilltop and mountain along our path was fortified, and heavy, bristling works confronted us at nearly every turn. Our chieftain had no desire to uselessly sacrifice his men by assaulting the strongly-intrenched positions of the enemy, but, instead, rapidly hurled one corps and then another upon either flank of the enemy, causing them to abandon their most powerful works and reluctantly retire southward toward Atlanta.

On July 12 Gen. Sherman reported to Gen. Grant as follows: "All is well. Have three places at which to cross the Chattahoochee in our possession, and only await Gen. Stoneman's return from down the river, to cross over in force and move on Atlanta." [6]

On the other hand, copies of Southern papers would occasionally fall into our hands containing long and minute descriptions of great victories which had crowned Confederate arms, and how Gen. Sherman's army of vagabonds had been defeated and was hastily retreating, a panic-stricken mob, back to the Ohio River. We were perfectly willing, however, that the enemy should keep right on winning their kind of victories, as such a course would soon bring the war to an end, and the armies of the Union would return home.

While we lay in camp on the Chattahoochee several of our comrades established a medium of exchange with the rebs on the opposite side of the river. We would meet each other in the middle of the river and trade coffee for tobacco. The latter was a very scarce commodity with us, and as coffee was highly prized by the rebels, they would gladly make the exchange, which would take place after the shadows of night had fallen.[7] It was amusing to see a comrade stick to his choice morsel as long as there was any taste to it, after which he would dry it and smoke it in his pipe, and as he finally knocked out the ashes would draw a long sigh.

About July 12 the 32d Ohio, with which we had been associated since November 1863, was transferred to the Fourth Division, Seventeenth Corps, to give Col. Potts a chance to command a brigade.[8] The other three regiments of our brigade — 20th, 68th and 78th Ohio — had been associated at Bolivar, Tenn., in the summer of 1862, and it is a very remarkable fact that they served their first enlistments, veteranized, returned from veteran furlough, and were again brigaded together, so to remain to the close of the war, thus forming and cementing a comradeship that will last forever.[9]

Early July 16 we started in the direction of Roswell on the Chattahoochee River. The object was to cross the river, and if possible plant ourselves on the east side of Atlanta. After a march of about 20 miles under a hot July sun we camped one mile from Marietta.

The following day we marched to Roswell, 10 miles east of Marietta, and the same evening crossed the Chattahoochee on a pontoon bridge, going into camp for the night. From Roswell our line of march was about 20 miles in a southerly direction to Decatur, a little village on the Augusta Railroad, eight miles from Atlanta. We arrived at Decatur on the evening of July 19.

The next day an incessant crash and roar of artillery and musketry on our right told us that a battle was being fought at a place which afterwards was known as "Peach Tree Creek."[10]

We devoted a portion of our time while near Decatur to tearing up and thoroughly destroying the railroad and bridges. We also picked blackberries, which grew in profusion around us.

Notes to Chapter 9

1. Those killed were Pvts. Jacob Friend, Co. A, and Anthony G. Seibert, Co. F. *Ohio Roster,* vol. V, p. 798, 801.

2. Federal troops assaulted or demonstrated at three different points along the Kennesaw line on June 27, suffering most heavily at the Confederate-held "Dead Angle." Total Union losses exceeded 2,500, while Gen. Joseph E. Johnston's Army of Tennessee lost fewer than 600 men. Baumgartner, p. 166.

3. After marching from Brush Mountain to Nickajack Creek, Pvt. Andrew Altman, Co. D, commented: "i believe this is the most miserablest State that I ever was in. we are a going threw the worst part of it so the Citazens say." Altman to his father, July 7, 1864, CAC.

4. That day Pvt. Elisha M. Ogle, Co. K, wrote to his good friend Simeon Gillis, who lost a leg the previous year at Champion Hill: "We are not in Atlanta yet but think will be before a great while. we have got the rebels across the Chatahoochee and are getting ready to cross. They evacuated their last line of works on this side night before last and went across the river and I dont know how much farther as there appears to be nothing but a skirmish line on the other side. theirs and our skirmishers are keeping up a continual shooting and popping, but are not hurting very many. There was two wounded in our regt. one in Co. 'I' and one in our co. we were on picket along the river bank and were firing across the river at each other and they shot T[hompson] Mizer [of Co. K] through the leg giving him a severe though not dangerous wound. the other man had one of his fingers shot off.

"We have been having a pretty good time of it lately. we have almost everything that is necessary to make us happy. In the first place the weather is hot enough to cook army beef which you know is pretty warm, and then we have the most amusing enemy that ever was seen. they have been in the habit of giving us a morning and evening entertainment of shell and a midnight entertainment of musketry. Then we have musquitoes to bite us[,] flies and giggers to tease us and scorpions to sting us. Then we have a great variety of nice things to eat. we have pork[,] coffee and hard tack for breakfast[;] coffee[,] hard tack and pork for dinner and hard tack[,] pork and coffee for supper. this with beef occasionaly makes up our living but we get plenty of it so we do fine. ..." Ogle to Gillis, July 11, 1864, Gillis Family Papers, CAC.

Eleven days later while on the skirmish line during the battle of Atlanta, Ogle, a 24-year-old Williams County farmer, was shot "directly through the head, the ball entering below the right eye, and passing out back of the left ear. He was left for dead on the field of battle, and was so reported to his comrades." Ogle survived the grevious wound and seven months' captivity in Andersonville prison, which he escaped until hunted down five days later. Two more months of imprisonment followed at Macon, Ga., before he was paroled in April 1865. Between 1878 and 1884 Ogle and his former Co. K comrade Simeon Gillis partnered in operating the *Bryan Press* in Bryan, Ohio. E.M. Ogle CSR, RG 94, NARA; Weston A. Goodspeed and Charles Blanchard, editors, *County of Williams, Ohio. Historical and Biographical* (Chicago: F.A. Battey & Co., 1882), p. 581-582.

5. Johnston's removal by Confederate President Jefferson Davis occurred July 17, 1864.

6. According to Sherman, this report was sent July 13 to Gen. Halleck in Washington, not Grant. Michael Fellman, editor, *Memoirs of General W.T. Sherman* (New York: Penguin Books, 2000), p. 443.

7. One particular incident of fraternization on the 68th Ohio's front occurred after dark July 11, as described by Pvt. Andrew Altman, Co. D: "I was out on the scremish line a shooting at the rebs. ... they were on one side of the river and our boys on the other and last night I stood piquett and our boys and Co. F got to talking with them and they agreed to not shoot at one an other and so our boys went to the river and traded the rebs their canteens for tobaco." Altman to his father, July 12, 1864, CAC.

8. The 32nd Ohio's transfer was ordered July 10 and it joined the 4th Division's 1st Brigade July 17, when Potts took command. *OR,* vol. XXXVIII, pt. 1, p. 109; pt. 3, p. 590.

9. Chaplain Thomas M. Stevenson, 78th Ohio, wrote that the 20th, 68th and 78th Ohio "have become banded together as firmly as brothers; all have shared equally in dangers and hardships, in honors and triumphs." Thomas M. Stevenson, *History of the 78th Regiment O.V.V.I.* (Zanesville, Ohio: Hugh Dunne, 1865), p. 263.

10. North of Atlanta July 20, nearly 20,000 Confederates attacked the Army of the Cumberland, which repulsed several charges made during two hours of fierce fighting. Hood, in his first battle as Army of Tennessee commander, lost close to 4,800 men. Long, p. 542.

10

'The tidal wave of war beat with wildest fury'

Early in the afternoon of July 20 our division moved forward along the railroad in the direction of the defenses of Atlanta. After marching about three miles, the enemy was discovered to be posted about half a mile in our front in a strip of heavy timber.

The Fourth Division now came up and immediately deployed into position on our right, after which it advanced upon the enemy, driving them pell-mell about one mile to a range of hills. In the meantime our division was rapidly moving forward and swinging as a pivot on the left of the Fourth Division. We moved forward across an open plain to the timber beyond, and just as the sun was sinking we came to a halt on the banks of a creek, from the opposite side of which came rebel shot and shell whizzing all around us. Night now coming on, we lay down in line of battle.

The next morning, just as the great orb of day commenced to lighten up the eastern horizon, a general advance was ordered against the enemy, who were in position on what afterwards became known as "Leggett's Hill." [1]

Our lines were quickly formed, our flags unfurled in the early morning breeze, and our comrades as they saw the colors sparkle in the morning sun realized in them everything we held dear in government, and again resolved to follow the grand old flag on to victory.

We moved across the creek and up the slope toward the enemy, who had been reinforced during the night, and were prepared to dispute every inch of ground. Our division, however, with the First Brigade in front, moved forward on the double-quick, driving the enemy from the hill and taking about 100 prisoners.[2]

The rebels again being reinforced made an attempt to retake the hill, but at this opportune moment the muskets of the Fourth Division, which was rapidly moving on our right, gave tongue, causing the enemy to retreat in wild disorder.

Before 10 o'clock Gen. Leggett had a battery in position on the hill and was throwing shells into Atlanta, one and a half miles distant. The position thus secured was one of great importance, as the occupation of the hill forced the enemy to give up his line of works in our front and fall back toward Atlanta. The balance of the day was spent in extending our lines and strengthening our position against an assault by the enemy.[3]

Early July 22 we discovered that the enemy had withdrawn from our front, and while engaged in preparing our breakfast we were aroused by the well-known voice of Col. Welles, shouting "Fall in men, fall in!" That earnest voice called us to our feet in an instant, and grabbing muskets we formed in line and were soon marching rapidly to the rear to repel, as we supposed, an attack by rebel cavalry upon our corps hospital and Seventeenth Corps headquarters.[4]

Upon reaching the new position imagine our surprise to find in our front, instead of cavalry, a long line of rebel infantry, while at the same time another line of rebel troops was forming across the road in our rear. Our regiment was thus being sandwiched between two lines of the enemy, who appeared to have been wholly unaware of the position of our little Buckeye band.

From our position, being partly concealed in a dense copse, the commands of rebel officers could be distinctly heard, and prisoners were taken who unknowingly ran into our line. Still the enemy moved on; something must be done, and done quickly, in order to get out of a trap which was about to spring upon us. Those were anxious moments, which to waste meant a visit to some Southern prison-pen.

Col. Welles hastily surveyed the ground on our left, and a moment later whispered down the line, "Be cool, men, be cool! Forward by the left flank — march." We sprang to our feet and moved to the left on the double-quick, and dropping behind a rail fence which lay in our path, poured a volley into the enemy, who were forming in line in an open field on our right. The alarm thus given by the muskets of our regiment was immediately responded to by a battery of artillery. The battle of July 22 had opened in earnest.

The Third Division engaged the enemy so promptly that our regiment was enabled, by making a rapid move to the left and a wide detour, to pass around the enemy's right and again join our brigade and division on "Leggett's Hill."

Col. R.K. Scott, commanding our brigade, and Lieut. A.C. Urquhart, picket officer on Scott's staff, accompanied our regiment in the morning, but upon our return they took a shorter route than that followed by the regiment, and were taken prisoners. The next day, the next week, the next month we anxiously discussed the matter of their capture, whether they were living or dead, but could hear nothing until Sept. 28, when they rejoined us in camp near Atlanta, having been exchanged.[5]

Upon reaching our division we found our comrades hotly engaged with the enemy, who were advancing in solid columns to storm "Leggett's Hill." My pen utterly fails me in an attempt to describe in detail the events of that fearful struggle.[6]

Nearer and nearer came the line of rebel gray, indicating that they felt able to brush us away, but as they ran up against the muskets of Leggett's Division they were sent reeling backward, suffering great loss, our loss being slight, as we lay behind a hastily constructed line of fence rails and dirt.

The next attack came from the direction of Atlanta; a skirmish line followed by a heavy force was observed moving upon us from that direction. We now quickly changed front — as the first attack had been from the east — and again repulsed the enemy in handsome style. The enemy fell back, reformed their lines, and again returned to the attack, but again were repulsed and driven back, leaving their killed and wounded on the ground.

During the afternoon the enemy again advanced upon us from the direction of Atlanta, at the same time furiously attacking us on our flank, and using their heavy artillery. If ever we were in a position to fight like demons it was then. "Get into the works," shouted Col. Welles. "Which side, Colonel?" was asked. "I don't care which side," yelled our regiment's commander, "but get into the works!" And get into the works we did, but it was a puzzle to us to know which side of the works would be the safest, as the attack came from front and flank, which compelled us to fight first on one side of a barricade of rails and dirt, and then on the other. At one time a portion of our division was on one side of our works firing in one direction, while a little farther along the line the rest of the division was on the opposite side of the works, firing in another direction.

About this time Gen. Logan dispatched to Leggett a message saying: "General, it is all important that you hold the hill." The left of our brigade now swung back to the crest of another hill, the right still resting on the old works, where a few rails were hastily thrown together, and behind these we hugged the ground. Still on came the enemy, rolling and surging up against our lines in another determined effort to take "Leggett's Hill." But Leggett's men were just as determined that they should not have it. We saw them coming to take the hill, with officers in front, lines well dressed and following each other in quick succession.

Such a scene one does not often behold, even in the wild tumult of war, as here it was the tidal wave of war beat with its wildest fury against us. Volley after volley of musketry, accompanied by the bellowing of heavy guns, seemed to have no more effect than so much chaff would have done in the ranks of those advancing hosts.

On the enemy came until they became engaged in a hand-to-hand struggle with a portion of Leggett's Division. Wild yells rent the air, and bayonets clashed together as the combatants gave the glistening steel. Men with uplifted blades sought each others' lives, but the swift, unerring ball reached them before the blows were delivered, and they fell side by side. The crash of cannon and roar of musketry were deafening, and the enemy was hurled back only to spring forward with greater determination in a vain effort to burst Sherman's coils that were tightening around them.

As I glanced to the right or left I found it the same — a struggling, fighting mass of men, now partly hidden by clouds of powdersmoke and then again in plain view. Thus the battle raged till night dropped her mantle over the scene. Little by little the enemy was driven back, and when darkness fell they gave up the fight and quietly quit the field.

Wearied with the confusion and excitement of battle we threw ourselves down to rest, but not to sleep. The voice of a comrade is heard calling; we hurry here and there — now holding our canteen to the lips of a dying comrade, now endeavoring to smooth the couch of a wounded brother, and now hastily answering the voice of a friend, "Oh, give me water."

The morning of July 23 a muffled shout that was taken up by brigade after brigade, and division after division, rolled along the lines. There was no enemy in our front, and the victory was ours; but, oh, what a fearful loss of life there had been. The ground over which the enemy made their successive charges was thickly strewn with dead.

In front of Leggett's Division the rebel dead lay so close together that one could have walked for some distance stepping from one body to another. During the day the enemy asked for a truce,

Fatally wounded while commanding the Army of the Tennessee at Atlanta, 35-year-old Maj. Gen. James B. McPherson was the highest ranking Union casualty of the war. Gen. Sherman reflected: "McPherson was then in his prime, over six feet high, and a very handsome man in every way, was universally liked, and had many noble qualities."

Mass. MOLLUS, USAMHI

and there was delivered to them to be buried about 1,000 of their dead. These were collected from the ground in front of Leggett's Division, which went to show how well Leggett's lads had responded to Logan's battle cry, "McPherson and revenge!"[7]

July 23 was a sad day to us. There was no excitement to keep up our strength, as with mute lips we gathered together those of our own regiment who had fallen on July 22, and with many an aching heart laid them tenderly away.

Our total loss in killed and wounded was about 70. Yet it does not appear in Ohio's records that our regiment suffered any loss in wounded. This discrepancy, however, may to some extent be accounted for by the fact that during the last 18 months of our service a very small percent of our wounded was reported. Only those who were wholly disabled were sent to the hospital, while those who sustained less severe wounds remained with the regiment, and in many cases were doing duty before their wounds healed.[8]

The most severe loss we sustained on July 22 was our beloved commander, Maj. Gen. James B. McPherson. He had just left Gen. Sherman's headquarters, where he had been in consultation, and was hastily riding forward accompanied by one orderly, his other aides having been sent on different missions, when, while passing through a belt of timber, which but a few moments previous had been in our possession, he encountered a body of the enemy's skirmishers and was shot dead.[9]

The first time we heard of McPherson was at Corinth, Miss., he then being a colonel on Halleck's staff. In October following he was made a major general, and upon the organization of the Seventeenth Corps was made its commander. He remained in command of the corps, leading it in all its marches and campaigns until March 1864, when he took command of the Army of the Tennessee.

Gen. McPherson's death was soon known throughout his entire army on July 22, awakening, first, bitter grief, and then an honest thirst for vengeance. That afternoon "McPherson and revenge!" rang from right to left along the line. Thousands of the enemy went down before it, and at night the dripping earth bore mute testimony of the terrible vengeance his devoted army had visited upon his slayers.[10]

A braver man never drew a sword. In a fight where the pressure was the heaviest he was sure to be found, encouraging his men by his presence. He never used profane language; he needed no oaths to emphasize his orders, yet in the heat of battle his words rang out like a bugle-call. There he was in his element, and his clear eyes blazed like a meteor as he rode at the head of his columns, a hero admired and loved by his men. Full of honor and generosity, he finished his short, bright career. His fall was a sad calamity to our cause and our country.

Soon after McPherson's death his body was recovered and taken to Gen. Sherman's headquarters. Sherman ordered McPherson's personal staff to escort the body to the home of his boyhood in Clyde, Sandusky County, Ohio, where his remains now rest under a beautiful equestrian monument erected by the Army of the Tennessee.[11]

Notes to Chapter 10

1. Christened "Leggett's Hill" after the battle of Atlanta in honor of Brig. Gen. M.D. Leggett, this terrain feature was known locally as Bald Hill. Early on July 21 it was occupied by portions of Maj. Gen. Patrick R. Cleburne's Confederate division.

2. The 12th and 16th Wisconsin led the 1st Brigade's assault, suffering 258 casualties. *OR*, vol. XXXVIII, pt. 3, p. 571.

3. A few hours after Bald ("Leggett's") Hill was taken, 1st Sergt. John D. Travis, Co. G, wrote home: "We mooved up in the morning and formed our lines as flankers. Being on the left we formed at right angles with the line and the fight commenced. ... our Brigade was on the flank so we did not have much to do but those to the right of us had a pretty warm time. The fight lasted nearly all the forenoon. ... we are throwing up works as fast as we can. the boys have stacked their dry goods and are ready to pitch in." Travis to his brothers and sister, July 21, 1864, Travis Family Papers, BHL.

The morning of July 21, Confederate commander John Bell Hood ordered Lt. Gen. William J. Hardee's corps and Maj. Gen. Joseph Wheeler's cavalry to march south, then east, and attack the Federal far left flank and rear early the next morning. Corp. John Harker, Co. K, a Williams County farmer and former member of the 68th Ohio's color guard, recalled: "Having been on the picket line on the night of July 21, in front of Atlanta, a Captain came to me and asked how many men I had on post. I replied, 'The usual number.' He requested me to take two of my men and accompany him, he having taken the same number of men from another post. I asked him what he intended to do. He said he intended to capture a rebel picket post. We then crept toward the Johnnies, and they ran away. We stayed there all night and fortified the post. Then some reserve pickets were moved forward to keep up a scattering fire to the right of a large tree.

"We could hear the enemy moving to our left in large numbers, and the Captain said, 'Hold this post.' As the Captain was about to leave I asked him, as I already had twice before, if it would not be right for him to send Gen. Sherman word about the movement of the rebels. He assured me that Gen. Sherman knew his own business. So it proved that Hood moved around our flank, and I obeyed the orders of a superior officer, while our General and our men slept on unconsciously."

Harker was wounded in the head the following day. *OR,* vol. XXXVIII, pt. 3, p. 631; John Harker, "In Front of Atlanta," *The National Tribune,* Nov. 30, 1905; J. Harker CSR, RG 94, NARA.

4. The 68th Ohio mostly fought July 22 as a seven-company regiment. That morning three companies were detached — Co. A at 17th Corps headquarters as provost guards, Co. F as guards to the 3rd Division field hospital, and Co. I as guards to the corps hospital. George E. Welles to W.B. Welles, July 24, 1864 in the *Toledo Blade,* Aug. 2, 1864.

5. Adjt. Thomas T. Cowan of the 68th related three weeks after the July 22 fighting: "We have news of Colonel Scott. It is from a member of the 32d O.V.I., who was captured at the same time, but made his escape by jumping from the cars, while en route for Macon. He was piloted through to our lines by negroes. He reports the Colonel as 'all right,' and says that when he took his unceremonious departure, the colonel was cheering up the boys by having them serenade the rebels with the 'Star-Spangled Banner,' and such other little songs as they could undoubtedly appreciate. Of Lieutenant Urquhart, we can hear nothing." Cowan, Aug. 12, 1864 to the *Napoleon Press,* reprinted in the *Toledo Commercial,* Sept. 5, 1864.

Scott and 1st Lt. Abram C. Urquhart, Co. A, were confined at Macon, Ga. and Charleston, S.C. before their release Sept. 28, 1864. Scott resumed command of the 2nd Brigade, 3rd Division, 17th Corps, on Nov. 13, 1864. Urquhart mustered out Dec. 19, 1864. R.K. Scott and A.C. Urquhart CSR, RG 94, NARA.

6. The July 22 battle of Atlanta was perhaps the most noteworthy and fiercely fought of any in the 68th Ohio's entire service. The following descriptions are excerpts from letters written by regimental personnel within days of the battle:

Pvt. Andrew Altman, Co. D: "We had a devil of a big fight here day fore yesterday. The rebs Charged all a rounde on our lines but we held them level. There were 62 killed[,] wounded and missing out of the olde 68 ovi. Two of the Shephards was killed [1st Sergt. Webster C. Shepard and Pvt. Benjamin C. Shepard, Co. H. A third brother, Pvt. Robert P. Shepard, also of Co. H, survived]. They fired on us from 3 different sides and you may kno that it was a warm time. ...

"A tremendious fight it was. In stead of playing snake in the grass we played it in the corn field for we lay on the ground and fired, not any brest

Opposite: **Among those in the 68th Ohio killed July 22, 1864 was Co. H's orderly sergeant, Webster Clay Shepard, who was photographed during the regiment's veteran furlough just three months before his death. A schoolteacher originally from Athens County, Ohio, Shepard was staunchly patriotic and abhorred anti-war activity as promulgated by "Copperheads" in the Buckeye State. "I'll venture you may enquire from Dan to Beersheba for a man among these croakers who would die for slavery," he wrote to the *Napoleon Press* in August 1863, "and your search would be in vain. I think I know the secret of their opposition to the war. They are cowards, and I think this can be proven by the following fact, viz: When there were plenty of men to enlist in the North, very few opposed the war, but as soon as it began to be rumored that men would be compelled to go, hundreds were attacked with hostility to the war. Inform your acquaintances, if you have any of Butternut persuasion ... to be sure and have their peace made with their God, for, when the war is over, we will return to settle the account we have with them." Shepard and younger brother Benjamin, also killed July 22, were interred side by side in Marietta National Cemetery.**

L. M. Strayer Collection

works only 2 or 3 [fence] rails in front of us and only one line of us & the rebs was fore Regts deep in front of us and charged on us twice and we drove them back twice. They were drunk for they came up at a right sholder shift arms and said surender but we could not see it in that way. We were never drilled that way. ... we held our ground and chew cartridges for life. They came so close to the 78 ovi that they took a Captain by the coat colar and took him off with them. I got 3 pones of johney cake out of a dead rebs knap sack." Altman to his father, July 24 and 26, 1864, CAC.

2nd Lt. James F. Cosgro, Co. K: "Our company was out on picket when the fight began. We were within two miles of Atlanta at the time, and I tell you we were in a hot place. We were driven in by a Regiment who charged on us, but the boys gave them several volleys before we left. ... We fell back to the Regiment only to meet a worse fate. Here we found the regiment had been fighting about two hours. We had not been with them more than ten minutes when our brigade was ordered to form on a hill and hold it at all hazards, and nobly did the Second Brigade do its duty. Cheatham's Division of Hardee's Rebels charged us on an open field, but we repulsed them with terrible slaughter. The ground in front of our Brigade is literally *covered* with their dead. ... This was a little the warmest reception the rebels met with for some time. Some of the wounded say this is the first time they were ever repulsed. ... The boys of Co. K lost all their knapsacks and canteens. I must quit for the rebs are shelling us like *blazes.*" Cosgro to Edwin J. Evans, July 24, 1864 in *The Bryan Union Press*, Aug. 11, 1864.

Pvt. Andrew J. Long, Co. K: "Many acts of individual heroism and valor came under my own observation on [July 22]. I saw a private of the 13th Iowa, standing in an exposed position, fire several hundred rounds into the advancing columns of the enemy while at least ten men were loading their pieces for him, and when he finally became exhausted your humble servant, though endowed with less courage, relieved him by taking his place.

"It would almost be criminal while speaking in this connection to omit mentioning the conduct of the gallant Captain [John B.] Mills, of the 78th O.V.V.I. The rebels had succeeded in planting a flag on the works in front of the 78th, and under cover they were dropping into the ditch in such numbers that they would have been enabled in a short time to drive this gallant regiment from the ditch, as the position gave them an enfilading fire into our ranks. Seeing the danger at a glance, Captain Mills called for volunteers to aid him in driving the rebels from the ditch. Twelve men instantly responded, but finding this number insufficient, Col. [Greenberry F.] Wiles, of the 78th, ordered the Captain to take his own company (Co. C). Placing himself at their head, Mills charged upon the ditch and soon drove the rebels to the opposite side of the works and took a large number of prisoners. Among the number was a rebel captain, at whom Mills aimed a blow with his sword, but the rebel, throwing up his own sword, exclaimed: 'For God's sake, don't kill me; I am your prisoner.' He was immediately secured and taken to the rear by a young man named [Corp. Thomas C.] Elder, belonging to [Co. G of] the 20th O.V.V.I.

"Captain Mills now directed Captain [John] Orr, of the 78th, who had accompanied him, to remain on this side with a part of the men and prevent the rebels from recrossing the works, while he (Mills) with another party would cross the works and attack the enemy who were lying in considerable force on the opposite side. Again placing himself at the head of a number of volunteers belonging to the 20th and 78th Ohio (these two regiments being together at the time), Capt. Mills crossed the works and by a vigorous onset soon put the rebels to flight. Some of them finding their retreat cut off, were forced to recross the works, and surrendered themselves prisoners to Capt. Orr and his men. Capt. Mills pursued the rebels for at least 150 yards. In this hand-to-hand fight, with about twenty men, Capt. Mills took forty-two prisoners. Thus by the daring bravery and prompt action of one individual was an entire regiment saved from destruction. I am happy to state that the gallant Captain escaped unharmed." Long to William M. Starr, Aug. 17, 1864 in *The Bryan Union Press,* Sept. 1, 1864.

Within five weeks of the battle a 17th Corps Board of Honor, instituted by Maj. Gen. Frank P. Blair Jr., conferred gold and silver medals of honor (not to be confused with the Congressional Medal of Honor) to 13 Ohio, Illinois and Iowa officers and enlisted men belonging to the 3rd and 4th divisions, 17th Corps. Although no one in the 68th Ohio received one of these awards, three were earned in the 20th Ohio and three given to members of the 78th Ohio, including 49-year-old Capt. John Orr of Co. H. These medals bore the inscription "Atlanta, July 22" and were to be presented to the recipients "in front of their commands by their division commanders." *OR,* vol. XXXVIII, pt. 3, p. 556-558.

1st Sergt. John D. Travis, Co. G: "I have seen and passed through that which I hope will not be repeated very often. Yesterday morning our Regiment was husteled off to the rear to clean out as our Generals supposed a small force of Cavalry who had cut our communication to Decatur and had burned a portion of our train. So we marched out on double quick[,] formed our line of skirmishers and pitched in but soon found that we were ... nearly surrounded and cut off from the rest of the army. So we skedaddled back and succeeded just in time to save being gobbled. It was then discovered that [the Confederates] had swung [their] whole force around to the left and was coming up on our train, hospitals, ammunition and supplys. So we marched back on double quick to join our Brigade.

"I hardly think that so large an army ever changed fronts and formed lines quicker than the army of General Sherman did yesterday. But we just got back to our Brigade in time to assist in repelling a desperate charge that Johney Rebs were making on our line. Every man jumped to his place and as the Rebs advanced we gave them a volley that sent a portion of them back pel mel but there was a great many that did not get back that lay as they fell. The rebs came up in our rear and front. We were ordered to change front on the 10th company and charge and the rebs skedaddled back like sheep but it was seen that we would have to abandon our position for we were between two fires. So we limbered up[,] changed front to the rear and reformed our lines. The men in the front rank took the guns from the rear rank and they carried rails from a fence that we crossed and in less than 10 minutes we had lines formed with a few rails in front to protect our heads.

We were ordered to hold that position at all hazzards for if the rebs gained that position we were lost. So we lay flat to the ground and in a few moments the rebs massed their forces and charged down on us 3 colums deep. As they came over the hill they raised such a yell that would be enough to scare the devil. We let them come until they got within 50 paces of us when we raised and let into them and checked them. Our batteries opened on them and we had pretty hot work untill after dark when they fell back leaving hundreds of their dead around or close to us. At one time they charged [and] siezed our flags but we beat them back with our muskets. The 78th Ohio was just to our left. They had their flag taken but charged and regained it. The Captain of one of [the 78th's] companies is complimented for clipping a rebbels head off with his sword who had siezed the flag. Such fighting I never saw before although the most of the time we were protected by our breastworks. They shot shell[,] railroad spikes and horseshoes flew around our heads in every direction. There was only 7 companies of our Regiment engaged, 3 companies being on detached service.

"I cannot tell how many the Regiment lost. Our company lost 12. Our Captain [John C. Harman] was wounded [in the thigh]. Adelbirt [Pvt. Adelbert Coleman, Co. K] was wounded early in the fight and was left in the enemies hands. I did not see him but his company told me he was hit in the thigh. The Rebs at that time were charging on their company which was on the skirmish line and were retreating or falling back to join the column. They did not have time to carry him along for the rebs were so close and were ordering them to halt. [Coleman died Aug. 12 in Andersonville prison]. Elisha Ogle [Co. K] was shot [in] the head and fell in to the enemies hands. He had a verry valuable watch in his pocket but the boys had no time to get it. Captain [James H.] Long [of Co. K] was wounded in the arm and John Kollars was wounded. Orderly [Francis] Lesnet [Co. K] was killed. Our Lieutenant Colonel was wounded. His name is George E. Welles." Travis to his brothers and sister, July 23, 1864, BHL.

Lt. Col. George E. Welles: "This has been a terribly hard battle, and we have thrashed the rebs, but have lost many of our best officers and men. Colonel Scott's horse was killed, and he was taken prisoner. The rebel colonel who captured Colonel Scott was subsequently wounded, and is now a prisoner in our hands. He says that Scott was not hurt, otherwise than being bruised from the fall of his horse.

"Our brigade held its position all day, but was compelled to change to the outside of its works four different times. About three P.M. the enemy charged us both in front and rear, and we were compelled to leave our entrenchments. We moved back about five hundred yards and formed line in [a] cornfield on the crest of a little ridge, and had no sooner got the position than Cheatham's (reb) Division came yelling like devils, two brigades two lines deep right into our two little regiments, the 68th and 78th Ohio. We were all lying down in the corn, about 500 yards in front of the last line of works, and never fired a shot till the rebs came through the hollow and on to our ridge, but the minute they showed their heads above the top of the hill, we poured it into them. Some of them came clean over our men, and were shot right in among us. It was the hottest place I ever got into. It lasted about two hours, and during that time they and we kept pouring in the heaviest fire we could give. Night closed the fight, the rebs fell back, and we fortified, and are still on the same ground. You will probably see full descriptions of the battle, how it opened by the rebs, turning our left flank and coming in our rear, bending our lines back into the shape of a V, &c. Well this V ran out to a very sharp point, that a breast work in front of our brigade, *that we held all day,* part of the time on one side of the work, and part of the time on the other side until, as I said, they came for us from both directions. This was a vital point, and had we given way the whole thing would have gone up. Never did a regiment behave better than the 68th — the people of the Northwest may feel still more proud of them." Welles to W.B. Welles, July 24, 1864 in the *Toledo Commercial,* Aug. 2, 1864.

Welles received a slight arm wound as well as four bullet holes in his coat and one through his pants. *Toledo Blade,* Aug. 2, 1864.

7. During the July 23 truce, Gen. Leggett reported "between 900 and 1,000 dead rebels" were delivered to the enemy or buried on ground fought over by the 3rd Division. *OR*, vol. XXXVIII, pt. 3, p. 566.

Pvt. Edward A. Bigelow, who enlisted at age 15 in Co. F in December 1863, observed in a letter home: "In front of where our regiment was stationed during the fight, the ground is, or was literally covered with dead and wounded rebels, and it was almost impossible to walk about without stepping on them. A flag of truce was out yesterday for over an hour, exchanging the wounded and dead, and while doing so we exchanged six rebels for one Yankee, during the time they were permitted to remain." Bigelow to his father, July 24, 1864 in the *Toledo Commercial,* Aug. 8, 1864.

8. The 68th Ohio's losses July 22 ranged from 62 to 78, the higher number reflecting slightly wounded men who did not require hospitalization. Casualties in Leggett's 3rd Division were 137 killed, 308 wounded and 315 captured or missing. *OR*, vol. XXXVIII, pt. 3, p. 566

9. Among the best accounts of McPherson's last hours is Lt. Col. William E. Strong's "The Death of General James B. McPherson," published in *Military Essays and Recollections,* vol. I (Chicago: A.C. McClurg and Company, 1891), p. 311-343. Strong served on McPherson's staff as Army of the Tennessee inspector general.

10. Confederate losses July 22 have been estimated from 5,500 to 8,000. Albert Castel, *Decision in the West: The Atlanta Campaign of 1864* (Lawrence: University Press of Kansas, 1992), p. 412.

11. Clyde, Ohio's McPherson monument was unveiled July 22, 1881 by Gen. Sherman. Ceremonies were attended by 15,000 people, who were addressed by nine former Union generals. *History of Sandusky County, Ohio* (Cleveland: H.Z. Williams & Bro., 1882), p. 367.

11

'Amply repaid for the hardships of a long campaign'

Our division remained in the position it occupied July 22, strengthening our works and keeping a close watch upon the movements of the enemy, who kept up a continuous fire during the day. The night of July 24 our regiment advanced about half a mile and went on picket duty. Our duty was to signal should any hostile demonstrations be made by the enemy. The night passed by very quietly, and at the first break of day we returned to our intrenchments on "Leggett's Hill."

The morning of July 26 heavy firing took place all along the line. It was reported that the rebels were advancing in force, but this proved to be a false rumor and the excitement soon quieted down. Late in the evening we moved toward the right. We marched all night and part of the next day, making a circuit around the north side of Atlanta, and came to a halt on the west side of the doomed city. This move brought us to the right flank of Sherman's army, where we again took position. Skirmishing commenced immediately upon going into position, and between that and throwing up breastworks we managed to pass the day and succeeding night.

Early the morning of July 28 we moved forward to a new position and then engaged in throwing up another line of works. About 10 o'clock the enemy made a furious assault upon the Fifteenth Corps, but was handsomely repulsed with great loss. In this engagement, which was known as the battle of Ezra Church, only a part of Leggett's command was engaged, our brigade being held in reserve under orders to be ready to move any moment. Logan's Fifteenth Corps, however, proved to be more than a match for the flower of Hood's army; therefore, we were not called into action.[1]

During the succeeding days we changed our position in the line a number of times, the object being to get a little closer to the enemy.

One morning we were ordered to pick up our worldly goods and move to the right through a belt of timber and take a new position. It was a very dark night when we made this change, but the enemy seemed to know of it, as they treated us to a lively shower of shot and shell at short range, which made us feel a little more uneasy than when in the works we had left. In some way the idea got out that we had better move back from such close proximity to eternity. The idea was acted upon, and away we went at rather a rapid gait to the rear. Directly in our rear was an abrupt decline of about six feet, and a number of our comrades walked over this bank. It proved to be a friend worth more to us than riches, as that little bank protected us from a storm of iron hail sweeping over our heads and felling trees all around us.

Early July 30 our division was ordered to move about two miles and fill up a gap on the flank of the Fifteenth Corps. Soon after changing our position a spirited engagement took place, lasting about one hour, after which everything became quiet save for a scattering fire along the picket line.

Sunday, July 31, a spirit of conciliation seemed to pervade the men all along the line; cornet bands were entertaining each other with many choice selections, which came to us mellowed by the distance, and thus July 1864 passed into history.

During the long month of August we moved from one position to another, now throwing up a line of earthworks at one place, and now at another, in the meantime living on green corn that was found in abundance around us. This we served in every possible style. When found too hard to roast or boil, we would punch one-half of a discarded canteen full of holes with our bayonet, and with these improvised graters prepare our meal. I do not wish to convey the impression that Uncle Sam did not provide for our wants. Immense supplies of army rations were held in store subject to orders. The rustic living, however, offered us a change from army rations, which we enjoyed.

Aug. 1 brought heavy skirmishing along the lines. Late in the day an artillery duel took place, many of the shells going into Atlanta, two miles away. From the top of a giant oak near us one could plainly see into the city and observe the confusion created by the heavy cannonading.

Early Aug. 4 we were ordered to advance our lines, but our skirmishers met with such serious opposition that the attempt was abandoned. Late in the afternoon our regiment was ordered out to support the picket line, which was being warmly engaged.

The night of Aug. 6 we constructed a new line of works and set out two lines of pointed stakes at a half-pitch. After the work was completed one of our officers remarked: "Now the fool rebs can charge us if they want to."

Aug. 10 we were engaged in digging up the earth and building works for protection against an enfilading fire; meantime everything was in a perfect roar around us.[2]

Aug. 12 the rebels made an attempt to drive in our pickets, but the pickets did not drive, much to the inconvenience of the enemy. About midnight we received orders to move to the extreme right of our division, where a large detail was made to assist in constructing another strong line of earthworks. The following day we were engaged in building the strongest works we had yet constructed.

Aug. 20. Heavy columns continued to move by us, going to the right. We were ordered to make a demonstration on our front to keep the enemy from massing on our right. The night of the 22d we were intrenched behind the 14th line of earthworks that our regiment and brigade had constructed since June 10.

Gen. Sherman, being dissatisfied with the course of events, now resolved to raise the siege of Atlanta and move upon the railroads south of the city. This successful move began Aug. 25. We marched southward toward the [Atlanta & West Point] Railroad. We made a wide detour, cautiously feeling our way until noon of the 28th, when we reached the railroad near Fairburn. Here we employed our time in turning over the track. We then made bonfires of the ties. The rails were laid across the fire, and after becoming hot were seized at each end by willing hands and twisted around telegraph poles. We remained near Fairburn until the afternoon of the 30th, when we took up our line of march in the rear of our division, and about midnight went into bivouac near the Macon [& Western] Railroad.

The next morning we moved in the direction of Jonesboro and formed in line of battle on the left of the Fifteenth Corps. Just as we reached the position assigned us the enemy made a furious attack upon the Fifteenth Corps, but were repulsed with heavy loss.[3]

The evening of Sept. 1 we were ordered to move to the right in the direction of Lovejoy. Early the next morning our attention was called to the sound of explosions in the direction of Atlanta. The rebels were blowing up their munitions of war.

The enemy having left our front during the night, we were ordered to follow them. After a march of about six miles we were brought to a halt by bumping against the enemy in the vicinity of Lovejoy. That night and next day we were on the skirmish line. John Scott of Co. I was mortally wounded. Comrade Scott was the last man the 68th lost on the Atlanta campaign.[4]

It was while confronting the enemy at Lovejoy that we received the glad news, "Atlanta is ours, the campaign is ended." The wild cheering that rolled along the lines as the news was imparted to us made us feel amply repaid for all the hardships incident to a long and trying campaign.

We remained in camp near Lovejoy until the night of Sept. 5, when we started toward Atlanta. The next morning we were at Jonesboro, and on Thursday, Sept. 8, went into camp on the Rough and Ready road, three miles south of Atlanta. Here we remained until Oct. 4, taking a much-needed rest.

During the Atlanta campaign we were in line of battle nearly all the time, engaged in fighting or fortifying. For days and nights we never removed our shoes as we lay in our works, not knowing what moment would call us to resist an attack. Night after night the picket line would become warmly engaged, and volleys of musketry would be exchanged. Night after night the pickets watched while others slept, but in case our pickets were driven in those sleeping comrades were awakened by earnest but friendly kicks which never failed to arouse their bump of combativeness and put them in a fighting mood.

Sept. 12 our regiment held dress parade, this being the first time since the previous May.[5]

Sept. 28 Col. Scott and Lieut. Urquhart joined us, having been exchanged under the cartel of Gens. Sherman and Hood. Our regiment fell into line as they drew nigh, and then there took place a season of glad greetings.

As October drew near rumors began to reach us of an early move. Hood, with his army, was reported to be on the north side of the Chattahoochee River, striking out boldly for Tennessee. The railroads and our communications with our Northern homes had been destroyed, which for a time made matters look perplexing to us. It seemed as though we would be compelled to give up all we had gained during the summer. We knew not, however, of other plans that were taking form in the brain of our beloved leader, which electrified the Nation and made the holding of Atlanta of minor importance.

Courtesy of Margaret Wilkins

Oct. 3 we received orders to turn over all camp equipage, and at 4 o'clock the following morning we started in pursuit of Hood. We swept north through the suburbs of Atlanta and about 4 o'clock in the afternoon went into camp near Marietta, 22 miles from our camp of the morning.

The morning of Oct. 5 we marched through Marietta and about noon came to a halt near Kennesaw. North of us could be seen the smoke of the enemy's campfires. The battle of Allatoona was being fought. We could hear the bellowing of distant arms, and saw the Signal Corps on the top of Kennesaw flashing the message of our chieftain: "Hold the fort; I am coming."

"Oh, for a voice to reach them," said Sherman, as again and again the signal was flashed across the intervening space. At last there came a lull in the fight; the smoke lifted and the garrison at Allatoona caught sight of the signal flag on top of lofty Kennesaw. "Hold the fort; relief is coming," it said, and hold the fort those brave men did. [6]

The early morning of Sunday, Oct. 9, found us sweeping on through the narrow defile between Kennesaw and Brush Mountains. We moved over the ground we fought over the previous June, and in due time went into camp near Big Shanty, where a detail of 200 men was engaged in repairing the railroad, which the enemy had wrecked. We remained near Big Shanty until the night of Oct. 10, when we marched in the direction of Kingston. Heavy firing was heard in front and we hurried forward, to be on hand if needed. At daylight next morning we were at Allatoona, where cheer upon cheer rent the air in honor of Gen. Corse and his noble men, who for 10 long hours had withstood the fierce onset of the enemy.

From Allatoona we moved north along the railroad until about noon, when a halt was ordered to hold our State election. Late in the day we moved on and about midnight crossed the Etowah River. We went into camp near Cartersville.

Opposite: **Photographed shortly after his August 1862 enlistment, Henry County farmer Eugene M. Rugg belonged to Co. D and was appointed corporal on July 1, 1864. From October 1864 to April 1865 he served in the regimental color guard.**

Oct. 12 we passed through Kingston, 62 miles from Atlanta, and at dark camped four miles from Rome after a march of 20 miles. Late the following day we started in the direction of Resaca, 25 miles distant. We marched all night, and just at daylight stopped long enough to make coffee, after which we moved on and at night went into camp near Resaca.

This constant marching, early and late, began to tell on us. We would march through the day and then continue on through the night, stopping now and then to let the line close up, and then on again over hills and mountains, through fields and swamps.

Oct. 15 we crossed the Oostanaula River and approached Snake Creek Gap. Here we found trees felled into the road to check our progress, but we mounted the high ground and at night went into bivouac on the north side.

Sunday, Oct. 16, our line of march lay along the foot of a mountain to Gordon Springs, where we remained until Monday evening, when we turned to the left, ascended the mountain, and after a march of six miles halted for the night.

Oct. 18 we moved down the mountain side to the valley below. About 10 o'clock we marched through Lafayette, going in a westerly course, the enemy in full retreat, and we after them in hot haste. The following day we reached Summerville, and on the evening of Oct. 20 went into camp near Gaylesville, Ala. Since leaving Atlanta the enemy had led us on a wild chase of 170 miles, much of the way over mountain roads, which made the march very tiresome.

Gen. Sherman now became satisfied that Hood could not be made to fight. Therefore he ordered the pursuit of Hood's army to be discontinued, as he had no desire to wear out his army following a cowardly foe. He felt sure that Gen. Thomas could attend to Hood, so he began to perfect his plans for putting a cherished idea into effect.[7]

Oct. 22 our non-veterans, whose term of service had expired, were ordered to get ready for a march to Chattanooga, about 70 miles away, preparatory to being mustered out. During the time our comrades were making preparations for their march northward the regiment was preparing for a march southward, and all were seemingly too busy to even heave a sigh of regret that a comradeship extending over a period of three years was being sundered. However, our orders to march were countermanded, but our comrades moved on, and soon passed over the hills out of sight.

Oct. 25 our supply train reached us from Rome, Ga., laden

with rations, and we were once more relieved of the necessity of foraging.

Early the 28th a shout went ringing through the camp: "One hour for writing letters. It may be the last chance for some weeks to come." This extended to the army in camp around Gaylesville, and I doubt another more quiet hour in the army was ever witnessed, except when in slumber, as one and all were engaged in writing letters to some dear relative or friend. These letters conveyed the news that a great move would soon be made, and that some weeks might pass before they heard from us again.

The morning of Oct. 29 we formed in line and started in the direction of Atlanta, 100 miles southeast, keeping step to the merry music by our band. "Oh, ain't I glad to get out of the wilderness, down in Alabam." We crossed the Coosa River on pontoons that afternoon and went into bivouac for the night. The evening of the next day we camped at Cave Springs. Here we remained one day.

Nov. 1 we resumed our march by way of Cedar Town, Dallas and Lost Mountain, and Nov. 5 went into camp on Nickajack Creek, six miles south of Marietta, where we remained till Nov. 13. Our regiment was now supplied with new clothing and everything thoroughly overhauled.

The wild echoes of the struggle around Atlanta had died away. The banks of the Nickajack or Chattahoochee no longer resounded with the crack of rifles along the picket line, and the Yanks and Johnnies no longer sassed each other from the shadows on either side.

One evening the boys felled a large chestnut tree, when there came upon us a new enemy — an army of enraged bees — which put to flight the fellows who were after chestnuts. My comrades fell back in good order, and for a time were busily engaged in picking out this new enemy's bullets. After the bees quieted down and ceased to trouble us, we sought the sweetness in that tree, and ate heartily of the honey.

Nov. 8 we drew our pay and also held Presidential election, our regiment casting 381 votes; 316 for Lincoln and 65 for McClellan.

Nov. 13 we marched along the line of the railroad toward Atlanta, leaving the smoking ruins of bridges and culverts behind us, and about 8 o'clock in the evening went into camp one mile from Atlanta.

Notes to Chapter 11

1. For five days following the battle of Atlanta, Logan commanded the Army of the Tennessee. On July 27 he was replaced by Maj. Gen. Oliver O. Howard, and resumed command of the 15th Corps. *OR,* vol. XXXVIII, pt. 3, p. 4.

Portions of two Confederate corps unsuccessfully attacked Howard July 28 at Ezra Church, losing as many as 5,000 troops before withdrawing to Atlanta's fortifications. Federal casualties were fewer than 600. Long, p. 547.

2. "We now occupy works about one mile from the city," wrote the 68th's adjutant, Thomas Cowan, "and some three hundred and fifty yards from the rebel picket line. How long we will be allowed to occupy our present position would be hard to say. We have built four strong lines of works, each of which we have been compelled to give up to other troops, and move to a different part of the line. ... The boys are thoroughly worked down, but the discipline of the regiment is perfect, and scarcely a murmur is heard, all seeming willing to do whatever amount of labor the exigencies of the service may demand. ...

"Since [July 22] we have been in no regular engagement, although our present skirmish line will almost equal (so far as noise and amount of ammunition expended is concerned) a *small fight.* In fact, unless a fellow keeps a sharp lookout, it is neither pleasant nor safe to be out on the line in daylight, and we are not troubled, either by inquiring *'special correspondents'* or *'Our special artists,'* as all members of these honorable fraternities regard their precious pates too highly to expose them to a brisk fire." Cowan, Aug. 12, 1864 to the *Napoleon Press,* reprinted in the *Toledo Commercial,* Sept. 5, 1864.

3. Two depleted Confederate corps under Gen. W.J. Hardee's overall command assaulted the entrenched 15th Corps between Jonesboro and the Flint River. The piecemeal attacks failed miserably, resulting in 2,200 Confederate casualties versus 154 in Logan's corps. Casteel, p. 502-503.

4. A married Bowling Green, Ohio, farmer, Corp. John M. Scott, Co. I, was shot through the head Sept. 5 while on picket duty near Lovejoy's Station. His brother-in-law, Pvt. John Hutchison of Co. I, was given Scott's effects — a hat, jacket, extra pair of cotton drawers and flannel shirt, rubber blanket, tobacco box and sewing case — which were "to be by him sent to [Scott's] wife." He later was buried in Marietta National Cemetery. J.M. Scott CSR, RG 94, NARA; *Ohio Roster,* vol. V, p. 801.

5. Using paper confiscated July 22 from a dead Confederate's knapsack, Pvt. Andrew Altman, Co. D, wrote from Atlanta in mid-September: "I just came in off of piquett guard this morning. The whole regt was out last night and it was a nice moon light night as i ever saw in my life. ... we have not got any tents yet nor do not expect any Soon but we have our rubber Blankets stretched up for shelter. It has not rained since we have been here at this place." Altman to his father, Sept. 16, 1864, CAC.

6. As Hood moved north, a Confederate division under Maj. Gen. Samuel G. French confronted Brig. Gen. John M. Corse's Federal garrison at the fortified railroad pass of Allatoona, Ga., 18 miles from Kennesaw Mountain. Corse, signaled by Sherman to hold fast and believing large reinforcements were on the way, spurned a surrender demand by French, after which the Confederates attacked. Each side sustained between 700-800 casualties before French withdrew. The battle inspired a popular evangelical hymn "Hold the Fort, For We Are Coming." Long, p. 579-580.

French's lengthy account of the battle of Allatoona can be found in *Two Wars: The Autobiography & Diary of Gen. Samuel G. French, CSA* (Huntington, W.Va.: Blue Acorn Press, 1999), p. 223-284.

7. Maj. Gen. George H. Thomas had been sent to Tennessee by Sherman in late September to gather and organize Federal forces against a Confederate invasion of the state. Sherman, *Memoirs*, p. 512.

12

'The liveliest lot of Yankees the world ever heard of'

Orders were now read to us from Gen. Sherman that the Fourteenth, Fifteenth, Seventeenth and Twentieth Corps had been organized into an army for a special purpose far away in Dixie.[1] We did not know where we were going, neither did we care. We only knew Billy Sherman was to lead us on some great adventure. The common soldier is not supposed to know anything but to march, camp, dig trenches and fight. But they were no ciphers. They had a pretty clear opinion of the purpose of any campaign, though, like our leaders, were often at sea as to the ultimate result.

Some said we were going to Mobile, while others said we were going to Richmond. But when we started on a southeasterly course we became satisfied that we were going to Savannah, or some point on the south Atlantic coast.

Early in the morning of Nov. 15 there was a commotion in the camps surrounding us. Campfires blazed high, fed with rubbish and such equipage as had been cast aside. In the direction of Atlanta the smoke and flames from mills, machine shops and such other buildings as Sherman thought best to have destroyed leaped to the skies and rolled away over the doomed city. The bugle soon sounded, telling us to fall in. Lt. Col. Welles mounted his horse "Polk" and shouted, "Attention – battalion; shoulder – arms; right face, forward – march!" and one of the most brilliant campaigns of modern times — the march to the sea — began.[2]

We were happy that morning. Mules brayed, drivers cracked their long whips, and we shouted with joy as we turned our backs upon the smoking ruins of Atlanta and marched away, accompanied by the invincible hardtack, a testament and a Southern paper announcing Sherman's retreat from Atlanta. A number of recruits who had recently joined us lugged enormous knapsacks. About the second or third day out a murmur began to be heard when, upon investigation, they started to cast first this and then that into the bushes along the wayside. This operation was repeated the next day and the next, and in time they found themselves in light marching order, equal to the old vets.

Different corps marched by parallel roads. Each regiment was provided with one ambulance and one wagon; and in the center of each brigade, to better guard against an attack from the enemy, came our provision and ammunition train. The army was ordered to forage liberally, and each day 30 men were detailed from each regiment. Property was ordered to be protected where the line of march was not molested by armed bands of the enemy, or by the inhabitants burning bridges, obstructing the roads or otherwise showing their hostility toward our troops.

The evening of the 15th we went into camp 16 miles from Atlanta. Early the next morning we were in motion, and that day marched 18 miles through wood and field. On the 17th we marched about 15 miles, passing through the town of McDonough. The following day we marched 18 miles. About the close of the day we passed through Jackson, the seat of Butts County, when a halt was ordered to let the columns close up. Soon after we moved on, and about midnight we crossed the Ocmulgee River and went into bivouac till morning.

Thus far everything had gone well. The people appeared to be thoroughly frightened at the sudden appearance of Sherman's conquering heroes in the heart of Georgia. Some had been taught to believe that a Yank was a counterpart of the devil, and had horns growing out of his head.

I pause to remark that my readers will say, "Oh, how absurd!" Yet my comrades will bear me out in saying that colored people have gathered around us with the query, "Is yo'uns real Yankees?" Upon our replying in the affirmative, they would further question us: "Whar's yo'uns horns? White folks tole us yo'uns Yanks had horns."

Many of the citizens fled from their homes upon our approach, while those who remained gazed in silent awe as the army went sweeping by. The Governor of Georgia, Jeff Davis, Beauregard and many other leaders of the so-called Confederacy pleaded with the people of the state to arise and hurl the Yankee invader back. But against such an army as Sherman held in hand they must have felt that what little resistance they could offer would have been in vain.

Nov. 19 we marched 16 miles, being in the advance of the entire Seventeenth Corps. About 4 o'clock in the afternoon we passed through Monticello, Jasper County, and went into camp.

The next day we marched in the rear of the whole corps, having in our charge a drove of beef-cattle. During the day a number of cattle mired down in a deep, boggy swamp by the roadside, when a detail was ordered out to shoot them.

We were on the road all night of the 20th and until midnight of the 21st, when, having caught up with the advance, a halt was ordered until morning, we having marched about 26 miles.

Nov. 22 we left camp at the usual hour, and after a rapid march of 12 miles reached Gordon, 16 miles south of Milledgeville, where we remained a short time listening to Gen. Kilpatrick's guns near Macon, Ga., 12 miles south.[3] In the evening we gave the railroad our attention, to notify Gen. Kilpatrick of our whereabouts, and then rolled up in our blankets to wait the dawn of another day.

On the 23d we marched eight miles along the Georgia Central Railroad, utterly wrecking it as we moved forward, and in the evening went into camp on a large plantation.

All along our line of march we found the colored people bubbling over with delight, each endeavoring to outdo the other in some crude expression of frantic joy as they first beheld Massa Linkum's boys.

Upon one occasion Capt. Mooney of Co. C addressed an old colored man, who from all appearances may have been a centenarian: "Well, Uncle Ned, what do you think of us Yankees?" With a loud guffaw and doff of his cap, Ned replied: "Fore de Lawd, Massa, I dun don't know what to think, sah. Neber did I see so many white folks. Dey jus' trable and trable down de road all day."

"How many Yankees were there?" asked one of my comrades. "Bress mah soul," said Ned, "I dun don't know, sah, fo' sure. I guess dars about a million." "Oh, you old fool," said another, "you old nigger, you dun don't know nuffin nohow. Dars more dan a million fo' sure, sah. Guess dars 'bout five hundred."

Nov. 24 we acted as guard for our supply train. We marched 12 miles and went into camp. After supper we were ordered out on the railroad, and for a time were engaged in tearing up the track.

The next day we marched to the Oconee River, 10 miles distant, where we met with a body of "Georgia Home Guards" who disputed the crossing. Our artillery treated the woods on the opposite side to a vigorous shelling, after which the representatives of the cradle and the grave retired from our front. The next morning we crossed the river on pontoons laid during the night, and then hurried away four miles when a halt was called to let the column close up.

Early on Sunday, Nov. 27, our bugle sounded the advance and we marched off in the direction of Millen, 55 miles east of us. A portion of the time our brigade marched along the line of the Georgia Central Railroad, leaving smoking ruins behind.

Nov. 30, just as the shades of night began to wrap their mantle about us, we crossed to the east side of the Ogeechee River, and on the afternoon of Friday, Dec. 2, went into camp on Buck's [Buckhead] Creek, one mile from Millen.[4]

The month of December found Sherman and his soldiers in the best of spirits. Not so with Jeff Davis, Hardee, Beauregard and the rebel authorities of Georgia, who were almost frantic in their earnest appeals for help, couched in the following language: "Georgians, be firm. Let every man fly to arms. Remove all horses, cattle and provisions from Sherman's army, and burn what you cannot carry away. Burn all bridges and block the roads in his front. Assail the enemy in front, flank and rear by day and by night. You can destroy the invader by retarding his march. Act promptly and fear not."

The people failed to respond, which fact convinced us that the resources of the Confederacy were well nigh exhausted.

The days were warm and pleasant, and new scenes were continually opening up before us, which made our march through Georgia one grand excursion. With the exception of the engagement with the Georgia militia at the Oconee River crossing, we experienced no variation from the easy marches and pleasant bivouacs, interspersed with chickens and turkeys that our Commissary found, and the noted sweet potatoes that started from the ground. Our daily bill of fare consisted of fresh pork and chicken, cornpone and chicken, sweet potatoes and chicken, and for a change we always ate a little more chicken.

When our daring move first began, rebels North and South, and the traitorous press everywhere, declared that Sherman's army had gone into the jaws of death; that the citizens would destroy all manner of subsistence in our front, and that we would die of starvation in the swamps of Georgia. After long days and weeks of weary watching and waiting, the joyful news was flashed through to our Northern homes that Sherman's boys were on the

Atlantic coast, 300 miles from Atlanta, and so far from being dead, were the liveliest lot of Yankees the world ever heard of.

But I have left our regiment at Millen, where on the morning of Dec. 3 we were engaged in reducing to ashes the rebel stockade and prison where several thousand boys in blue had been confined, but who had been removed by the rebel authorities a few days before our arrival. From Millen we marched east 10 miles, and in the evening went into camp on a large plantation where, finding molasses in untold measure and kettles in abundance, we invited ourselves to an old-fashioned taffy-pulling party.

Dec. 4 we marched 12 miles, and toward the close of day were ordered out of line to go on guard at a large mill, where a detail was engaged in grinding corn for army use. We remained on guard until the next morning, when, after assisting to load the wagons with corn and meal, we formed in line and hastily moved forward.

Toward the middle of the afternoon we caught up with our advance columns, which were brought to a temporary halt along the bank of the Little Ogeechee by a body of the enemy on the opposite side. The enemy seemed to think there was but one place to cross the river, and that in their front; but a portion of our corps made a crossing two miles below, which caused the enemy to evacuate their works and seek safety in flight. Meanwhile, one of our batteries was engaged in feeling for the enemy, but eliciting no response, an advance was ordered, and about dark we crossed the river and went into camp in the evacuated works of the enemy.

Dec. 6 we remained quietly in camp resting ourselves and preparing for the last chapter of our march to the sea. The four corps were close together and thousands of campfires were in sight around us. The scene was a merry one, as we told stories and sang songs till the country fairly rang with the echo. Now and then some of the lovers of the dance would clear off a place, or lay down a floor from lumber found near by, and then get the colored boys who had joined us to entertain us with the plantation song and dance. The colored boy that could not dance was looked upon by his fellows as a "no 'count nigger, no how." The joy of the colored boys knew no bounds when permitted to dance before an admiring audience of "Massa Linkum's sogers," each trying to outdo the other in some artistic cut of the plantation pigeon-wing.

In the meantime the evening passed rapidly, our campfires burned low, and at last the great army lay in as sweet sleep as ever men enjoyed. But in the sweetest of our dreams the clear notes of a bugle would ring out. One could not help hearing it, in spite of his desire to do otherwise, and soon the camp was in motion. Then came the odor of boiling coffee, frying chickens, roasting sweet potatoes and whatever else our foragers might have brought in the previous evening.

Dec. 7 we moved at an early hour, marched 12 miles through swampy country, and about 9 o'clock at night went into camp. The roads were in a detestable condition, and the fences along our route were used to keep our wagons and artillery from miring down.

The following day we marched 10 miles, passing through Marlow. Trees had been felled in the road and our march otherwise obstructed. We, however, moved forward, turning aside now and then to escape being murdered by the vandals who had buried torpedoes in the road over which we were marching. Gen. Sherman ordered a body of prisoners, recently captured, to be brought forward, and compelled them to march in close column along the highway, so as to explode their own torpedoes, or to find and dig them up. It was amusing to note how gingerly they walked, but none were found other than six dug up by our men.

Meanwhile, our advance columns were busily engaged in skirmishing with the enemy, which, with slight intermissions, continued throughout the long day.

Thus far our approach to Savannah had not been stubbornly opposed. But it became more and more apparent as we moved along that the enemy intended to call us to a halt in the near future, and to do his best to prevent us from reaching Savannah, or even getting a foothold anywhere on the coast.

The morning of Dec. 10 we started out as usual for an all-day march, which would have taken us down to the sea; but after going five miles we were brought to a sudden halt and formed our first line of battle five miles from the city. In our front was a large rice field partly covered with water, on the opposite of which was a slight elevation, on which the enemy was intrenched.

No sooner had we formed our line, with the right of our regiment resting on the road over which we had marched from Millen, than we were awakened by a sullen roar followed by the familiar screech of a 24-pounder. The shot struck the ground near the right of our regiment, and, bounding, hit a colored boy who had joined us some days before. A number of colored boys standing near by observed the incident, and they, being superstitious, a general stampede was the result.[5]

Our artillery immediately responded to the enemy's guns, and for a time we were treated to a repetition of the scenes around Atlanta. During the day we were kept busy moving from place to place, the object being to learn the strength of the enemy confronting us. Late in the day we moved to the south side of the Georgia Central Railroad and went into bivouac for the night.

The country for some miles inland from Savannah was low and swampy, and because of this the advantages for supplying our wants through our foraging details were very limited. However, rice was found in abundance, some of which already was hulled and cleaned ready for use; but the most was still in the straw and stored away in buildings or stacked in the fields.

The stock of hulled and cleaned rice soon gave out, when we were compelled to hull and clean what was needed for use. Not being familiar with the rude devices used by the colored people in hulling rice, we made slow progress; in fact, it kept us pretty busy just to get enough hulled and cleaned to satisfy the pangs of hunger. After we had enough rice for a mess we would stop to rest, cook and eat it, and then go to work again to prepare enough for the next meal.

Those who never engaged in this work can form no idea how closely the hulls stuck to the kernels, or how much pounding it required to separate the two. Then the grain had to be separated from the chaff. After cleaning the rice we would put it into a camp-kettle together with a good-sized chunk of Georgia beef and make a rice soup. Thus for some days our bill of fare was the same.

A few miles to the south of us flowed the Ogeechee River, and at its mouth was the rebel Fort McAllister. Gen. Sherman began planning to capture this fort, which would enable our vessels at anchor off the mouth of the Ogeechee, laden with provisions for the army, to approach and land their stores.

Sunday, Dec. 11, heavy firing commenced early in the morning and continued throughout the day, but no general engagement was brought on. About the close of day we were ordered to move to the right flank. We quietly moved off under cover of the night, and after a zig-zag march of about four miles came up in the rear of the Fifteenth Corps, which was feeling the enemy's lines and cautiously forcing its way across canals and flooded rice fields in the direction of King's Bridge on the Ogeechee River. Heavy cannonading continued at intervals all night, many of the shells from the enemy's guns striking in our vicinity and doing us more or less injury. One large shell exploded near the 12th Wis. Battery, killing three of the battery boys and wounding others.[6]

The following morning, after enjoying a breakfast of Georgia beef, we marched to the right, as a command of the Fourteenth Corps came up during the night and occupied our position. We moved to the right about five miles and took up a new position on the right of the road leading from King's Bridge to the city of Savannah. Here we were engaged for a time in throwing up a line of earthworks along the edge of a flooded rice field about half a mile wide. On the opposite side of the field, on an elevation, was the enemy. The Fifteenth Corps, meanwhile, was working its way to the right, and on the evening of Dec. 13 captured Fort McAllister, and Savannah lay at our feet.[7]

Gen. Sherman was never so happy as when he observed from the roof of Cheeves' rice mill the parapets of the fort covered with his noble boys, as it gave him assurance of the success of his great march, so important in crushing the gigantic rebellion. Of this notable event our chieftain speaks as follows:

"At 2 o'clock in the afternoon we observed signs of a great commotion in the fort, which told us of the approach of Hazen's assaulting columns. The sun was sinking, and I was getting impatient. Another signal came from Hazen, and I replied, 'Go ahead,' as a friendly steamer was approaching from below. The officers on the steamers had seen us and signaled, 'Who are you?' The reply was signaled back, 'Gen. Sherman.' Again the signal came, 'Is Fort McAllister taken?' The reply was, 'No, not yet, but will be in a minute.' Just at that moment the boys in blue came out of the wood that enveloped the fort with colors flying and steady pace. The fort belched forth with heavy guns, and for a moment Hazen's assaulting columns were hid from view in the sulphurous smoke of battle. As the smoke lifted the parapets of the fort could be seen lined with the blue. We signaled the glad event to our friends on the gunboat, whose view of the fort was obstructed by a point of timber, 'Fort McAllister is taken! Hurrah!' "[8]

Gen. Sherman now made a demand for Savannah's surrender, but Hardee, who commanded there, stubbornly refused to comply. We therefore began to thoroughly intrench ourselves before the Monument City of the South, and engaged in the usual trying duties of a besieging army. Heavy siege guns were brought up from the Ogeechee River and placed in position, and everything was made ready to open fire upon the enemy.

On Dec. 15 a brisk cannonading took place between the opposing lines. In the meantime a large detail from our regiment was assisting to build a line of earthworks when the saucy enemy threw a number of shells among the working parties. But the boys hugged the ground and escaped injury.

Thus day followed day, and between a limited supply of rice and beef and a liberal sprinkling of rebel shot and shell, we managed to live till Dec. 18, when there came a glorious change. Coffee and hardtack, bacon and beans, took the place of rice and beef, and letters, big and sweet, fresh from our Northern homes, made the thought of rebel shot and shell a secondary one. For six long weeks we had been completely isolated from the outside world. What shouts of joy and thanksgiving rang throughout the North when it was learned that Sherman's army was in camp near Savannah, while our enemies cursed and wished the bottomless pit had swallowed us up.

Dec. 20 our field artillery kept up an incessant bellowing, accompanied by the thundering of heavy siege guns, carrying projectiles to all parts of the enemy's line, bursting with terrific violence and striking dismay into every heart. We remained in great expectation, watching the enemy's works and the dirt fly in the air as the heavy shells landed, wondering how long flesh and blood could endure such a rain of death and destruction.

This one-day reign of terror convinced Hardee, commanding the Confederate forces, that to attempt to hold the city any longer would only subject it to certain destruction and inflict untold misery and distress upon its inhabitants. Early the next morning our pickets noticed an unusual quiet all along the enemy's works. Not a human being was visible where for some days previous an active army had been intrenched. Only here and there stood a heavy piece of ordnance like a lone sentinel watching our every move.

It required but a moment to fathom the meaning of the deathlike silence, and then our skirmishers moved forward. With a loud shout they were soon over the silent works of the enemy. Bugles rang out in the early-morning air. Orderlies rode here and there, and soon a long line of men with glistening muskets was moving forward with quick and steady tread. The enemy had disappeared from our front, and Sherman's boys were after them. We crossed the low, swampy ground in our front, and passed through the enemy's works. Dashing on, we learned that under cover of night Hardee had moved his army across the Savannah River and marched off in the direction of Charleston, S.C., leaving every evidence of a hasty and timely evacuation behind him.

We moved on straight to the city, the termination of our march to the sea. Here and there as we moved forward inhabitants hastened around a friendly corner. The windows were curtained, but many careworn faces could be seen watching us through partly-closed doors. The people of Savannah had never seen an army of Northern soldiers, so they thought best to study us awhile before venturing out among us.

Immediately following the enemy's evacuation our regiment was detailed to duty in Savannah as provost-guards. We were assigned quarters in Warren and Oglethorpe Parks, where we remained for some days, holding the post of honor in the city. Gen. Sherman soon formulated a plan of government, when matters began to settle down to a new order of things, and peace and quiet reigned everywhere.[9]

Savannah is an old city, and the most beautiful place it had been our fortune to visit during our entire service. The city in its best days had a population of about 20,000. Its buildings were of brick and wood; its streets regular, crossing each other at right angles, and at many crossings were located small public parks, of which there were 24. Many of these parks were lined with beautiful trees, while others contained large marble shafts erected to the memory of noted men in American history — Warren, Oglethorpe, Pulaski and others.[10] But the most interesting place to me was a quiet cemetery called "Bonaventura," where quaint marble slabs overgrown with moss stood like sentinels over the tombs of men of former times. The gray moss hanging ghostlike from the highest trees to the ground gave the place a truly weird appearance.

On Dec. 24 we heard of the battle between Gens. Thomas and Hood at Nashville, Tenn., and that Hood had been whipped and his broken columns driven in confusion across the Tennessee River.[11] That same day some of the boys made an effort to find something in the city for breakfast on Christmas morning. But becoming disgusted at the high prices, they returned to camp and contented themselves with hardtack, coffee and bacon.

On turning to my diary I find the following prices in Confederate money. (The Confederate dollar was then worth just 4 cents in gold): One apple, 50 cents; one loaf of bread, $1.40; a dozen eggs, $5; ham, per pound, $8; sugar, per pound, $25; butter, per pound,

$30; Chickens, $50; flour, $400 a barrel.

Early the morning of Dec. 27 we received orders to rejoin our brigade, one mile outside of the city, where we made our camp, there to remain until Jan. 4, 1865.

While at Savannah our regiment lost some of its valuable officers by reason of expiration of term of service.[12] In the meantime a large number of commissions was received, and the 68th was supplied with a fine corps of young and enthusiastic officers — men who had seen service in the ranks — to take the place of those whose terms had expired.

Dec. 28 the Seventeenth Corps was ordered out on grand review, but a storm coming up, the order was countermanded and we returned to our camp. The next day we marched in review through the city. The Fourteenth, Fifteenth and Twentieth Corps had previously marched in review, and the grand display by Sherman's legions must have deeply impressed the citizens of Savannah of the utter hopelessness of the Southern cause. They could not understand how it was that Sherman's army had retreated from Atlanta, his broken columns rapidly falling back across the Tennessee River, and then that same army thundering at the doors of Savannah, while Gen. Hardee hurried off into South Carolina to get out of its way. "Why, torment their lying hides!" said one old Union man of Georgia. "They tell us Sherman's army is falling back; at the same time the durned fool rebels are retreating so fast that you could play checkers on their coat-tails."

Early one morning the men in camp around Savannah began firing their muskets, and for a time it appeared as though a warm engagement with an enemy was taking place. The noise and confusion extended to all the camps around the city, from which the crack of small arms was heard ushering in the year 1865.

Notes to Chapter 12

1. For the Savannah Campaign, Sherman organized his troops into two wings — the left (14th and 20th corps) commanded by Maj. Gen. Henry W. Slocum, and the right (15th and 17th corps) commanded by Maj. Gen. O.O. Howard. The 17th Corps was led by F.P. Blair Jr., whose three divisions were commanded by Maj. Gen. Joseph A. Mower and Brig. Gens. M.D. Leggett and Giles A. Smith. A cavalry division, reporting directly to Sherman, was commanded by Brig. Gen. Judson Kilpatrick. Sherman, *Memoirs,* p. 536.

2. Col. R.K. Scott had resumed command of the 2nd Brigade, 3rd Division, 17th Corps, which now was composed of the 20th, 68th and 78th Ohio, and 17th Wisconsin. *OR,* vol. XLIV, p. 21.

3. Kilpatrick's cavalry division consisted of two brigades and an artillery battery. *OR,* vol. XLIV, p. 25.

4. On Dec. 2, while helping to tear up tracks of the Augusta & Savannah Railroad just north of Millen, Loop injured two fingers of his right hand. "It was splintered up and he carried it in a sling for a long time," recalled Corp. Daniel W. Jones, Co. E. M.B. Loop pension records, RG 94, NARA.

5. This incident occurred along the Georgia Central Railroad near Pooler's Station. Gen. Sherman himself was an eyewitness, as he later wrote: "I ... walked down to the railroad-track, at a place where there was a side-track, and a cut about four feet deep. From that point the railroad was straight, leading into Savannah, and about eight hundred yards off were a rebel parapet and battery. I could see the cannoneers preparing to fire, and cautioned the officers near me to scatter, as we would likely attract a shot. Very soon I saw the white puff of smoke, and, watching close, caught sight of the ball as it rose in its flight, and, finding it coming pretty straight, I stepped a short distance to one side, but noticed a negro very near me in the act of crossing the track at right angles. Some one called to him to look out; but, before the poor fellow understood his danger, the ball (a thirty-two-pound round shot) struck the ground, and rose in its first ricochet, caught the negro under the right jaw, and literally carried away his head, scattering blood and brains about. A soldier close by spread an overcoat over the body, and we all concluded to get out of that railroad-cut." Sherman, *Memoirs,* p. 557.

6. Loop evidently was mistaken. The 12th Wisconsin Battery roster shows no one killed Dec. 11, 1864. *Roster of Wisconsin Volunteers, War of the Rebellion, 1861-1865,* vol. I (Madison, 1886), p. 246-250.

7. Troops of Brig. Gen. William B. Hazen's 2nd Division, 15th Corps, successfully assaulted Fort McAllister at a cost of 134 casualties. The fort's capture opened river communication with the Union fleet just off the coast. Long, p. 609.

8. The Sherman quotation is a condensed paraphrasing from his *Memoirs,* p. 559-560.

9. Brig. Gen. John W. Geary, a 20th Corps division commander, was appointed military governor of Savannah during the city's Federal occupation. He was a former territorial governor in Kansas, and after the war served two terms as Pennsylvania's governor. Warner, *Generals in Blue,* p. 169-170.

10. Joseph Warren, Revolutionary War general killed in the 1775 battle of Bunker Hill, Mass.; James Edward Oglethorpe, British philanthropist, colonist and founder of Savannah in 1733; Casimir Pulaski, Polish army officer and Continental Army general mortally wounded in the 1779 siege of Savannah.

11. The battle of Nashville was fought Dec. 15-16, 1864, resulting in the decisive, crippling defeat of Hood's Army of Tennessee.

12. Officers leaving the 68th Ohio included Capts. Patrick Mooney, Co. C, and Wesley Bowen, Co. F. Col. Scott also departed, being ordered Dec. 26 "to attend to Rosters of Ohio Regts in 3 div. 17th A.C. at Columbus, Ohio." He was replaced Dec. 27 as 2nd Brigade commander by Col. Greenberry F. Wiles, 78th Ohio. R.K. Scott CSR, RG 94, NARA; *OR,* vol. XLIV, p. 823.

13

'A seven weeks' tramp through swamps and tar camps'

Soon after reaching Savannah Gen. Sherman began to map out a plan to join Gen. Grant in Virginia, and assist him in the battles against Lee at Richmond. Gen. Grant thought it best to have Sherman's army transported to the James River by water, but Sherman preferred to march. So, on Jan. 3, we received orders to be ready to move on the following day, destination Beaufort, S.C. We left Savannah the next morning and marched to Thunderbolt Bluff, five miles below the city, where we camped for the night.

Early on the 5th we embarked on an ocean steamer, the whistle blew, the great wheels began to revolve, and we started on our voyage. We moved out on the smooth waters of the bay, and in due time reached a point where we noticed a radical change in the color of the water from a dirty yellow to that of the deep green of the broad Atlantic.

We continued on our course all day and night, and as morning dawned we saw nothing but water, water. Few of my comrades felt like calling for rations. A favored few of the boys engaged in singing "A life on an ocean wave," while others, between a spasmodic effort and a groan, declared they were going to die right there. A thick fog hung over the water until about noon, when it lifted, and soon after we landed at Beaufort.

We remained at Beaufort two days, and when not otherwise engaged we occupied our time in raiding along the sea shore, searching for the festive oyster, in which we found more enjoyment than chasing after rebels. It required a good bit of skill to scoop Mr. Oyster out of his house and home and take him prisoner, but after a little practice we did very well in our new vocation of capturing natives of South Carolina.

Jan. 8 we left our camp in the suburbs of Beaufort and marched four miles into the country, where we remained until Friday, Jan. 13.

Jan. 13 we marched in the direction of Pocotaligo, 24 miles from Beaufort. After six miles we reached the channel dividing Beaufort Island from the mainland, where a halt was ordered to wait for our pontoons. Soon after dark the pontoons came up and were laid to bridge the channel. Meanwhile, our regiment and the 78th Ohio were taken across the channel in skiffs. After crossing we marched two miles into the country and went into bivouac.

Early the following morning we moved cautiously forward, and about noon found the enemy intrenched behind a strong line of earthworks, but after two hours' maneuvering the rebels left on the double-quick, with our boys in hot pursuit. Just as the shades of night began to deepen we again came up with them, intrenched behind another line of works.

A halt was ordered to wait for the dawn of another day, while our boys constructed a line of earthworks confronting the enemy. But when Sunday, the 15th, dawned upon us, we found the enemy gone. We were immediately ordered forward, and about noon reached Pocotaligo, a little village on the railroad running from Savannah to Charleston, where we remained, with the exception of an occasional scout, until Monday, Jan. 30.

Near our camp was an old saw mill, and some of the boys who claimed to know all about engines built a fire in the furnace. The fire grew hotter and hotter; the steam moaned and sputtered, but the wheels refused to move. At last, one of the boys gave the fly-wheel a lift and the fun began. The engine threatened to run itself to kingdom come, and there was no one there who knew how to stop it. We began to think that it was getting ready to run out of the building and chase us out of South Carolina. But just before it started, one of the boys ventured near enough to touch a lever, after which all was still. The boys now gathered around the engine and discussed its running qualities, but no one said "go!" to the old thing again.

Jan. 17 our brigade was ordered out for the purpose of reconnoitering the adjacent country, to learn of the movements of any armed bodies of the enemy operating around us. After a march of five miles we encountered a force of the enemy near the Salkehatchie Swamp, where we remained overnight. They opened fire upon us and continued to throw shells at intervals throughout the night, but doing our regiment no injury. The next morning we returned to our camp near Pocotaligo, where we turned our attention to constructing a line of earthworks.

Jan. 20 we were sent out on another reconnaisance to feel for the enemy. It was said the rebels were approaching from Charleston 30,000 strong to whip Sherman's army in detail. But the whipping failed to come off, so we returned to our camp, remaining there for some days in idleness. These were cold and stormy, with not one single ray of sunshine to gladden our hearts, which made us almost feel that the Supreme Ruler had forbade the sun to shine upon South Carolina because of its treason.

Jan. 25 we were ordered to turn over our tents and surplus baggage, the same to be sent to Beaufort and again join us at some place further north.

The next day our brigade was ordered out with the pontoon train to bridge a stream in our front. The bottoms being overflowed for a mile on each side, we returned, reaching our camp about midnight. A bitter north wind accompanied by heavy rain beat upon us the whole night, and having no tents we suffered from the cold, there being no fuel to build a fire and the mercury below freezing.

Monday, Jan. 30, we marched five miles in the direction of River's Bridge on the Salkehatchie.

Feb. 1 the great march through the Carolinas began. We moved out of camp in a cold rain and marched 17 miles, going into camp about 10 o'clock at night. The country was one vast sheet of water. But in spite of wind and water we were feeling gay and happy, as we started out on a seven weeks' tramp through the swamps, cities and tar camps of the Carolina states.

When this march began our enemies were in the utmost confusion. They had been defeated everywhere — in the Atlanta campaign and on the march to the sea. Wade Hampton was now dispatched from the Army of Northern Virginia with a great flourish of trumpets, to raise men and horses with which to stay the progress of the invaders.[1]

Early Feb. 2 our brigade took the advance and marched miles through a beautiful country. Just before night we encountered a force of the enemy posted behind a swamp. A strong skirmish line was ordered forward, and with the assistance of a battery we soon cleared our front, after which we went into bivouac.

The next day we marched five miles, being in the rear of the entire column. About 3 o'clock in the afternoon we came up with our advance, whose skirmishers were having a warm tussle with the enemy, and went into camp under orders to be prepared to move at any moment. We, however, remained quiet until after dark, ate our supper and were preparing for a night's rest when Lt. Col. Welles shouted, "Fall in, men! Fall in!" The mutterings told how little we enjoyed it, but once in line an advance was ordered, and, wrapped in darkness, we moved rapidly toward the front. We marched two miles and formed in line of battle fronting River's Bridge, where we lay on our guns until morning.

This move was a mystery to us. But as morning dawned all was made plain, as over on the north side of the Salkehatchie was the enemy intrenched behind a line of works, ready to dispute the crossing. A lively exchange of compliments between the opposing artillery now took place. Meanwhile, one division of our corps moved down the river, and under cover of timber crossed on pontoons, then turned on the enemy's flank and sent it reeling backward, broken and bleeding.[2] The enemy at once abandoned the works along the Salkehatchie, and retired to the defense of the South Carolina Railroad, a line of great importance [running between Charleston and Augusta, Ga.].

In this action our regiment was very fortunate, suffering no loss; but some of our companion regiments did not fare so well.

Feb. 5 and 6 found us on the road moving forward, but we made slow progress, owing to a number of bridges — spanning streams from four to ten feet deep — which the enemy had destroyed, and which required our attention so as to enable our artillery and trains to follow us. We made a short halt on the night of the 5th, then moved on, now repairing a bridge that had been wrecked, and now building a causeway across some swamp, until night again spread its mantle over us, when we would go into camp.

Feb. 7 we were ordered to march at 7 o'clock in the morning, but were not in motion till 4 o'clock in the afternoon, when we moved forward four miles and camped near the [South Carolina Railroad].

An incident in connection with the capture of the railroad is well worth relating. Gen. Howard, in command of the Army of the Tennessee, felt confident that the enemy would make a bold stand in defense of the railroad. Upon our approach the General ordered the columns to deploy so as to be ready for battle. Sitting on his horse near the head of the column, expecting at any moment to hear a loud crash of musketry, his quick eye caught sight of one of our foragers mounted on a mule and riding at breakneck speed down the road from the front. The forager rode up to the General and at the top of his voice delivered his message, as follows: "Hurry up, General! Hurry up! We have got the railroad and can hold it, if you hurry up."

Sure enough, a number of foragers looking for supplies had advanced to the railroad, routed a body of the enemy found there, took possession and held it until the advance came up. While our foragers were engaged in providing food and forage for the army, they did not lose sight of the fact that they were Union soldiers battling for their country, and often the information furnished to our Generals by them proved of great importance.

Early the following morning we moved along the railroad, thoroughly destroying it as we went forward, and at night camped near the little village of Midway.

The work of destruction having been completed, the next morning we were ordered to the front. We left Branchville a few miles to our right and marched in the direction of Orangeburg. Early in the day the Third Division passed the Fourth Division, which for two days had been in advance making it interesting for those who dared to obstruct their progress.

A march of eight miles brought us to the South Edisto River, where a rattling fire of musketry told us the enemy was disputing the crossing. One of our batteries delivered a number of well-directed shots into the enemy's ranks, which caused a general stampede. Soon after dark our pontoon train came up from the rear and bridged the river. Our brigade was ordered to its support, where we remained during the night.

About noon the next day we crossed the river and marched four miles, when a halt was ordered until the next morning. In order to be prepared should the enemy make a night attack, we constructed a line of works all along our front. But everything remained quiet through the night, save the steady tramp and whispered commands to troops coming up from the rear.

Feb. 11 our brigade moved out of camp at 6 o'clock in advance of the entire Seventeenth Corps. We marched about 12 miles with skirmishers well thrown out, and late in the afternoon discovered the main body of the enemy intrenched on the north bank of the North Edisto River near Orangeburg.

Early the following morning our division was ordered down the river four miles, where we crossed the main channel on pontoons moored to the trees, then stepped off into the waters of a February river and waded across the bottoms waist deep to the high grounds on the north side.

While our advance columns were making this crossing, Gen. Sherman rode up and dismounted near our regiment. The General walked back and forth along the river bank, apparently oblivious to his surroundings, when a crash of musketry reached his ears. With flashing eyes he asked, "In what direction is that firing?" "Directly in front, General," was the response. Sherman resumed his beat. Then another report of musketry assailed his ears. "In what direction is that firing?" he asked again. "Further in front and to the left," was the reply. "Amen," remarked Sherman, and hastily crossing the pontoon bridge he was soon falling over submerged cypress trees equal to any Corporal. However, he returned to the south side and mounting his horse, rode rapidly away to the left.

After emerging from the overflowed river bottoms we moved forward to the support of our advance columns, which were anticipating a vigorous opposition, as it was reported that the enemy was in considerable force all along our front. But only feeble resistance was met, and that evening we went into camp in the suburbs of Orangeburg.

During the morning of Feb. 13 we visited the large Orangeburg Asylum housing about 300 orphan children. It seemed that the governor of the home had informed the children upon our approach that we were Northern soldiers, which greatly excited their curiosity. They gathered around us and in childish simplicity asked all manner of questions, such as, "Is it true; are you people real Yankees?"

From Orangeburg we marched 15 miles along the railroad in the direction of Columbia, making an occasional halt long enough to destroy any Confederate stores or manufactories that lay in our path. We found the roads in good condition.

Feb. 14 we marched 18 miles. A portion of the way our line of march was along a railroad, and about dark, just as a cold rain began to fall, we camped in a dense pine forest. Strange as it may appear, with wood in abundance all around us, not a stick or a rail could be found with which to build a campfire.

Seven o'clock the next morning found us moving on. We marched 10 miles around to the left of the Seventeenth Corps, and toward night camped near Congaree Creek, five miles from Columbia. Before we had time to make coffee we were ordered forward to support our cavalry, who were having a warm time with the enemy at the crossing. A bridge having been partly destroyed by the enemy, our cavalry forded the creek at the same time we crossed over on the partly wrecked bridge.

After crossing we proceeded to establish ourselves behind a quickly constructed line of works, where we remained until morning. Great importance was attached to this move to get possession of the west bank of Congaree Creek — a branch of the Congaree River — as thereby a shorter road could be opened to Columbia. It was thought that the enemy would make a desperate stand in defense of Columbia, but the next morning they were gone. The bridge being repaired, we were ordered forward, and after a march of five miles went into camp on the bank of the Congaree River opposite Columbia.

While resting on the banks of the Congaree, with the once-proud city of Columbia at our feet, a company of officers, including our gallant "Tecumseh," was standing hard by observing the bustle and excitement in the city, when one of the officers remarked: "If those fellows should throw a few shells this way wouldn't there be a scattering among us?" To which remark one of our officers was said to have responded: "I wish they would. I should like to have an excuse for destroying that city. Yonder is where treason to our country had its birth, that has cost our nation thousands upon thousands of lives, and billions of treasure."

During our short stay along the Congaree a number of the boys visited Camp Sorghum, a rebel prison pen where Union prisoners had been quartered. We observed the surroundings, which impressed upon us the inhuman treatment to which our men had been subjected by the rebel authorities. With pleasant, shady groves upon two sides, yet the camp was situated on a barren hillside, and protection from the sun and rain could be secured only by burrowing in the ground.

The afternoon of Feb. 17 we moved three miles to the left, where we crossed the Saluda and Broad rivers which form the Congaree at Columbia, then turned to the right, and about 10 o'clock at night went into camp in the city. Before we reached our camp site there was a mighty fire raging in the city. How the fire started is well known. Wade Hampton wantonly ordered the torch applied to cotton stored there, and instead of defending the city he made a great bonfire for our entertainment. It was said that Sherman burned Columbia. The statement, however, was characteristic of rebels who were in the last ditch, who made their boast that

L. M. Strayer Collection

Following duty with the 15th U.S. Infantry, John G. Bigham was appointed surgeon of the 68th Ohio in December 1864 and served with the regiment through the Carolinas.

they would burn their bridges and cities before the Yankee invaders.[3]

Shortly after going into camp a number of my comrades visited the burning city. It would take pages to describe the helpless misery which the inhabitants of Columbia endured on that fateful night as block after block was consumed by the flames. Long, livid tongues of fire reached out everywhere and desolation followed to mark its path. The falling of brick and stone walls; the screaming of old and young as they saw their houses swept away, made an awful picture — the result of treason, indelibly stamped upon each and every heart.

Some writers have said that the Seventeenth Corps did not enter the city at all. Our division of the Seventeenth Corps, however, went into camp near Columbia, and the next morning marched through the desolated streets, down beyond the smoking ruins and tottering walls to the northern part of the city, where a halt was ordered to complete the destruction of foundries, machine shops and other Confederate property that had escaped Hampton's torch. After finishing the work assigned to us, we took up our line of march along the railroad in the direction of Winnsborough, and toward night went into camp five miles from Columbia.

Sunday, Feb. 19, we remained in camp, enjoying a rest. During the day our foragers were driven in by the enemy's cavalry, who in turn ran up against our pickets, when a warm engagement ensued. Just at the close of day our brigade was ordered forward two miles, the object being to cover our front and look after any rebel force operating in our vicinity.

Early the following morning we were ready and eager to move on. Our line of march lay along a line of railroad, the destruction of which had long since become a skilled vocation.[4] The problem of converting a railroad into a wreck was an easy one, and required no special talent. Late in the day, after a march of 12 miles, we went into camp.

Feb. 21 we left the railroad at Winnsborough and marched 16 miles in a northeast direction, facing all day long a deluge of rain, which continued through the night. The next day our division was assigned to the rear of the Seventeenth Corps. After marching a short distance we came up in the rear of the Fifteenth Corps, when a halt was ordered for the day.

From Atlanta Sherman's army marched on parallel roads, the Fifteenth and Seventeenth corps on the right, and the Fourteenth and Twentieth corps on the left of one common center. Upon approaching a river — one that required the pontoons of two corps to make a crossing — the head of column would diverge to the right or left, and if upon reaching a road leading to the river it was found to be clear of troops, they were entitled to the right of way.

Feb. 23, after a march of three miles, we reached the Wateree River where we found the Fifteenth Corps engaged in crossing. Late in the day we were informed that Charleston, S.C. had been evacuated by the enemy, and that our troops were in possession.[5]

About 10 o'clock in the evening we were ordered forward, crossed the river, and after a march of one mile went into camp. The following day we marched 12 miles and made our camp near the village of Liberty Hill. Early in the morning a cold rain commenced to fall, which continued throughout the day, thoroughly soaking us, and in that condition we remained through a long, cheerless night.

Feb. 25 our division marched in the rear of the corps. We left camp at an early hour and marched 12 miles over execrable roads, reaching camp just at dark. Rain was still falling, and we were compelled to weather through another stormy night.

Sunday the 26th the sun came out beautiful and warm. We moved out of camp at 8 o'clock and after a march of 10 miles reached Brush Creek, where we remained over night. At daylight the following morning we were in motion, our division still in the rear. But after a march of 10 miles we came up with the advance column, in camp on Lynch Creek.

Feb. 28 we left our camp early, our division leading; marched 17 miles and about 4 o'clock in the afternoon went into camp. Here we remained the two succeeding days waiting for Sherman's left to move forward.

About this time a number of men, who had been captured by the enemy, were found brutally murdered along our line of march. This fact so enraged Sherman that he notified Hampton that his only alternative was to retaliate man for man. Hampton replied that he would put to death two prisoners held in his hands for every one Sherman should shoot in retaliation. As to the execution of Sherman's order, I am not prepared to say. Hampton relented, and no more of Sherman's men were found murdered by the roadside. But at one place four men were found hanging to the trees, and at another place several cavalrymen were found with throats cut from ear to ear.[6]

March 3 we marched 15 miles to Cheraw on the Big Pee Dee River, where we were engaged until evening of the next day destroying all Confederate stores and munitions found there.

On March 5, after a march of four miles, we were halted and ordered to construct a line of works as the enemy, 20,000 strong, was reported on our front. The following morning we turned to the right and marched 10 miles to Bennettsville, where was found buried a large quantity of cornmeal and bacon, which we appropriated, as for days the question of rations had been an important one.

March 7 our division, still in the advance with little opposition, marched 10 miles, and about four o'clock in the afternoon went into camp. The next day we marched 14 miles, and just at dark crossed the Little Pee Dee River and camped on the soil of North Carolina.

The next morning we marched in the direction of Fayetteville, on Cape Fear River, reaching that place the afternoon of March 11.

Sunday we remained in camp enjoying a rest. But about noon we were startled by the shrill whistle of a steamboat. In a moment we were all attention, prepared to skedaddle from a rebel monster coming up the river to annihilate us. We watched the course of the river, and at last blue smoke began to curl above the tops of the trees lining the shore, and a moment later the steamer came into full view; but instead of a rebel gunboat there floated at her mast our grand old flag. The steam-tug *Davidson* had come up from Wilmington, N.C. to bring us news from the outside world.

It was a great mystery to us how our Government, isolated as we were, had been informed of our whereabouts so as to be able to communicate with us.[7]

March 13 we marched down the river three miles, when a halt was ordered. At first dawn we crossed the river, and after a rapid march of about five miles went into camp.

March 15 our brigade was assigned to duty as train guard in the rear of the entire corps. A heavy rain fell at intervals throughout the day, but being accustomed to such conditions we moved on, covering 14 miles that day.

Sherman knew that Johnston was rapidly concentrating his army, and that we would probably meet him somewhere before we reached Goldsboro. Sherman hoped to be able to reach Goldsboro and unite his forces with those of Gen. Schofield, who had moved up from Wilmington, and then turn and destroy Johnston with one mighty blow.[8] Johnston, however, did not intend to let Sherman unite with Schofield if in his power to prevent it. So on the 16th he hurled Hardee's Corps upon Sherman's left flank near Averysboro. But in turn Slocum turned one of his divisions loose upon Hardee's flank, catching it, in military parlance, "in the air," and sending Hardee reeling backward toward Smithfield.[9]

During the day our division was engaged in bridging a swamp, using for that purpose rails and saplings, so as to enable our teams to follow us. About dark, our work having been completed, we again moved forward, and after a march of seven miles a halt was ordered till morning.

March 17 we moved out of camp at 7 o'clock. The roads were found in much better condition than on the previous day. We marched 17 miles and about midnight came up in rear of the advance columns. For some distance our line of march lay through a North Carolina tar camp, the burning pine trees lighting up the country for miles and making a scene long to be remembered.

The following day our division took the advance, some other command being train guards. After a march of 12 miles a halt was ordered. In the meantime heavy cannonading took place on our left, which indicated some opposition in that direction, but as night came on the firing ceased.

March 19 we met with little resistance. We marched 12 miles, all the time hearing the roar of heavy guns on our left.[10] Away off in the direction of Goldsboro was also heard the heavy thundering of artillery.

We broke camp at 3 o'clock next morning, marched 17 miles, and about 6 o'clock in the evening went into position and threw up a hastily constructed line of works. Heavy skirmishing continued the greater part of the night, and as morning dawned the firing increased in volume. About noon we moved forward half a mile, meeting with slight opposition. Simultaneously with our movement, the enemy furiously assaulted the Fourth Division, but was handsomely repulsed. Our skirmishers now becoming warmly engaged, our regiment was ordered out to their support. Heavy firing continued until about midnight.

The morning of March 23 revealed the fact that the rebels were retreating in disorder, burning bridges behind them and leaving their dead and wounded on the field.

The next day we marched 14 miles and about sundown crossed Mill Creek, making camp on the banks of the Neuse River. The following day we crossed the river on pontoons, marched through

Goldsboro and camped one mile north of the city. On the 26th we moved our camp three miles east of Goldsboro, on the Kinston pike, where we remained until April 10.

Shortly after reaching Goldsboro a congratulatory address by Gen. Sherman was read, assuring us a season of rest. We had marched about 400 miles through a hostile country, a portion of the way flooded with water and traversed by many large rivers. Important lines of railroad had been crippled, cities captured and a vast amount of Confederate property destroyed. A strip of country 40 to 60 miles wide had been laid waste and the Southern people made to feel the horrors of a war which they had brought upon the country.

Sherman's army, as well as our regiment, was in splendid condition physically, but another as ragged a body of men never had an existence. The morning after our arrival at Goldsboro our Adjutant, Henry Welty, reported "35 men barefooted, 43 men bareheaded, and 270 wearing some article of citizen's clothing." [11] After a few days we drew a supply of clothing and soap, and soon made ourselves the best-looking regiment from northwestern Ohio.[12]

On Friday, April 7, our old commander, Maj. Gen. M.D. Leggett, joined us direct from his home, and mounting his horse rode through our camps shouting: "Richmond is taken!" We had previously heard such a report, and when Pap Leggett confirmed it there arose a mighty confusion, our regiment trying to surpass all others in boisterous cheering. We continued to yell until an Orderly rode up and told us to hush, as we were disturbing our sick comrades down at Goldsboro.[13]

About this time our old Colonel, R.K. Scott, again joined us and assumed command of our brigade.[14]

On April 10 we started toward Raleigh, the capital of North Carolina. Our brigade moved to the right flank, and after a march of 12 miles went into camp near Little River. The following morning we crossed the river and marched 10 miles, making our own roads through fields, swamps and forest.

April 12 we moved four miles, when a halt was ordered. During the day the following special field order, No. 54, was issued us:

Headquarters Military Division of the Mississippi,
Smithfield, North Carolina, April 12, 1865.

The general commanding announces to the army that he has official notice from General Grant that General Lee surrendered to him his entire army, on the 9th inst., at Appomattox Court-House,

> Virginia.
>
> Glory to God and our country, and all honor to our comrades in arms, toward whom we are marching! A little more labor, a little more toil on our part, the great race is won, and our Government stands regenerated, after four long years of war.
>
> W.T. Sherman, Major-General commanding.

It would be difficult to describe the joy which the news of the surrender of Lee's army excited among us. We had not yet tired of cheering over the fall of Richmond, and upon this last news being imparted to us we just let out another notch.

The next day we moved forward in a high state of enthusiasm to do the work assigned us. We marched 16 miles, and on the following day, after a rapid march of 20 miles, passed through the capital city of North Carolina and went into camp. We found Raleigh abandoned by Johnston's army, which had hastily retreated 20 miles northwest.

Another day found us in motion in the direction of Johnston's army, but about noon we came to a halt. During the morning thunder was heard, which developed into a heavy downpour of rain. We stood around patiently enduring the elements, when hark! The sound of distant cheering assailed our ears. Regiment after regiment took up the shout as some joyful news reached them. We were in suspense. What did it mean?

An officer dashed up to Lt. Col. Welles, spoke a few words and then spurred his horse onward. Feeling anxious to know the cause of the cheering we gathered around our boy Colonel, and when all was quiet he said: "Comrades, Johnston has sent in word that he would like to know the terms of surrender." Then there occurred loud and prolonged cheering. The victory for which many had hoped and prayed was almost within our reach; h-u-r-r-a-h!

For some days following we remained in camp patiently awaiting the result of an armistice between Sherman and Johnston.

April 17 there came a report that plunged us into deepest sorrow. The noblest heart in America had ceased to beat. Our beloved President had fallen by the hand of an assassin. How we were shocked by the receipt of such sad news. It completely overwhelmed us, and many sat down and wept tears of pain and sorrow. The whole army was hushed with a death-like stillness, and here and there threats of dire vengeance were heard. Only the great, magnanimous spirit of freemen held Sherman's army in check.[15]

April 24 occurred a grand review of the Seventeenth Corps. We marched in close column, and as we passed the reviewing stand there stood the hero of Appomattox beside our leader W.T. Sherman. After the review we returned to our camp, wondering why Gen. Grant was with us, and if he was going to assume command of Sherman's army.[16]

By way of digression, about this time a charge was made against our commander, an accusation that almost implied disloyalty. The press took up the cry till an impartial public would have inferred that our chief was a traitor. This was brought about by one high in office giving to the public a telegram which he had formerly sent to Gen. Grant, implying that Sherman had seen it and had instructions respecting the course [of negotiations with Johnston] he was to pursue. To this our chief replied: "I was not in the possession of such instructions; I never saw them, and I have reason to believe that the —— —— knew of that fact." This reply by our commander, to one whose only purpose it seemed was to humble him in his hour of triumph, was one that the party high in office never answered.[17]

The reading of history makes us feel indignant. Those, however, who sought to injure our chief passed away unhonored, while Sherman, with Lincoln, Grant and many others, live on among a grateful people whose hearts enshrine the memory and whose tongues prolong the praise.

April 25 the truce between Sherman and Johnston having expired, an advance was ordered. Johnston, hearing that Sherman's army was approaching, asked for another meeting with Sherman to take place at noon on the 26th.[18]

The army was halted to await the result. Early on the morning of the 26th Gen. Sherman went forward by rail — the railroad having been repaired — to meet Johnston. Late in the day we heard the train returning. All was now silent expectation, and our hearts were beating fast in anticipation of glorious news. We gathered along the railroad, but the train swept by and came to a stop further down the road. We listened, and soon a loud shout was heard that grew in volume as it was taken up by other commands.

What joyful news those shouts conveyed to us. Johnston had surrendered, the war was at an end. The old woods around us fairly rang with a confusion of voices as we chased each other around big campfires and shouted ourselves hoarse, then wrapped up in our blankets to dream of home, sweet home.

Notes to Chapter 13

1. Maj. Gen. Wade Hampton, a native South Carolinian and commander of the Army of Northern Virginia's Cavalry Corps since mid-May 1864, was ordered to his home state with part of his command to reinforce Gen. Joseph E. Johnston. On Feb. 15, 1865, Hampton was promoted to lieutenant general. Warner, *Generals in Gray,* p. 122-123.

2. Two brigades of Mower's 1st Division, 17th Corps, carried the Confederate works at Rivers' Bridge, losing 125 killed and wounded. Rebel losses were estimated at 20 killed and 150 wounded. Gen. O.O. Howard rated the captured position "as good for defense as any I ever saw, with abatis or slashing covering its front, and that undescribable river [Salkehatchie] with its swamp to discourage every approach." *OR,* vol. XLVII, pt. 1, p. 91, 194.

3. Who burned Columbia remains one of the Civil War's biggest controversies. For a recent dispassionate appraisal, see Tom Elmore, "The Burning of Columbia," *Blue & Gray Magazine,* vol. XXI, Winter 2004.

Five weeks after the 68th Ohio left Columbia, Pvt. Andrew Altman, Co. D, wrote his father: "You had ought to seen the happy soldiers at Columbia SC when it was on Fire. The boys like to see a southern town go to ashes." Altman to John Altman, March 26, 1865, CAC.

4. The Charlotte & South Carolina Railroad.

5. Confederate evacuation of Charleston occurred Feb. 17-18. The city immediately was occupied by Union troops of the Northern District, Department of the South, commanded by Brig. Gen. Alexander Schimmelfennig. *OR,* vol. XLVII, pt. 1, p. 1018-1020.

6. On Feb. 22 Gen. Kilpatrick, Sherman's cavalry commander, reported that "An infantry lieutenant and seven men were murdered yesterday ... after they had surrendered. We found their bodies all together and mutilated, with paper on their breasts, saying, 'Death to foragers.' Eighteen of my men were killed yesterday and some had their throats cut." Two days later Kilpatrick related that 21 Union infantrymen were found in a ravine three miles from Feasterville, S.C., "with their throats cut and stripped of their clothing," while a 92nd Illinois mounted infantryman was discovered hanging from a tree. Taking these reports at face value, Sherman ordered Kilpatrick to "at once shoot and leave by the roadside an equal number of their prisoners, and append a label to their bodies stating that man for man shall be killed for every one of our men they kill." This order was forwarded Feb. 24 to Gen. Hampton, who, replying on the 27th, refuted Sherman's claim that Federal foragers were killed after capture. He informed his opponent he knew nothing of such deaths, and assured Sherman "that for every soldier of mine 'murdered' by you, I shall have executed at once two of yours, giving in all cases preference to any officers who may be in my hands." *OR,* vol. XLVII, pt. 2, p. 533, 544, 546, 554-555, 596.

After another corpse of a 3rd Division, 17th Corps, forager was found March 1 with a smashed skull, retaliation ensued the next day when a Confederate prisoner, chosen by drawn lots, was executed by firing squad. For an account of this incident, see Mark L. Bradley, *Last Stand in the Carolinas: The Battle of Bentonville* (Campbell, Calif.: Savas Publishing Company,

1996), p. 55-57.

7. From Laurel Hill, N.C. on March 8, Sherman had sent two disguised scouts down Cape Fear River to communicate with Federal military authorities at Wilmington, "and to report our approach." Sherman, *Memoirs,* p. 649.

8. Maj. Gen. John M. Schofield commanded the Army of the Ohio, and on Feb. 9, 1865 assumed command of the Department of North Carolina. *OR,* vol. XLVII, pt. 1, p. 3, 57.

9. Hardee's delaying action at Averasboro, N.C. stalled the Federal advance for 24 hours. He was opposed by portions of Slocum's 14th and 20th corps, and Kilpatrick's cavalry, inflicting 682 Union casualties at a cost of 500 irreplaceable Confederates. Bradley, p. 132.

10. The opening of the battle of Bentonville, N.C., fought March 19-21. It was the last significant engagement between the forces of Sherman and Johnston, costing the Union more than 1,500 casualties and the Confederates some 2,600, many of whom were captured. Long, p. 655.

11. A schoolteacher and resident of Defiance County, 1st Lt. Henry Welty, Co. A, was promoted the 68th Ohio's adjutant on Oct. 24, 1864. The following May he was named the 2nd Brigade's acting assistant adjutant general. H. Welty CSR, RG 94, NARA.

12. From Goldsboro, Pvt. Andrew Altman, Co. D, wrote home: "Sherman has brought his children out of the wilderness all right. We was on this Campaign for 57 days be fore we got any Comunications but now we can get hard tack a plenty. We have been a having a good time part of the time and some harde times with the good times. We foraged a bout all our living excepting shugar and coffee. Meet & sweet potatoes we got a plenty, meal and flour — the pan Cakes had to suffer. Many a mile we came as many Swamps we waded and many a crook and bend we made. Billy [Sherman] did not get lost or get scart, the rebs Charged our lines 7 times in one day [at Bentonville] and had to scratch gravel and skedadle away. Now as olde billey stops to let his army rest he Cloathes them and feeds us the best [he can]. ... We have not lost a man on the trip that i know of. The boys are well and hearty and think the time coming when this war shall and must close." Altman to John Altman, March 26, 1865, CAC.

13. The Confederate government evacuated Richmond, Va., on April 2. Union troops occupied the city the next day. Long, p. 663, 665.

Due to illness, Leggett had relinquished 3rd Division command to Brig. Gen. Manning F. Force on Jan. 15 at Pocotaligo, S.C. Force, former commander of the 20th Ohio who was severely wounded in the face during the battle of Atlanta (later receiving the Medal of Honor), led the division until Leggett's return at Goldsboro. *OR,* vol. XLVII, pt. 2, p. 56; Warner, p. 155.

Toward war's end, an arrow was selected as the badge of the 17th Corps. Gen. Force, according to Sergt. Osborn H. Oldroyd of the 20th Ohio, "suggested the arrow to Gen. Frank P. Blair, commanding the corps, giving the meaning as follows: 'In its swiftness, in its surety of striking where wanted, and in its destructive powers when so intended.' Gen. Blair adopted it, adding laughingly, 'The arrow denotes their swiftness, the point their firmness whenever they strike, and the feathers their liking for chickens.' " Oldroyd, p. 193.

14. A month later Scott was promoted brigadier general, to rank from

Jan. 12, 1865. Warner, p. 428.

15. Lincoln was shot in the head April 14 at Washington's Ford Theater, dying at 7:22 the next morning.

16. Grant arrived at Raleigh at 6 a.m. April 24, informing Sherman that his initial terms of surrender offered to Johnston had been disapproved by President Andrew Johnson. Grant was under orders to direct military movements, but left it to Sherman to carry them out. Long, p. 681.

17. The high official Loop referred to was Gen. Henry W. Halleck. For Sherman's perspective, see his *Memoirs*, p. 700-728.

18. The two generals met at James Bennett's farmhouse near Durham Station, N.C.

14

'Over all obstacles to this joyful end'

The next day, April 27, we marched back to Raleigh and went into camp two miles west of the city, where we remained until April 29. Soon after returning to Raleigh our wagons were loaded with supplies necessary for a long march across the country to Washington, 280 miles by our line of march.

Early on Saturday, April 29, we turned our backs upon Raleigh, N.C. and started northward. Early the evening of the first day out we went into camp 14 miles northeast of Raleigh, where we remained over Sunday.

May 1 we again moved forward, and on the night of May 3 camped on the banks of Roanoke River, where we found the advance of the Fifteenth Corps laying pontoons.

The Fifteenth and Seventeenth corps moved on parallel roads and the Fifteenth Corps, having reached the river first, we made camp until they crossed over. We had never been on such a march before, as only such fires were permitted as were necessary to cook our rations. There was no enemy hovering on front or flank, therefore no heavy detail was made each night for picket guard.

May 5 we crossed the Roanoke, and after a tiresome march of 26 miles crossed the North Carolina border and went into camp on the soil of Virginia.

The people along our line of march had never seen an army, much less a Northern one. In many places they congregated by the roadside and closely observed us as we passed, and I suppose were surprised to find that Yankees were a little more than half human, barring a want of soap.

The next day we crossed the Nottoway River and marched some distance over what was known as the Boydton Plank Road.

May 7 we began to observe signs of the terrific struggle between the armies around Petersburg. We passed through a little village named Dinwiddie, and toward the close of day crossed Appomattox Creek and made camp.

It was with deep interest that we gazed here and there at the landmarks covering years of war.

The following day we passed through Petersburg, and the night of May 9 went into camp one mile from Richmond. Here we remained two days, visiting many places of interest in the city, including Libby Prison.

Gen. Halleck was in command at Richmond, and upon our arrival — in the absence of our leader — ordered the army to march in review past his headquarters. This only added fuel to the fire in the heart of Sherman and his men, who had not forgotten Halleck's course in the Raleigh episode. Sherman, upon being told of Halleck's order, promptly revoked it and informed Halleck in words more forcible than polite that if he could not march his army through Richmond without being subject to his orders, he would march his army around it. Sherman meant what he said. Halleck took him at his word; the order was not put into effect and we went on our way rejoicing.

Friday, May 12, we crossed the James River, marched by the famous Libby Prison and on through the streets of the city, and toward night went into camp near a line of old earthworks 10 miles from Richmond. Early the next morning we moved on, and as the day began to wane went into camp near Hanover Court-House.

On the 14th we crossed the Pamunkey River, and on the 16th came to the high ground above Fredericksburg. Here our attention was called to the famous stone wall behind which [Longstreet's] rebel legions took refuge from the guns of Burnside's army. A profound silence prevailed as we moved down the slope leading to the city. The ground, as well as the buildings on either side of our line of march, bore silent witness to the fearful storm of shot and shell under which 10,000 of Burnside's men went down.[1]

Late in the afternoon we crossed the Rappahannock River, mounted the high ground on the north side, and went into camp.

May 18 our route lay for some distance along a high range of Virginia hills overlooking the historic field of Manassas. In the evening we crossed Occoquan Creek, and on the following day went into camp two miles from Alexandria.

Our march from Raleigh was ended, and we were once more promised a season of rest. Weary and foot-sore we made our camp on a level plain near the base of Arlington Heights, where we remained three days.

Early one morning we could have been seen climbing the side of Arlington, that we might enjoy a view of the surrounding country. In due time we reached the top, when an enthusiastic shout of thanksgiving escaped us as our eyes beheld the scene. On our right the proud Potomac swept onward down the valley to the sea. But the great crowning glory of all — a sight that made us feel amply repaid for all our trials — was the Capitol Building of our nation rising in grandeur far above all its surroundings. The massive white walls and great dome glistened in the sunlight, and above it floated the beautiful and glorious flag of our country.

As our eyes feasted on the majestic scene before us, a voice seemed to whisper in our ears: "It would have been a sad day to our country had the scene been otherwise, and our own starry banner stricken from its proud place in the galaxy of nations." Through hardships endured and death in every shape encountered we had pressed forward over all obstacles to this joyful end.

May 20 a number of our comrades, wounded and sick, who went to the hospital during the Carolina campaign, again joined us. But there were others who came not; yet we hope to be able to say "Good morning, comrades" when the reveille shall sound in camp on the other shore.

On May 23 we marched through Alexandria and went into camp on the banks of the Potomac opposite the capital of our country, preparatory to the Grand Review in which we were to take part. This parade was the closing act of the great war for the nation's life.

The Army of the Potomac preceded us, and on May 23 marched in review past the White House, where upon a stand erected for the occasion sat the President, surrounded by his Cabinet and the Generals of the war. Those proud warriors were the survivors of many hard-contested fields. They carried with them the marks of Gettysburg and the battlefields of Virginia, where the dripping earth told of their valor. Their work was done, and they would soon be permitted to go home and rest upon their laurels.

Long before sunrise Wednesday, May 24, we were busily engaged in preparing for the review. At 7 o'clock we were in motion. We crossed Long Bridge and closed up in mass near the Capitol grounds. At 9 o'clock the signal gun was fired, when the head of Sherman's army began its march down Pennsylvania Avenue.

In this review of Sherman's army there was no great desire on the part of the officers or men to make an attempt at military display. However, we moved as if by machinery, with lines well dressed, but the long, swinging step of those accustomed to long journeys was wholly maintained, which fact was made the subject of much discussion by military critics.

Never before was such a scene witnessed on the American continent. The whole length of Pennsylvania Avenue, extending about one mile, was a dense mass of living, surging humanity.

Suspended over our heads were all sorts of mottoes and banners. We felt proud as we read here and there, "All honor to Sherman and his noble men," which brought up feelings of sadness as we thought of comrades who were peacefully sleeping in Southern graves, and wished they could be with us to behold this joyful day. Oh, that our beloved martyr, President Lincoln, might have been spared to see his soldier boys come marching home.

Bullet-riddled battle-flags, ragged and tattered from long exposure, brought forth loud and prolonged cheering from the thousands on either side. Thus we moved on, and the greatest day of our long service passed into history.

Of this notable event Sherman speaks as follows:

> Punctually at 9 a.m. the signal gun was fired, when, accompanied by Gen. Howard and my staff, I rode slowly down Pennsylvania Avenue, the crowds of men, women and children almost obstructing the way. We were closely followed by Gen. Logan and the head of the Fifteenth Corps.
>
> When I reached the Treasury Building and looked back, the sight was simply magnificent. The column was compact, and the glittering guns looked like a solid wall of steel moving with the order of a pendulum.
>
> We passed the Treasury Building, in front of which was an immense throng of people, for whom extensive stands had been prepared on each side of the Avenue.
>
> As I neared the brick house opposite the lower corner of Lafayette Square, someone asked me to notice Mr. Seward [the Secretary of State], who, still feeble and bandaged for his wounds [inflicted the same night Lincoln was shot], had been removed there that he might behold the troops. I moved in that direction and took off my hat to Mr. Seward. He recognized the salute, and returned it, and then we rode on past the President, saluting with our swords.
>
> All on his stand arose and acknowledged the salute. Then turning into the gate of the Presidential grounds, we left our horses with orderlies, and went upon the stand, where I found Mrs. Sherman and son. Passing them I shook hands with Presi-

Abraham Lincoln Presidential Library

Shortly after the Grand Review, Gen. William T. Sherman (center) was photographed in Washington with some of his top lieutenants. From left, Gens. John A. Logan, William B. Hazen, Jefferson C. Davis and Henry W. Slocum.

dent Johnson, Gen. Grant, and each member of the Cabinet. I then took my post on the left of the President, and for seven hours stood, while the army passed in the order of the Fifteenth, Seventeenth, Twentieth and Fourteenth corps.

It was in my judgment the most magnificent army in existence; 65,000 men who had just completed a march of nearly 2,000 miles in a hostile country, and who realized that they were being scrutinized by thousands of their fellow countrymen. The steadiness and firmness of the tread, the careful dress on the guides, the uniform intervals between the companies, and the bullet-riven flags, festooned with flowers, all attracted universal notice.

Many good people up to that time had looked upon our Western army as a sort of mob. But the world then and there saw and recognized the fact that it was an army in the truest sense, well-organized, well commanded and disciplined; and there was no won-

> der that it had swept through the South like a tornado.
>
> For seven long hours the steady tread of the Army of the West resounded along Pennsylvania Avenue. The meantime not a soul of that vast crowd of spectators left his or her place, and when the rear of the column had passed by thousands of the spectators still lingered near to express their sense of confidence in the strength of a Government which could claim such an army. [2]

After the review we went into camp on the Tennallytown road, three miles northwest of the city, where we remained until June 6.

After getting well settled in camp we were given permission to visit the city, but what a contrast we found. The countless thousands who were in the city on the day of the grand review were gone, and stillness reigned everywhere, except the hurried steps of pedestrians who, like ourselves, were taking in the sights of our nation's capital.

We visited the public buildings, including the Capitol, Patent Office, the Treasury and Smithsonian Institution. Everywhere long folds of black drapery met our eyes, which impressed upon us the severe loss our country had sustained in the death of Lincoln.

We gazed in silent admiration upon the Washington family relics. Here was Washington's Bible and camp chest, his hat, coat, pants and boots, and the bed upon which he died. There was the saddle upon which he had ridden when Commander-in-Chief of the Army; the holsters, pistols, sword, and also the tea set, drapery and furniture of the Washington family.

There was also the table upon which the Declaration of Independence was written. Franklin's printing press claimed a conspicuous place, yonder the reclining figure in bronze of a celebrated Indian chief, and many other things which I would tire my readers to enumerate.

We also visited Ford's Theater, and saw the box where sat our beloved President when the assassin stealthily crept upon him and delivered a shot that plunged our country into the deepest sorrow. Thus day followed day, each one ushering in some new scene of joy or sadness.

On Friday, June 2, Gen. Sherman's farewell address to his army was read to us.

During the early days of June rumors began to reach us, which betokened an early move. Day after day our attention was called to the movements of different commands around us, and the fact soon became clear that the Army of the Tennessee was being transferred by railroad and river to Louisville, Ky., preparatory to being mustered out.

On the morning of June 6 we moved out of camp and marched through the Capitol City to the Baltimore & Ohio Railroad, where we loaded ourselves on cattle-cars bound for Parkersburg, W.Va. A railway journey in box cars was as uncomfortable as could well be, but the delightful change from our long and tiresome marches we heartily enjoyed.

Our route lay north to Relay, Md., 10 miles from Baltimore, when we turned west, and as the somber shadows of night enveloped us we crossed to the south side of the Potomac River at Harpers Ferry. In vain we peered into the darkness to catch a faint glimpse of the historic town where John Brown struck the blow that sounded the doom of human slavery.

Morning found us at Cumberland, Md., where we were most kindly received and made to feel immediately at home, while the dear ladies of the Christian Commission supplied a nice warm breakfast.

In due time we moved on, and early the morning of June 8 reached Grafton, W.Va., where the Christian Commission again entertained us. The same evening we arrived at Parkersburg, on the Ohio River, where a mighty shout went up in thankfulness as we once more caught sight of our own dear Buckeye State.

We remained at Parkersburg until the next morning, when we marched through the city to the river and went on board the transport *Bertha,* bound for Louisville, but after a run of about 30 miles we were transferred to a boat named *Wren.*

During the day we passed Camp Carrington, on the Ohio side near Gallipolis, when a number of comrades who had seen three-months' service in the 21st Ohio, hastened to the top of the boat to behold their camp ground of four years previous.[3]

The evening of the 10th we passed Cincinnati, and soon after a sigh of regret escaped us as the showy hills of Ohio disappeared from sight.

Sunday, June 11, just as the sun began to lighten up the Ohio, our boat tied up at Louisville, where, after a ride of 860 miles by rail and water, we landed and marched through the city to a camp three miles down the river. Our camp was not a pleasant one, being wet and swampy; so on the following day we moved to a beautiful grove on the bank of the Ohio four miles below the city.

On the 14th we again moved camp; marched back through

the city and made camp two miles southeast. While here we got more and better rations than had been furnished us for some time; besides, we were able to purchase a variety of food in the city, and although prices were high we fairly reveled in the good things of life.

In spite of our surroundings, good food, clean clothes and a pleasant camp, yet we chafed under its restraint. We could be contented so long as we were engaged in active service, but when the object for which we had donned the coat of blue had been accomplished, and the dove of peace had again returned and perched upon our victorious banner, we did not care to remain longer in the service, but wished to return to the homes we had left in 1861-62.

June 15 our regiment held a meeting to select delegates to a state convention to be held at Columbus, Ohio, on June 21. Gen. Scott, our old Colonel, was present and made a speech, after which by a motion made and sustained, Lt. Col. George E. Welles and Sergt. Nason were chosen as delegates to represent us.[4]

Numerous incidents occurred while in camp near Louisville, but in vain do I try to refresh my memory of events that would be interesting. I do remember, however, that a number of comrades went down to the city and attended the theater where Maggie Mitchell, a noted theatrical star, was playing a two-weeks' engagement.[5] It was from her lips that we first heard the words set to music of a song composed by Adjt. Byers, of the 5th Iowa.[6]

Night after night Miss Mitchell's musical voice was heard in response to a call from her many admirers, and each night she was nearly buried in an avalanche of flowers, which had been prepared for the occasion. Strong men wept with joy, and the Opera House fairly trembled with vibration as Miss Mitchell threw her whole soul into the song's chorus, "When Sherman Marched Down to the Sea."

June 21 Uncle Sam kindly remembered us with a very liberal sprinkling of greenbacks.

One evening a great crowd of men of Logan's old command raised the yell, "Rally to Logan's headquarters." Logan was a great favorite, and we thought he ought to make us a speech. We soon reached his tent and began to yell "Logan! Logan!" but an orderly came out and informed us that the General was in the city. The cry was then raised, "Rally to Leggett," and away we went, shouting at the top of our voices until we brought up in front of Leggett's tent. The General, realizing the object of our visit, came out and in a few chosen words said: "Be patient, men. I beg you, be patient. Your muster rolls are in actual preparation, and in a few days you will be returned home." That was enough, and after giving Gen. Leggett three rousing cheers we joyfully returned to camp.

July 4 Gen. Sherman paid us a visit. Our division was formed in a hollow square, and as Sherman, accompanied by Logan, rode into the center there was much cheering, after which the General gave us a farewell address of some length, passing in review the camp, the march and the fierce surge of battle, closing with: "Dear comrades, as you are soon going to your homes, I again urge upon you, be as good citizens as you have been good soldiers, and your General will meet you again in the sweet by-and-by."

He then bid us a tender farewell, after which with uncovered head he rode slowly away amidst a sea of upturned faces whose eyes were bathed in tears. A deep silence prevailed. The memory of the past and the bright hopes of the future crowded upon us as we retired to our camp.

During our stay at Louisville a regular system of regimental drill and discipline was maintained until Monday, July 10, at which time the long-talked-of muster-out rolls were signed, and we were ordered to report near Cleveland, Ohio, for final payment and discharge from the service.

Ours was a merry regiment when on the morning of July 11 we formed in line and marched to Gen. Logan's headquarters. Lt. Col. Welles stepped forward and spoke for the regiment: "Gen. Logan, we are discharged from our country's service, and come to bid you good-by. We realize that we cannot burst asunder the ties that have bound us together in the past without a sigh of regret; yet we are rejoiced that we are now returning to our homes to again engage in the vocations we laid aside in 1861. And now, General, on behalf of the 68th Ohio, we bid you an affectionate farewell."

Logan responded in a few well-chosen words, after which with a voice filled with emotion he bade us good-by. We also called upon Gen. Leggett, and the blessing and counsel he gave us I trust we have carried through life.

We then marched through the city and boarded an Ohio River steamer, the *St. Charles,* bound for Cincinnati, 130 miles up the river. The next morning we reached Cincinnati. We marched to the Little Miami Depot, and were soon rolling away toward Columbus. Early in the evening our train reached the state's capital city, where a stop was made long enough to get supper.

On the morning of July 13 we arrived at Cleveland, being accompanied from Columbus by the 55th Ohio. Upon our arrival we were waited upon by a delegation of enthusiastic citizens who escorted us to the City Park, where breakfast awaited us.[7] Soon after, we marched out to old Camp Taylor, two miles from the city. Here we remained until July 19.

During our service covering a period of nearly four years we were on the soil of every Southern state except Texas and Florida.

At the beginning of our service we were presented with a beautiful flag by the citizens of Henry County, Ohio. The flag was returned to our admiring donors by Lt. Col. Welles on behalf of the regiment, and is now in the possession of the family of Joseph Stout, of Napoleon, Ohio. Mr. Stout was one of the principal donors, a highly-respected citizen of Henry County, and a staunch friend of the 68th.

Our regimental colors were turned over to the Adjutant General of the state and were deposited in the State Archives. Upon our regimental flag by authority from Department Headquarters were inscribed the following names:

Fort Donelson, Pittsburg Landing, Siege of Corinth, Iuka, Hatchie, Raymond, Jackson, Champion's Hill, Big Black, Vicksburg, Monroe, Meridian, Kennesaw, Nickajack, Atlanta, Jonesboro, Lovejoy, Savannah, Pocotaligo, Salkehatchie, Orangeburg, Cheraw, Columbia, Bentonville and Raleigh.

Our last evening together at Cleveland was rather less cheerful than many others covering a period of months and years, realizing something akin to pain, knowing that on the following day we must part, perhaps forever. While we all rejoiced in the thought of returning to the homes and friends we had left in 1861-62, yet we knew too well that the ties of comradeship which were forged around our campfires could not be sundered without many a sigh of regret.

Upon our muster-out of service Lt. Col. Welles issued a farewell address [a printed copy of which appears at right].

On July 19, 1865, we as citizens of the Republic were sweeping westward over the Lake Shore & Wabash Railroad. The 68th Ohio Infantry, battered and war-worn, was on its way home. As our train steamed on and comrades came in sight of familiar places their excitement grew intense. Many of the men pulled their hats

Soldiers of the 68th Regt. O. V. V. I.

COMRADES: The time for parting has at last arrived, and we will soon part from each other, probably never to all meet again on this earth. But before parting with you, I, who have had the honor of associating with you, and in part sharing your labors, privations and hardships, and I trust, also of your well earned laurels, and honors, and for the last two years had the honor of commanding you; I say before bidding you farewell, I wish to thank you one and all, both officers and men, for the uniform kindness and consideration which you have ever evinced towards me; for the promptness and cheerfulness with which you have obeyed my every order and instructions, and last but not least, for the invariable courage and gallantry which you have ever displayed in all the terrible conflicts in which you have been engaged. Yours is a proud record; not a blot or even a suspicion rests upon your fair fame: Ever the first into battle and the last ones out; Never driven from a position which you desired to hold, but always onward and forward to victory.

To you—the men who have carried their knapsacks and guns proudly and triumphantly through every Rebel State but two—who have marched so many weary miles on foot, through almost impenetrable swamps, and over almost impassable mountains, and traveled so many thousands of miles on crowded steamboats, and suffocating cars—enduring all these things without murmuring or complaining—to you, I say, belongs the honor and praise for the proud record which we, as a Regiment, boast of to-day. And to you, my brother officers, I wish to express my sincere thanks, for your courtesy, and kind and respectfull treatment, and acknowledge that to your counsel, assistance, and labors, I feel I am indebted for whatever reputation I may have as an officer; and all the honor I shall ever wish to claim will be that I was one of the old 68th Ohio.

God bless each and every one of you, both officers and men. Farewell.

GEO. E. WELLES,

Lt. Col. Com'd'g 68th Regt. Ohio Vet. Vol. Inf.

Center for Archival Collections, Bowling Green State University

over their eyes and settled themselves down in their seats while a volcano of emotion raged in their bosoms. Brothers were there who went out nearly four years previous with a brother by his side; but that brother was now sleeping in a far-off Southern grave. Oh!

how could he go home to mother without his brother? And there was another pale, gloomy thought, that of the wife who in 1861 had said "Good-by, my dear husband," but whose white, quivering lips could never say "Welcome home."

The city or village near our homes was called out by the conductor. Crowds of people that had been notified of our coming were at the depot, bands were playing, banners waving, men cheering and loved ones in all attitudes of joy, excitement and expectancy. Hardly had our train come to a stop before we were going in all directions, catching up wives and mothers, sisters and sweethearts, laughing, crying, cheering and trying to bear up under our own happiness.

From the best authority I am able to obtain, I find that our regiment left the state of Ohio on the 9th day of February 1862, 940 strong.

There were recruited for the regiment during its service about 390 men, making a total of 1,330 men who saw actual service in its ranks. During the winter of 1863-64 about 310 men who had seen two years' service re-enlisted in the veteran service, making a total enlistment of those who saw service in our ranks about 1,640 men.

Our total loss, including those slain in battle, died of wounds and of disease, was about 294. These comrades who gave their lives for the flag they loved, whose names can be found inscribed on our Roll of Honor,[8] are peacefully sleeping at the following places:

Marietta, Ga., 52; Vicksburg, Miss., 47; Shiloh, Tenn., 39; Corinth, Miss., 24; St. Louis, Mo., 22; Memphis, Tenn., 16; Chattanooga, Tenn., 8; Cairo, Ill., 12; Cincinnati, Ohio, 10; New Albany, Ind., 8; Fort Donelson, Tenn., 6; Keokuk, Iowa, 6; Louisville, Ky., 5; Columbus, Ohio, 5; Andersonville, Ga., 4; Nashville, Tenn., 3; Covington, Ky., 3; Arlington, Va., 3; Napoleon, Ohio, 3; Defiance, Ohio, 2; Wauseon, Ohio, 2; Woodville, Ohio, 2; Camp Dennison, Ohio, 2; and one each at Bolivar, Tenn., Evansville, Ind., Holly Springs, Miss., Madison, Ind., and Antwerp, Bryan, Cleveland, Florida, Monroeville, Providence, and Pioneer, Ohio.

Our loss by companies was as follows: Field and staff, 1; Co. A, 31; Co. B, 25; Co. C, 26; Co. D, 20; Co. E, 30; Co. F, 24; Co. G, 41; Co. H, 26; Co. I, 26; and Co. K, 44. Total, 294.

Besides these there were discharged by reason of wounds and disabilities: Field and staff, 6; Co. A, 26; Co. B, 24; Co. C, 25; Co. D, 28; Co. E, 27; Co. F, 20; Co. G, 40; Co. H, 27; Co. I, 23; and Co.

K, 30. Total, 276. A number of these disabled comrades returned to their homes to die.

There were discharged previous to July 10, 1865 by reason of general orders, resignation, or upon expiration of term of service, about 240 comrades.

Mustered out of service at Louisville, Ky., on July 10, 1865, about 500 men.

In conclusion, it may be remarked that Ohio's record shows about 50 of our comrades unaccounted for. This casts no shadow upon those who died in the service or were honorably discharged, but rather upon those who neglected their duty to report these men.

Besides these there are about 60 others whose names appear on our rolls, but who never saw service in our ranks. Some never reported for duty, and others were discharged from Camp Latty by civil authority.

Notes to Chapter 14

1. The Federal defeat at Fredericksburg, Va. Dec. 13, 1862 cost Maj. Gen. Ambrose E. Burnside's Army of the Potomac 12,653 casualties. Long, p. 296.

2. Condensed by Loop, Sherman's account is from his *Memoirs,* p. 731-732.

3. Camp Carrington, located just north of Gallipolis near the Ohio River, was named for Henry B. Carrington, Ohio's adjutant general from 1857 to 1861, when he was commissioned colonel of the 18th U.S. Infantry and in November 1862, a brigadier general of volunteers. During the war a U.S. general hospital also was established at the camp's site. Reid, vol. I, p. 931.

4. 1st Sergt. Edwin J. Nason, Co. C, a schoolmaster from Antwerp, Paulding County, was elected the 68th's alternate delegate to the state convention. E.J. Nason CSR, RG 94, NARA.

Welles was promoted colonel June 16, 1865, but never mustered at that grade. Two years later he received a brigadier general's brevet for "meritorious services" to date from March 13, 1865. G.E. Welles CSR, RG 94, NARA.

5. New York-born actress Margaret Julia Mitchell, affectionately called "Maggie" by theater audiences from 1851 to 1892, was best known for her title role in the play *Fanchon the Cricket,* which she first performed onstage in New Orleans in 1860. *Dictionary of American Biography*, vol. 13 (New York: Charles Scribner's Sons, 1934), p. 57.

6. 1st Lt. Samuel H.M. Byers, adjutant of the 5th Iowa Infantry, had been captured Nov. 25, 1863 in the battle of Missionary Ridge outside Chattanooga. His confinement in four different Southern prisons ended Feb. 17, 1865 when Sherman's troops entered Columbia, S.C., and a few days later Byers joined Sherman's staff at the general's invitation. He was impressed by the song "Sherman's March to the Sea," which Byers composed during imprisonment at Columbia. Richard A. Baumgartner & L.M. Strayer, *Echoes of Battle: The Struggle for Chattanooga* (Huntington, W.Va.: Blue Acorn Press, 1996), p. 310-311.

7. A Cleveland newspaper reported that the 55th and 68th Ohio, "after a short rest at the depot, were escorted to the Park by the Reception Committee, preceded by a band of music." It noted the 68th arrived with 450 men and 22 officers. *Cleveland Herald,* July 13, 1865.

8. The 68th Ohio's Roll of Honor can be found in *Ohio Roster,* vol. V, p. 796-803.

BIBLIOGRAPHY

Manuscript materials

Altman, Andrew. Letters, Center for Archival Collections, Jerome Library, Bowling Green State University, Bowling Green, Ohio.

Bruner, Jacob. Letters and Papers, Archives-Manuscripts Division, Ohio Historical Society, Columbus.

Bundy, Eli M. Letters, CAC.

Gillis, James F. and Simeon. Diaries, Gillis Family Papers, CAC.

Harrison, Eugene Beauharnais. Diary, Civil War Miscellaneous Collection, U.S. Army Military History Institute, Carlisle Barracks, Pa.

Ogle, Elisha M. Letters, Gillis Family Papers, CAC.

Scott, Robert Kingston. Letters and Papers, MSS 176, OHS.

Travis, John D. Letters, Travis Family Papers, Bentley Historical Library, University of Michigan, Ann Arbor.

Newspapers & periodicals

The Bryan Union Press

Cleveland Herald

Defiance Democrat

Henry County Signal (Napoleon, Ohio)

Napoleon Press

The North-West (Napoleon, Ohio)

Ohio State Journal (Columbus)

Paulding Independent

The Perrysburg Journal

The Press and Leader (Bryan, Ohio)

Toledo Blade

Toledo Commercial

The Weekly Bryan Democrat

Dwight, Henry O., "A Soldier's Story. The Affair on the Raymond Road," *New York Daily Tribune,* Nov. 21, 1886.

Elmore, Tom, "The Burning of Columbia," *Blue & Gray Magazine,* Winter 2004.

Gillis, Simeon, "The First Gun at Shiloh," *The National Tribune,* Aug. 15, 1901.

Harker, John, "In Front of Atlanta," *The National Tribune,* Nov. 30, 1905.

Loop, Myron B., "Sounding the Alarm. The 68th Ohio's Trying Time at the Battle of Atlanta," *The National Tribune,* Dec. 1, 1898.

——, "Champion Hills. Stirring Description by a Comrade of the 68th Ohio," *The National Tribune,* Dec. 29, 1898.

——, "Would Try It, Anyhow. How Co. B, 68th Ohio, Lost the Honor of Capturing Fort Donelson," *The National Tribune,* Feb. 16, 1899.

——, "Campaigning with the Buckeyes. Ten Thousand Miles with the 68th Ohio," *The National Tribune,* Sept. 27–Dec. 13, 1900.

——, "Rounding-up the Confederacy. Veteran Campaigns of the 68th Ohio," *The National Tribune,* May 9–July 11, 1901.

Richardson, Lay W., "He Knew Lincoln," *The National Tribune,* Aug. 4, 1910.

Government records & publications

Compiled Service Records of Volunteer Union Soldiers who Served in Organizations from the State of Ohio. Records of the Adjutant General's Office, 1780-1917, Record Group 94, National Archives and Records Administration, Washington, D.C.

Hewett, Janet B., editor, *Supplement to the Official Records of the Union and Confederate Armies,* part II, volume 53, serial no. 65, Wilmington, N.C.: Broadfoot Publishing Company, 1997.

Official Army Register of the Volunteer Force of the United States Army, 8 volumes, Gaithersburg, Md.: Olde Soldier Books, Inc., 1987.

Official Atlas of the Civil War, New York: Thomas Yoseloff, Inc., 1958.

Ohio. Roster Commission. *Official Roster of the Soldiers of the State of Ohio in the War of the Rebellion, 1861-1866,* 12 volumes, Akron, Cincinnati, Norwalk, 1886-1895.

Roster of Wisconsin Volunteers, War of the Rebellion, 1861-1865, 2 volumes, Madison, 1886.

Terrell, W.H.H., *Report of the Adjutant General of the State of Indiana,* 8 volumes, Indianapolis: W.R. Holloway, State Printer, 1865-1868.

United States War Department. *The War of the Rebellion: A Compilation of the Official Records of the Union and Confederate Armies,* Washington: Government Printing Office, 1880-1901.

Other works

Baumgartner, Richard A., *Kennesaw Mountain June 1864,* Huntington, W.Va.: Blue Acorn Press, 1998.

Baumgartner, Richard A. & Strayer, Larry M., *Echoes of Battle: The Struggle for Chattanooga,* Huntington, W.Va.: Blue Acorn Press, 1996.

Bowersox, Charles A., editor, *A Standard History of Williams County, Ohio,* 2 volumes, Chicago: The Lewis Publishing Company, 1920.

Bradley, Mark L., *Last Stand in the Carolinas: The Battle of Bentonville,* Campbell, Calif.: Savas Publishing Company, 1996.

Castel, Albert, *Decision in the West: The Atlanta Campaign of 1864,* Lawrence: University Press of Kansas, 1992.

Cohen, Stan, *The Civil War in West Virginia: A Pictorial History,* Missoula, Mont.: Gateway Printing & Litho, 1976.

Dictionary of American Biography, volume 13, New York: Charles Scribner's Sons, 1934.

Dyer, Frederick H., *A Compendium of the War of the Rebellion,* 2 volumes, Dayton, Ohio: Press of Morningside Bookshop, 1979.

Fellman, Michael, editor, *Memoirs of General W.T. Sherman,* New York: Penguin Books, 2000.

Gladstone, William A., *Men of Color,* Gettysburg, Pa.: Thomas Publications, 1993.

Goodspeed, Weston A. & Blanchard, Charles, editors, *County of Williams, Ohio. Historical and Biographical,* Chicago: F.A. Battey & Co., 1882.

Headley, Joel T., *The Life of Ulysses S. Grant,* New York: E.B. Treat & Co., 1868.

Henry County, Ohio, volume 1, Napoleon, Ohio: Henry County Historical Society, 1976.

History of Defiance County, Ohio, Chicago: Warner, Beers & Co., 1883.

History of Sandusky County Ohio, Cleveland: H.Z. Williams, 1882.

Hunt, Roger D. & Brown, Jack R., *Brevet Brigadier Generals in Blue,* Gaithersburg, Md.: Olde Soldier Books, Inc., 1997.

Johnson, R.U. & Buel, C.C., editors, *Battles and Leaders of the Civil War,* 4 volumes, New York: The Century Company, 1887-88.

Killits, John M., editor, *Toledo and Lucas County, Ohio 1623-1923,* Chicago: The S.J. Clarke Publishing Company, 1923.

Long, E.B., *The Civil War Day by Day: An Almanac 1861-1865,* Garden City, N.Y.: Doubleday & Company, Inc., 1971.

Long, E.B., editor, *Personal Memoirs of U.S. Grant,* Cleveland: The World Publishing Company, 1952.

Military Essays and Recollections, volume I, Chicago: A.C. McClurg and Company, 1891.

Morrow, O. & Bashore, F.W., compilers, *Historical Atlas of Paulding County, Ohio,* Madison, Wis.: The Western Publishing Company, 1892.

National Cyclopaedia of American Biography, volume XII, New York: James T. White & Company, 1904.

Oldroyd, Osborn H., *A Soldier's Story of the Siege of Vicksburg,* Springfield, Ill.: H.W. Rokker, 1885.

Reid, Whitelaw, *Ohio in the War. Her Statesmen, Generals and Soldiers,* 2 volumes, Cincinnati: The Robert Clarke Company, 1895.

Roberts, Robert B., *Encyclopedia of Historic Forts: The Military, Pioneer, and Trading Posts of the United States,* New York: MacMillan Publishing Company, 1988.

Sauers, Richard A., *"To Care For Him Who Has Borne the Battle": Research Guide to Civil War Material in the National Tribune,* Jackson, Ky.: History Shop Press, 1995.

Schenkman, David E., *Civil War Sutler Tokens and Cardboard Scrip,* Bryans Road, Md.: Jade House Publications, 1983.

Stevenson, Thomas M., *History of the 78th Regiment O.V.V.I.,* Zanesville, Ohio: Hugh Dunne, 1865.

Ward, Steven H., *"Buckeyes All": A Compendium and Bibliography Ohio in the Civil War (Revised),* volume 3, Dayton, Ohio, 2004.

Warner, Ezra J., *Generals in Blue: Lives of the Union Commanders,* Baton Rouge: Louisiana State University Press, 1993.

——, *Generals in Gray: Lives of the Confederate Commanders,* Baton Rouge: Louisiana State University Press, 1959.

INDEX

Page numbers in boldface italic indicate photographs.

About the Editor

Wisconsin native Richard A. Baumgartner is a former newspaper journalist whose published works include:

Buckeye Blood: Ohio at Gettysburg
Blue Lightning: Wilder's Mounted Infantry Brigade in the Battle of Chickamauga
Yankee Tigers II: Civil War Field Correspondence from the Tiger Regiment of Ohio
Kennesaw Mountain June 1864
Echoes of Battle: The Struggle for Chattanooga
Echoes of Battle: The Atlanta Campaign
Fritz: The World War I Memoir of a German Lieutenant
The Passage: A Tragedy of the First World War

He is a recipient of the Richard B. Harwell and Alexander C. McClurg awards, a past contributor to *Military History* magazine and was a consultant for the Time-Life Books series *Voices of the Civil War.* A full-time researcher and writer, he lives in Cabell County, W.Va.